Face to Face with Political Islam

Face to Face
with
Political Islam

FRANÇOIS BURGAT

published with the assistance of
The French Ministry of Culture

Published in 2003 by I.B.Tauris & Co Ltd
6 Salem Road, London W2 4BU
175 Fifth Avenue, New York NY 10010
Website: http://www.ibtauris.com

Published with the assistance of the French Ministry of Culture

In the United States and Canada distributed by Palgrave Macmillan, a
division of St. Martin's Press
175 Fifth Avenue, New York NY 10010

First published in French as *L'islamisme en face*, copyright © Editions La
Découverte, Paris, 1996

ISBN   hardback 1 86064 212 8
       paperback 1 86064 213 6

A full CIP record for this book is available from the British Library
A full CIP record for this book is available from the Library of Congress

Library of Congress catalog card: available

Typeset in Goudy by Dexter Haven Associates, London
Printed and bound in Great Britain by MPG Books Ltd, Bodmin

CONTENTS

GLOSSARY OF ACRONYMS

AIG   Armed Islamic Group
CEDEJ   Centre de Documentation Economique et Juridique
CIA   Central Intelligence Agency
ETA   Euskadi Ta Askatasuna
FFS   Socialist Forces Front
FIS   Front Islamique de Salut
FLN   Front de Libération Nationale
Hamas   Islamic Resistance Movement
IMF   International Monetary Fund
IRA   Irish Republican Army
ISA   Islamic Salvation Army
MAJD   Mouvement Algérien pour la Justice et le Démocratie
MDA   Mouvement pour la Démocratie en Algérie
MIA   Armed Islamic Movement
MTI   Mouvement de la Tendance Islamique
PA   Palestinian Authority
PAGS   Partie de l'avant garde socialiste
PLO   Palestine Liberation Organisation
RCD   Rassemblement Pour la Culture et la Démocratie
UGTA   General Union of Algerian Workers
UN   United Nations

AUTHOR'S ACKNOWLEDGEMENTS

I am indebted to many people: my close family, who have had to test my metaphors and put up with my moods, the CNRS and, especially, the CEDEJ in Cairo, which have granted me immeasurable freedom to carry out my research, and all those, including Adel Hussein, Rached Ghannouchi and Tareq al-Bishri, who agreed to talk to me on Islamist soil about the material which is essential to this book and its *raison d'être*.

I also recognise the small number of colleagues who have on occasion allowed me to feel less isolated in what my hypotheses could have turned into a solitary endeavour, whether these people preceded, accompanied or just supported me.

I again recognise all those who study the same subject but with differing sensibilities, hypotheses and occasionally different convictions. In a profession where life is all about difference, the authors' identity has been shaped by their viewpoints.

But my greatest debt, for which I will be eternally grateful, is to those who knowingly shrugged their shoulders, who laughed sceptically, to the defamation and ironic insinuations, the pitiful recommendations and other methodological smoke-screens that were disguised as good advice. At a time when it was necessary to be prudent, it was this that spurred me on.

Finally, a very special mention for the invaluable Ali Ben Si Ali, to whom this book is partly devoted, whose premature death added to the deaths of thousands Algerians who have never merited our concern.

PUBLISHER'S ACKNOWLEDGEMENTS

The publisher would like to thank Anna Enayat and Daniel Neep for all their editorial work on the book.

Who could possibly declare their support for butchers, rapists and murderers? Especially when those murderers are 'Islamic crazies', a description which brooks no consideration of history? Cloaked by the term 'Islamic extremism', they are hidden beneath this atavistic symbol of all oriental fanaticisms. It is a term well suited for providing racist prejudice with an inscrutable alibi of legitimacy founded on ethical and secularist grounds.

Pierre Bourdieu[2]

After the attacks of 11 September 2001, people have quite rightly condemned those responsible for the tragedy which struck the US. Yet violence has been the tool of all religions and ideological persuasions in the Middle East.[3] No one side has ever had a monopoly over its employment: regimes and political actors across the spectrum have practised and legitimised violence in its various forms. Many analysts have moreover neglected to scrutinise the role of Western foreign policy in indirectly contributing to this violence. Instead, they examine the historical sources of the Islamic faith for the motives of the attack, in the misapprehension that this violence must be rooted in religion. Many have failed to recognise that its causes are mainly political. In the post-Cold War era, the 'Islamic threat' has come to replace Communism as the West's new global adversary. So-called experts label certain local political actors as 'Islamic extremists', a term wielded so heavy-handedly that efforts to place these actors in their wider historical and political context are rendered futile.

Rather than being determined by doctrinal belief, the forms of action favoured by Islamic movements have been directly inspired by dominant political actors at both local and international levels. In the context of domestic power struggles within each state, forms of actions favoured by the opposition are most often adopted as a response to violence originating from the state itself. Every time that parliament has been made a real arena for political activity (in Jordan, Yemen, Lebanon, Kuwait etc), all opposition groups, including Islamists, have reinserted themselves into the system without causing any major upheavals. The violence of the opposition in many respects reflects the violence inherent to the ongoing dynamic of domination which characterises the political field as a whole.

In Palestine, the frustration with the peace process once confined to people discredited as 'enemies of peace' has now spread to all sections of society. In Iraq, 'strategic' air strikes and the economic embargo have caused immeasurable human casualties, in addition to shoring up the regime of Saddam Hussein and putting an end to internal moves towards democratisation. In the Arabian peninsula, US policy has supported what are effectively long-lived dictatorships: political protection, blind acceptance of autocracy and lucrative weapons deals are offered to Saudi Arabia in return for maintaining high levels of cheap oil production.[4]

Such policies serve to fuel the anger, alienation and resentment felt by a generation deliberately excluded from the domestic political process and marginalized by the global struggle between rival states. Unrepresentative Arab states would be unable to withstand domestic pressure to reform were they not beneficiaries of the West's unconditional support in their 'struggle against fundamentalism', a struggle whose name is easy to invoke when it comes to the repression of local dissidents.

Islamic extremists: Not all 'religious nuts'?

Can 'Islamism' only be characterised as a religious fundamentalism hostile to democratic values and religious tolerance?

Take any interview given by Osama bin Laden, currently considered to be the most dangerous Islamist.[5] A preliminary observation is that, although religious rhetoric is indeed pervasive, the demands and ambitions of this 'religious lunatic' are of a political rather than religious nature. 'The current price of oil [is the product] of pressure exerted by the American administration on Saudi Arabia to keep the market flooded and keep prices low [...] In ten years, the USA has stolen several million dollars from Muslims.'

> In our eyes, the USA is directly responsible for all the victims killed in Palestine, Lebanon and Iraq [...] The attacks are a reaction to these provocations, aimed at expelling the American soldiers who proudly march the length of our country, whilst our university professors languish in prison.

Islamic movements are all affected by a degree of specificity arising from their national circumstances. But they are also, as this book seeks to demonstrate, the common product of one underlying historical dynamic.[6] Much more than a hypothetical 'resurgence of the religious', it should be reiterated that Islamism is effectively the reincarnation of an older Arab nationalism, clothed in imagery considered more indigenous. The effect of the move to 'religious' language has of course made it easier to condemn a West seen not as Christian, but as de-Christianised and materialistic. As it is considered to be native, this language has been more than sufficient in meeting the need of formerly colonised peoples to re-distinguish themselves from the West, giving them a sense of being different from it. The indigenous vocabulary of Islamic culture increasingly seems more appropriate than imported concepts, such as Marxism, as a way of expressing nationalist sentiments.

This 'genealogy' of Islamism helps us better understand why the resurging popularity of Islamic terminology has inspired not just one, but an infinite variety of political projects. The victory of President Khatami in Iran meant that, ironically, the 'theocratic dictatorship' founded by Khomeini was the very first state in the region to witness a credible change in leadership through the ballot box. All the 'modernist' generals who ruled secular countries such as Algeria, Egypt and Tunisia, failed to achieve such a feat. In the 1990s the tone of statements made by various Islamic groups involved in direct action has not been well publicised, out of a desire not to 'serve the purposes' of these groups or simply because no-one wanted to listen to what they were saying. Islamic rhetoric primarily serves to protest the current impasse in relations between a large part of the Muslim world and the West – especially the US. The partial alignment with the Israeli camp and the support given to discredited regimes, however alien they might be to the to the values that the US claims to defend, have widened misunderstandings of all kinds. This has all contributed to the current situation of widespread violence, initially perpetrated against the Israelis and now against their allies, at the heart of their homelands.

If the nationalist, anti-imperialist and identity-related aspects of Islamism are accepted, a whole series of methodological consequences are imposed on analysts. It is well documented that religious discourse can be used to condone and sanctify violence, although it is in no way the cause. The Quran can 'explain' Osama bin Laden no more than the Bible can 'explain' the IRA. Islamic studies is an important discipline, but it should not be used to understand the mundane, political currents which shape the modern world.

Having said that, it is also impossible to interpret Islamism with recourse to nothing other than the dominant terminology used by Western social science to do so. All too many people have adopted and continue to adopt these shortcuts. Capable of illuminating some of the secondary factors in the resurgence, a purely socio-economic analysis fails to grasp the essential dynamics of the Islamist phenomenon. It can only reveal the contingency and diversity of its social base, and contributes little to our understanding of the underlying processes at work.[7]

Finally, it has often been thought that any discourse using an Islamic vocabulary was necessarily incompatible with the universality of Western modernity. This book hopes to underline the fact that, in reality, the attitude of Islamic movements toward 'modernity' is open to change and far from being monolithic. Its truly 'extremist' fringes have often succumbed to the easy temptation of indiscriminately rejecting the West's contribution to social and political modernisation under the pretext that this contribution is a continuation of the West's 'imperialist' phase, even extending to the categories of its language. However, these fringes are a minority:[8] the composition of the Islamist movement is considerably more complex. The values of modernity are much less renounced than rewritten in the terminology of the symbolic system of Islam, a fact which helps to extend the reach of such modernisation rather than to interrupt it or obstruct its progress. The example of the women's movement is notable in this respect: it has been well documented that dynamics of gender re-empowerment have been pursued from within the process of re-Islamisation itself.

The lens of the 'fundamentalist threat' still monopolises interpretations of the struggles as diverse as the Algerian civil war and the Arab–Israeli conflict. Obscuring the incoherence of Western foreign policy and the complicity of Arab regimes in fuelling the 'threat', this reading hinders any more realistic analysis of the sources of violence and the means to absorb it. The 'ideologisation' of terror reinforces perceptions of the Islamic resurgence as a purely religious phenomenon, when it evidently serves as a vehicle for broader cultural demands, in addition to political ones (nationalist, anti-imperialist and even 'democratic'). By confining itself to this misleading perspective, the West is depriving itself of understanding that at least a part of the demands voiced by this generation of Islamists is no more illegitimate than those expressed by their nationalist fathers in their time (who also had recourse to violence, *mutatis mutandis*). The West has to acknowledge its shortcomings in the face of increasingly violent attacks. The chilling efficiency with which these attacks were carried out must be the first consideration. The West then needs to rethink its 'counter-offensive' quite carefully. When the time for explanation and strategy comes, it is to be hoped that hot-headed passions are put to one side, and rational analysis is allowed to come to the fore.

François Burgat
Sanaa, Yemen
September 2002

Notes on Foreword

1   The English 2002 edition of *Face to Face with Political Islam* has undergone the following revisions: the conclusion of the 1996 French edition has been omitted and a new foreword and conclusion have been added.
2   'L'intellectual négatif', *Liber*, the supplement of Archive des sciences sociales, College de France, Paris, January 1998.
3   Michel Foucault, *Dits et Ecrits III*, Gallimard, Paris, 1996, p.776.
4   See, for example, the well-documented account of a former French ambassador, Jean Michel Foulquier, *La dictature protégée*, Alan Michel, 1995.
5   See, for example, the interview given to Peter Arnett and Graham Fuller in Imad Nadhaf, *Usama bin Ladin, 'One in a Million'*, Mu'assassat al-Iman, Dar al-Rashid, Beirut, 1998. Also, the interview given to al-Jazeera TV in 1998, in Jamal Abd al-Latif Isma'il, *Bin Ladin, al-Jazeera wa Ana*, S.E., 2001.
6   See also François Burgat, *L'Islamisme au Maghreb, la voix du Sud*, Karthala, 1988; Payot, 1995.
7   The profile of bin Laden's closest henchmen, not to mention bin Laden's personal wealth, serves to illustrate the pitfalls of 'materialist' interpretations. Aiman Zawahiri, the head of one of the most revolutionary Islamist groups, was born by the Nile. Trained as a surgeon and married to a philosopher, the leader of Tanzim al-Jihad is the son of a university dean and a professor. His genealogy underlines the fragile and artificial division erected between 'institutional, Islamist and informal (Sufi)' versions of Islam: he is a descendant of a Sheikh al-Azhar on his father's side and, on his mother's side, a rector of Cairo University who was also an ambassador for his country and the leader of a Sufi brotherhood.
8   The Taliban provides an example of this trend. One of the best analysts working on Afghanistan has taken care to point that 'other than in the popular imagination of both Western and Muslim countries (which is not entirely without relevance), their rise to power does not seem to herald more revolutions of the same kind'. Gilles Dorronsoro, *La Révolution afghane: des communistes aux tâlebân*, Karthala, Recherches Internationales, CERI, 2000.

Introduction

Face to Face with Political Islam gives further weight to research whose first results were presented in *The Islamic Movement in North Africa: the Voice of the South*.[1] The problematic of the first book has been retained here. The six-year period between publications, however, has witnessed important changes to large parts of the political landscape of the region (most notably with the '*glasnost*' of Algerian politics in 1989, the Gulf War and the unblocking of Arab–Israeli negotiations), which have prompted a serious rethinking of the first conclusions. The critiques of the first book – which were often useful – from both within and without the academic scene, and equally the reactions of the 'Islamist subject',[2] had to be considered and analysed. Moreover, the book led to academic work which is today the focus for a great deal of discussion and on which, without meaning to be confrontational, it has been necessary to clearly state a position.

After I established myself in Cairo, my hypotheses began to definitively exceed the territorial scope of *The Islamic Movement in North Africa* to include Sudan, Lebanon, Jordan, Yemen and the rest of the Arab world. Rather than relying on analysing only written works from these countries, I again sought direct contact with the 'players' on the Islamist scene, the backbone of the approach in *The Islamic Movement in North Africa*. Even if the content of these dialogues is less systematically reproduced, the attempt is still made to give '*homo islamicus*' a free voice, with the minimum possible mediation – although the objective of curbing the tendency to demonise seems today to be even further from being fulfilled. Whenever this becomes unavoidable, certain definitions from the first work have been restated, although the basic argument of *The Islamic Movement in North Africa* has not really been altered.

1

However slow and difficult, the irresistible process of the remoulding of the Arab political landscape is inexorably poised to slip from the hands of those who, since independence, have held sway over the destiny of the region. Various phenomena and observations suggest that, far from being weakened by this delicate 'democratic transition', the forces of the Islamist movement have every chance of playing a key role in it.

This new political generation is almost exclusively perceived as a symptom of social disease, both in the West and in the Arab world. The terminology used to describe potential parliamentary majorities of the south to their enforced partners north of the Mediterranean is almost identical to that used almost 15 years ago to describe the splinter group of assassins who killed Anwar al-Sadat.

Whether conscious or not, this lack of nuance has severely handicapped all attempts to understand the Islamist phenomenon, in the same way that understanding the European parliamentary left would be handicapped if the movement's goals were presented as being synonymous with the principles of some minor organisation, such as the tiny French militant group Action Directe.

In other words, either decolonisation has indeed produced a generation of fanatics on the Arab shores of the Mediterranean, and it is now right to question the validity of the discourse on which this decolonisation was founded, or, if this is not the case, it has become urgent to acknowledge that the political forces labelled 'Islamist' ready to emerge from Arab ballot boxes cannot be reduced to a simplistic, Western view. From where does the recurrent difficulty the West has in understanding the changes in Arab neighbours stem? What does such deep-rooted change mean to the stability of the Mediterranean and of the world? The aim of this book is to find an answer to these two questions.

The complicity of subject and object?

Do we have the right to be in 'agreement' with what we seek to analyse as 'behaviour'? Does the convergence of all or part of the Islamist discourse with the results of impartial observation necessarily discredit such results? Does prolonged direct contact with the subject of analysis inevitably cloud the results of scientific observation?

Let us first recall a little-known fact. Throughout the 1980s the exponents of political Islam knew the (frequently unobjective) analyses of Western academic observers better than they knew their own faces or the shape of their microphones. During this period, much of the huge volume of writing on the 'return of Islam' was in fact produced by those who had never met the people whose mentality they sought to explain to the entire world. However, others, to whom I was drawn at an early stage, wanted to go to the heart of Islamist rhetoric in order to understand it. They therefore systematically sought contact with those who produced it.

There are many benefits to this approach, including the discovery of new, totally unmediated material and, of course, uncensored information. But that is not of paramount importance. Establishing contact with subjects, showing them your respect and eventually gaining theirs in return, allows authors to avoid the myriad of fantasies that are the product of the mutual misunderstandings and sometimes wrongly reproduced in the name of 'science'. By being conscious of and able to internalise the angles of observation of the subject of study, one can enrich one's own understanding and explore new avenues of interpretation. Inevitably, as a result of these numerous contributions, one might come to adopt certain parts of schools of thought other than the Orientalist model. Does this handicap analysis?

In the name of sacred epistemological principles, those who display this 'involved empathy', which has already demonstrated its uses, are often accused of complicity with the discourse of the subject. Innumerable sins are attributed to those who have the gall to sacrifice indispensable scientific distance and 'go deep into the lair to look at the dragon'. At the very least, they have abandoned 'scientific prudence'; at worse, they have become 'advocates', 'spokesmen', 'drummers' and – why not – even the 'accomplices' of their subjects. Aren't they doing all the manipulating? Just what does all this supposed collaboration mean?

Do we actually realise the extent to which direct contact with a political actor reaps more than perusal of that actor's discourse? From the physical appearance and the style of dress of interlocutors to the tone of their voice and the framework within which they express themselves, their family environment, the books in their library or the confidences of their neighbours, tête-à-têtes yield much more than the limited, one-dimensional image created by the juxtaposition of the elements of their discourse, a fortiori within the narrow framework of the written world. The suburbs of Cairo, which hide many of those who have escaped the countless police raids against Islamist activists, and the villages of the Sa'id, the birthplace of the Gama'a Islamiyya movement, without doubt provide more information on the political culture of Sheikh Omar Abd al-Rahman's disciples than the Parisian interpretation of the fatwas, supposed or real, issued by the sheikh.[3] Sometimes silence is more important than words, allusion more meaningful than the explicit. Once the tape recorder has been turned off, an off-the-record conversation about the World Cup and one or two remarks about a referee's performance often say more about an individual's ability to internalise the demands of a pluralist culture than taking their beliefs on the matter at face value.

A reminder is unfortunately necessary: if there has been a methodological error, it has not been made by those who have taken the trouble to meet with Islamists before discussing Islamist issues, but by those who for so long thought that they could forego such an enterprise.

The scientific status of a discourse, in its strictest sense, is generally agreed. It is an obvious fact that you must not 'take their word for it'. One of the basic laws of good methodology is to exercise extreme caution when dealing with discourse from a subject in general, and when the subject speaks about him- or herself in particular. However, let us ensure that this does not lead to such an inflexible reading that, in each of the areas where this is an issue – for example in Oriental studies, in Europe or French cuisine – it does not condemn Orientalists, Europeans or eminent French chefs to the sidelines, or limit their participation in a debate which concerns them to silent contemplation.

However, it is necessary to establish, or re-establish, the difference between the actual 'discourse' of the actors and the presentations made by those observer-participants of a particular group with academic pretensions. The difference between the position taken by a player to values that are considered positive ('I am a democrat', 'ours is a liberal party') and the analyses of an ethnic, ideological or scientific community by one of its members is absolutely essential.

In the case of academic works produced by participators in Islamist activity, the question of whether they are scientifically admissible should not even arise – no more than, say, the question of the credibility of an Orientalist analysing the conditions of his work in the scientific field, a Frenchman conceptualising French foreign policy or a journalist writing the history of his newspaper. For a long time this question has been clearcut and, with all due respect to those who want to smother any sympathy towards the discourse of the subject, the answer can be nothing but affirmative.

When discussing discourse in the strictest sense, it will evidently have to be considered as such: its authors will be judged on their actions rather than their words. Care will be taken never to build up these words as proof. On the contrary, one will try as carefully as possible to decode each of the presuppositions which determine their exact meaning. Again, this should be done in all circumstances and without exception, something which is not always the case: too often this cardinal rule of methodology regarding 'the discourse of the subject' fluctuates according to the content of the discourse or the degree of proximity and allegiance of the audience. When an Islamist takes a position on democracy, the judgement of his proposal can thus vary completely according to its content. If the Tunisian Rached Ghannouchi declares that 'democracy is a part of Islam' or that it 'constitutes one of its fundamental values', few will believe that he has real democratic convictions. One should rather consider it as a mere 'discourse', a position of 'circumstance', something that is said 'because there is a vested interest in saying it at a given moment but which, if the case arises, can easily be withdrawn in another context', 'the positive side' of an inevitable 'doublespeak', which is the prerogative of all those practising political Islam as a minority. This duality will not even be considered as revealing an ambivalence, since it is implicit in this type of 'argument' that only the 'negative side' of such double language is meaningful. There is no point in even replying to such proposals, as you would fall into the 'trap' of this double discourse. Such prudence is praiseworthy. When he did not give the 'hard-line' response that his interlocutors expected by right from a 'fundamentalist leader', Abdelfatah Mourou, former Secretary-General of the Mouvement de la Tendance Islamique (MTI) in Tunisia, was regularly referred to as 'Mr Valium'.[4] It has been the same for the Algerian Abbassi Madani and Hassan Turabi of Sudan, and many others whose nuanced and moderate speeches – which do not count – have less access to the media than those of their colleagues or adversaries who play the role intended for them.

Let us look at this from another angle, by examining what happens when Ali Benhadj, the leader of the Front Islamique de Salut (FIS) in Algeria, distances himself from democratic terminology[5] ('today is a victory for Islam, not for democracy', 'Democracy is against Islam'), or when he criticises any of the values held dear by the listener. Curiously, his proposal will no longer be a 'discourse': it is no longer something its author 'has a vested interest in saying at this moment, but which he can withdraw in another context, if the case arises'. It is no longer about 'words' whose allusive and circumstantial character must be system-atically considered. Here the 'discourse' becomes 'proof', and timeless proof: a case of 'if he said it, it must be true', applying equally to those who sympathise with Benhadj – preferably forever. The methodological prudence that was initially demanded and which is, however, vital to understanding the significance and scale of this need to distance oneself is forgotten. The Islamists say 'Islam is Islam', which means that their modern day reading of Quranic references ignores history. This is the proof that Islamists from Casablanca to Tehran and from 1979 to the year

3000 'will never change'. They say that they prefer 'Islam to democracy': this proves that they will always be tyrants. They say they oppose secularism: this proves that they oppose reason and that, beneath the minarets, obscurantism will hold sway eternally. And so on.

Evidently, the trap of 'being too sympathetic to the discourse of the subject' has undermined analyses. But the victims are perhaps not always those one might think.

'Islamism': Neither too much nor too little

The propensity of the West and its media to see the Arab world only through the 'distorting lens of Islamism' has often been denounced. In socio-political analysis of the region, there has been endless discussion of the dangers of over-emphasising the importance of the religious factor, and of the dangers of 'essentialising' Islamic doctrine into the sole frame of reference which determines individual and collective behaviour, without even mentioning non-Muslim minorities. Therefore, pleads Georges Corm,[6] 'In order to analyse the Arab East, Western political science must rid itself of all the obvious prejudices of Islamic Studies and Orientalism. It must re-establish both the history of the people who are part of the geography and of the provincial history...and the Islamic abstraction to understand these people in their human multi-dimensional specificity: that of language, of morals and customs, and the diversity of ethnic and provincial territories.'

Since millions of 'Muslim' individuals are less accessible to observation than the verses of their doctrine, geographic and linguistic barriers continue to encourage a tendency in Western observers to over-emphasise the factor of religion. The exegesis of the Quran, (that is the relatively accessible ethical ideal followed by the millions of people of the Muslim religion or culture) thus often replaces socio-economic and socio-historical investigation, which would by itself explain the attitudes of each of these individuals in determined political contexts. It is easier to study one eternal and intangible Islam than all the thousands of interpretations. This reveals an evident drift that rightfully continues to be condemned. The suras of the Quran and the spiritual leaders of radical Islamism, Ibn Taymiyya (1236–1326)[7] and Sayyed Qutb (1906–66)[8] – or those of other real or supposed doctrinal credos of some or all Muslims – are charged with explaining a terrain that can only be grasped through the innumerable parameters of political sociology.

'Ah! It is both refreshing and reassuring to read indigenously produced works stripped of all neurotic fascination!' commented Ghassan Salamé, not unjustly, on reading a collective work, *Religion in the Arab World*, written by local authors.

> This is neither wayward Orientalism, nor that kind of unconsidered journalism embellished with a style more befitting Foucault. It is plural, fumbling, and certainly insufficient in more than one point, but it has the merit of breaking (unintentionally) the sacred alliance which unites the most outspoken Islamism and the most folkloric Orientalism in a historically incorrect, ideologically charged and intellectually ephemeral affirmation of Muslim ontologism.[9]

Indeed it is an invigorating critique. Is it nevertheless true that it is the old line of demarcation between insiders and outsiders which separates today highly respected work from that of the lesser players in Arab social sciences?

The better-informed 'Arab' approach to Islamism is naturally less susceptible to the fantasy which affects a major part of Western output. Produced locally, its critical potential is greater. While the impact of the denunciation of Islamist abuse is devalued by Western approximation, its criticism is given special weight by the informed rigor of someone like Fouad Zakariya.[10] Nevertheless, there is a scientific price to pay for this precious intimacy with the region: its very inscription in the political – and indeed ethnic and religious – landscape can also be a source of distortion. Zakariya pays the price of his (admittedly courageous) inclusion in the Egyptian political debate each time he refuses to accord the dress-code of Egyptian Islamists the same status as identity symbol that he grants to the garments of their Iranian counterparts. The shortcuts often taken by the Arab left to describe the Islamist phenomenon (a CIA device to combat Nasserism or Ba'thism) and the extreme reluctance of non-Muslim Arabs to accept the depth of feelings of identity tapped by the Islamist rhetoric, are clearly not much different from the *a priori* reductionism of certain Orientalists.[11]

Some highly respected figures seem to have finally come to regret that the great French figures in Islamic studies have, until now, given birth to a rather dull generation of intellectual heirs – weak political analysts working on the Arab world. One factor of this is the intrusive use of the 'Islamist' parameter, which masks the historical depth, the spiritual richness and diversity of Muslim thought, thus risking projection by the analyst of an image of Islam that is dangerously impoverished. For the fiercest of its attackers, the 'Islamist syndrome' that political analysts sometimes suffer from is brought on by nothing but their own lack of intellectual rigor, their lack of culture in some way echoing that of their subject of analysis. Is this really the case?

When the great generation of French Islamic studies was in a position central enough to control the system, it did not safeguard its own reproduction. But is this the real debate? Was the Islamism of the 1970s and 1980s really built on the scientific foundations of Islamic studies? Is it not true that, when examining the essence of the turbulence generated by the rise to power of the 'Islamists', one encounters certain trivial and temporary political problematics that have little to do with the points of reference and ambitions of Muslim thought through the ages? To analyse the elections of 12 June 1990, which confirmed the supremacy of the FIS in Algeria over all other political parties, must we really examine the core treatises of Islamic studies? In the 1960s, the observers of the Arab political scene had some difficulty explaining why many movements derived from old-style, European scientific socialism flourished there. They did not feel obliged to debate it, to invest all history with Marxist philosophy. On the same political scene, today's observers of Arab politics must make sense of an Islamic vocabulary that is continually changing. This mission does not necessarily mean mobilising all the resources of the history of religious thought. It would never strike a political analyst to deny that the history of Muslim thought is manifestly richer, more complex and more ambivalent than the Islamist slogans would lead you to believe. No analyst is ambitious enough to appreciate the value of the actors in the political game, recognise their authenticity or make exceptions: 'They do not represent true Islam!'. More modestly, analysts attempt to understand the mechanics of how a political ideology works – that is they accept the investigation of one particular representation, by definition both reductive and deforming, of historical reality and of whichever body of references it gave birth to.

Having repeated that more of the laws which govern the conduct of *homo orientalis* are inscribed in manuals of political sociology than in the holy books, there is nevertheless nothing to prevent the improvement of these books of sociology through observation in a field other than the West. There is also nothing that forbids us to ignore the limits of provinces, nations or regions in order to construct a grid of reading of the Arab region as a whole. This is where the Islamist paradigm is located. Here the same dynamic can be clearly perceived throughout, despite exceptionally diverse human and geographical contexts, and this pushes some political actors to reintroduce the traditionally dominant references of religious culture into the system of representation. From Algiers to Amman, passing through Cairo, this dynamic gives those who are able to exploit it a capacity for mobilisation and communication superior to that of other groups. Without prejudging the existence and strength of other dynamics of transformation – underestimating the formidable differences which separate the thought of Ali Benhadj from that of Ibn Khaldun or Ibn Sina, forgetting the distance between the hills of Amman and those of Algiers, of Bugeaud from Bonaparte, of French colonisation from the British mandate, the Hashemite throne from the Front de Libération Nationale (FLN) and the Muslim Brotherhood from the FIS – there exists a group of political forces whose convergence is sufficiently explicit that the academic observer is bound to construct them into an 'Islamist' grid of reading of contemporary Arab politics.

The intention in this book is in the first instance to set out the elements of the mobilising formula of Islamism, having pinpointed some of the obstacles that our Western outlook presents to its rational understanding. The second part aims to identify the real political origins of those acts of violence which are too systematically interpreted as a political expression of the process of 're-Islamisation', to the detriment of the essentialism that often affects the external view. Finally, the third part considers the capacity of the Islamist upsurge to dialogue with the dynamic of modernisation (for example democracy and the status of women etc) of the societies that it permeates.

CHAPTER ONE

Arabs – from *'Fellaghas'* to 'Fundamentalists'

One of the two faces of [Algeria], a hard and even tragic country, marked by the wind of unhappiness, has obstinately turned towards happiness, towards the sun and towards modernity and this, in spite of everything, is embodied in France.[1]

What makes up the political realities of Islamic Arab countries today? Is it possible to answer this question in a coherent and objective fashion? In other words, is there a pattern that links the recent manifestations of political, social and economic evolution that we have witnessed in countries as diverse as Lebanon, Saudi Arabia, Yemen, Algeria, Egypt and Palestine? Is there a single key that allows us to make sense of the myriad of causes of the short-lived fleeting victory of the FIS in the Algerian elections of December 1991, the Iraqi invasion of Kuwait in 1990, the reunification of the two Yemeni republics a few months earlier, the dying embers of the war in Lebanon, the attacks on tourists in Egypt, or the supposed belligerence of Hamas (Harakat al-Muqawama al-Islamiyya, or the Islamic Resistance Movement) in Palestine?

Aside from obvious national peculiarities, the first point of reference for those seeking such a key should be history. It cannot be stressed enough that in order to understand current political realities in the Arab world, as in the rest of the world, a comprehensive knowledge of its history is essential – certainly its more distant history, where the first references to its political field are to be found and where the most precious symbolic traits of its collective identity are rooted. Also, and perhaps above all, modern history has a direct influence over recent political, economic and social events, even if it has now disappeared from public consciousness. When discussing the Arab world, however, the average man on the street will not refer to either recent or more distant history, as his knowledge of both is poor. Paradoxically, the popular view of the more distant history of the Arab world as peopled by a few despotic caliphs accompanied by arabesques and harems is less inaccurate than the view of modern history, which is dictated by much more recent events. More distant history, although well-documented, remains insufficiently known. Yet, despite its proximity, the ignorance of modern history is even more widespread.

The return of history

Of course, *homo politicus occidentalis* has a good excuse for his ignorance. At school we have learnt about the Roman Empire in great detail, but have clearly been taught little about Muslim Andalusia and even less about the exact conditions under which the Western powers seized control of Arab territories.[2] At best, people in the West have been given a one-sided view of the impact that their commercial, military and later political and cultural penetration has had on the ruins of the Ottoman Empire. This view has underlined the benefits of the ruptures that were introduced to the heart of dormant societies and emphasised the powerful dynamic of scientific, political and social modernisation that men of knowledge and colonial soldiers throughout the East carried in their saddlebags.[3]

The collective ignorance of the West has naturally overlooked the negative side of this clash of civilisations, notably the exact conditions under which territories were made available for colonisation and the manner in which the new masters manipulated the balance between ethnic and religious groupings in order to assert their control. The disturbing effect of the marginalisation of cultural and linguistic codes within these societies went virtually unnoticed.

Yet it is the aftershock of this history, which is 'old' even though it happened recently, that is surely screaming out from the headlines of our newspapers. The inevitable detachment of the West unmasks the fragility of relations of power which mark certain inter-state boundaries and on occasion exists within these boundaries (most notably in the Arab East), the tensions that exist between religious groups which are more or less a direct result of its past influence. The distance adopted by the West high-lights some of the distortions that were at times consciously fabricated to justify, ease or underpin its presence but were indirectly caused just as much by the mere fact of that presence. Once this has been accomplished, or appears to have been accomplished, regional dynamics, petrified in the

Western 'mould', follow a course which is forcibly neither more 'natural' nor 'better', but is nonetheless different.

The pursuit of this profound process of 'repositioning' also explains the re-emergence of ideological references that the West finds hard to recognise. It is not its 'Arab policy' of the past century, but the universalist monopoly of its political thought, that the West is trying to reinstate. 'Islamism', the language through which the Arab world articulates its opposition to the West, characterises the wave of exorcism that is now sweeping across the former territories dominated by the West.

For the moment, this phenomenon, which is now on the verge of producing parliamentary majorities, is seen in the West as the most likely reason for 'deviations' and other social and political deadlocks. The discourse of the 'fundamentalists' of today, a new version of that of the 'dirty Arab nationalists' of yesterday, resembles that used for those who have long been described as 'fellaghas' (the term used by the French to label the Algerian nationalists during the 1954–62 war of independence) – virtual terrorists. The largest of these groups, the Algerian FIS, has, de Barrin says, recruited from the 'hordes of people on the margins of society'.[4] Is this correct? And if not, what lies at the root of this recurrent difficulty in recognising the changes in our Muslim environment?

Two symbolic episodes have alerted Western consciousness to the phenomenon of 'Islamic Resurgence', both brought about the physical or political death of Third World leaders whose international (rather than domestic) record, which has received rather less attention from the West, seemed most closely to accord with our political mindset and sensibilities. Mohammad Reza Pahlavi, the Shah of Iran, and Anwar al-Sadat, the President of Egypt, appeared to be more 'conciliatory' and more 'understanding' than their fellow statesmen of the Middle East. Crucially, they both sought to anchor their legitimacy outside Islamic terms of reference (in the case of the Pahlavis to the Achemaenids, in that of Sadat to the Pharaohs), to civilisations that are far too old to harbour any trope of continued confrontation with a 'Christian' or 'Western' other in their collective consciousness.

After the spate of 'nationalisations', which coincided with its improving relations with our then communist enemies, the restless Third World seemed to embody the hope of a return to old-style collaboration, thanks to these new mediators, whose wives smiled on the front covers of our magazines. Anwar al-Sadat, a liberal and pacifist entrepreneur, named Man of the Year by *Time* magazine in 1977, succeeded Gamal abd al Nasser, the pro-Soviet leader and arch-enemy of our Israeli ally who had nationalised the Suez Canal. In Iran, Shah Mohammed Reza was the active partisan of a 'White Revolution' and of industrial culture, whose father Reza had replaced Mohamed Hisayat Mossadegh, an impertinent challenger who objected to the Anglo-American oil system. In their time, Sadat and the Shah of Iran were, without doubt and not by chance, the Third World heads of state most respected by the European public.

In 1979, the radical departure of the first state-like expression of Islamism soon obscured the rupture represented by the downfall of Mohammad Reza Pahlavi. Within the terms of reference of its political culture, the West presented a one-sided account which kept refusing to consider the symbolic import of this 'revolution', whether good or bad. But for millions of people, this event, which marked the dawn of the fifteenth century of the *hejira*, has taken on a quite different meaning: namely that the limitations created by the hegemonic pretensions of Western culture over a society to which it was alien could be superseded.

Two years later, in 1981, the assassination of a new head of state, a familiar face on our television screens (a man who had displayed the courage to welcome the dethroned Shah, whom none of his former allies in the West had dared to acknowledge), reaffirmed an already well-anchored impression. Even those first academic observations that did break out of their narrow scholarly context did not really manage to inform the debate surrounding the event on a broader popular level. They proposed an analysis remarkably well-adapted to the subject: the radical expression of a political upsurge within a highly frustrated social environment. The thesis that has become the media reference for the Western Orientalist scene admirably fulfils its role of introducing the revolutionary expression of a tiny section of the Egyptian Islamist current.[5] This was the theory which imposed itself on the media to the detriment of other approaches, not because of its undoubted qualities or its objective limits, but because it did not upset the unconscious expectation of opinion.[6] If the image of Sadat the Pharaoh (as his enemies called him) was quickly buried, his assassins and their system of references have nevertheless remained as the explanation for the entire Islamist phenomenon.

Since then the Western view has essentially not changed. Islamism has replaced the former bugbears of political independence and nationalist conflict. And there it has remained. It has become increasingly difficult to discuss Islamism except over the grave of Mohamed Boudiaf, the sympathetic and modernising head of state who was assassinated by a group of bearded villains. When, 10 years after its first publication, Gilles Kepel revised his *The Prophet and the Pharaoh*, he saw in Mohammed Boudiaf a successor to Anwar al-Sadat, and in his assassination the only possible paradigm of 'Islamist violence'.[7] Can we ignore the fact that the

Algerian president 'who thought he could fight the war without the army'[8] died at the hands of the very people who had brought him to power? Is it possible to ignore the strength of the dynamic that affected the international Islamist movement between the assassination of Sadat on 6 October 1981 and that of Boudiaf on 30 June 1992? The answer generally given is 'yes' and the old, simplistic analysis has been retained, unaltered:[9] an Islamist is someone who adheres to *fatwas* permitting *jihad* and who willingly assassinates likeable leaders once they are branded as impious.

Added to this blurred picture are the images that the pro-Western Arab regimes present to foreign observers of how they are transforming their political arena. In this undemocratic, uncommunicative environment, reports from the heart of Muslim societies have not been transmitted through the media without being sensationalised. The cracks in the foundations of regimes that are friends of the West are caused by the deformed echo of the repression they force on their Islamist opposition. In the Arab world itself, the systematic demonisation of Islam in opposition and the tendency to criminalise its manifestations are in part mitigated by the image of the Islamist activists in mosques, welfare associations and trade unions. But in the West, analysis is increasingly replaced by the discourse of the embattled regimes. Scarred by a violence that is more often than not perpetrated, as will be seen one day, by these regimes and not against them, the extremist dregs of the Islamist movement have been presented as its recognisable face, although this is far from being the case.

Those who had the privilege of attending Khomeini's funeral on 5 June 1989 were solemn. A huge, unruly crowd thronged around the large platform where the coffin lay. Overcome by the heat and by grief, they were doused with water by the Tehran fire department as a preventative measure against sunstroke. This distraction aside, the event was a wave of human emotion. Two television crews sought refuge on a container. Then, once again, the game of filming, of 'reporting', began. Whether the government or foreign television was filming, no-one could have conjured up, in such tragic circumstances, a picture of undiluted calm. In a radius of some tens of metres, these overheated bodies came alive, and excitement seized the small group. The close-up allows grotesque enlargements of the grimaces, while isolating them from the rest of the crowd, which, though moved, was entirely detached from this organised hysteria. No director could ignore such wonderful images and no editor could afford to lose them to another channel.

In Algeria in 1990, when kalashnikovs were not the currency, a few Shiite–Lebanese guns could nevertheless help to 'explain' Islamism in Algiers.[10] The day after the FIS electoral victory a few months earlier, 'frightened women' were anxiously sought in the Hotel Saint-Georges in Algiers – with considerable difficulty: there were social engagements to go to and dinners and drinks to attend.

The system feasts on facts and eschews hindsight. How do you describe 'nuance' for the news? How do you describe history in a two-minute piece?

The distorting lens of the outsider

In order to communicate with any sort of interlocutor, you do not approach his or her neighbours, and definitely not his or her enemies. It is far more effective to talk in person and preferably to make eye contact. So why is this generally not the case when discussing Islamism?

The itinerary of a foreign observer who has travelled to Cairo in order to understand Islamism consists predictably of a variety of meetings with mediators whose ratio, if not whose number, remains fairly constant: three government representatives, because first you must know the official version, then three Christians (are they not directly involved?) and finally three left-wing intellectuals. After all, many shared memories unite us with these frequently important faces from the Arab political class. The most intrepid will go as far as actually meeting one Islamist.[11] The demands of pluralism are in this way respected and the visitor leaves convinced that he has based his opinion on a broad sample of perceptions.

He will only have met the three staunchest political opponents of the Islamists – the three discourses that are most likely to discredit them. Yet he will leave without questioning his sample – he won't even think of it – 90 percent of which, in all probability, represents no more than a tenth of the population at a time when it is not inconceivable that Islamists account for nearly 90 percent of it. There are so many traps to avoid.

Media distortion reached new depths during the Algerian crisis in 1992. In the space of a few months, misinformation from the Algerians and the naivety and political will of the West combined to allow a handful of skilful communicators to acquire a virtual monopoly over the representation of the Algerian population on our television screens. It took many more months before a portion of public and intellectual opinion got wise to this particular embargo on information.

Even when more direct contact with Islamist figures is sought, they are chosen for their exotic dress or the radicalism of their discourse, not for their communication skills. If an Islamist is shown pointing his finger at the moon, then the West prefers to show only his finger. The literalism of the most radical leader of the FIS in Algeria, Ali Benhadj, is more prized than the subtle, elevated views of Malek Bennabi, who was one of Benhadj's first intellectual references. You will no longer find a 'proper' spokesman of the Egyptian Muslim Brotherhood in Assyut: its spokesman there is 'far too polite to be honest'. And when Abbassi Madani, the leader of the FIS, declares that he considers the choice of the language of a child's education to be sacred and entirely up to the parents, that his own children were brought up with the French language and that it is inconceivable that he would violate this essential freedom, the correspondents of all the press agencies present prefer to focus on an ironic denunciation of the fact that the children of a spokesman of Arab-Islamism have been partly educated in a foreign language.[12] The least repulsive expressions of Islamism are therefore systematically ignored, replaced by people viewed as more 'authentic', and certainly more in keeping with the unconscious expectations of public opinion.

When villages in upper Egypt are filmed for Western television, the distance between the viewer and the transmitter is in essence more social and cultural than truly 'political'. When the television channels claim that they are aware of the essence of the Islamist movement, they often elect to concentrate on its most frustrated fringes – the highly conservative peasants of remote rural areas in Egypt or young people in the suburbs of Algiers who have been expelled from university – without locating them in the social and cultural context of which they are the product. The former French television channel La Cinq was often to be found in the backstreet cafés of Marseilles sounding out the partisans of the FIS. What would happen if an Arab television station, wanting to inform its viewers of the opinion on Islam of an important French political grouping chose to broadcast at peak viewing time material recorded in a backstreet café? The authorised spokesmen of the Islamist movements, who can reduce these distances, are all-too-often viewed as too diplomatic, and are dismissed when they do not conform to the image expected of them.

Exoticism is thus guaranteed. But the value of the observation, which unconsciously leads the television viewer to transform a circumstantial expression of the phenomenon into its essence, is perhaps undermined. The differences between the two cultural environments, which are already considerable, if only because of the distance separating them, are artificially exaggerated. The radicalism of the most rural branch of the Egyptian Islamist movement, the Gama'a Islamiyya (which has strong support in upper Egypt) and the frustration of its activists cannot, however, be explained in the abstract. The natural reserve displayed by these men in the face of Cairene practices such as mixing of the sexes is, for example, largely shared by those secular activists who are brutally extracted from the rural context.

But the distortions also affect media other than television, which has an overwhelming demand for brevity. And they are not always unconscious. The author was once asked by a high-profile illustrated journal of political geography to provide a brief account of the Islamist movement in Egypt, which was printed at the top of a page that was left half blank – proving that there was no lack of space – and yet from which all references to repression were removed. And just for good measure, the article was illustrated by a photograph of the Sheraton Hotel, which was destroyed in 1990 by the foolhardiness of one of its service staff. The caption nevertheless read: 'Terrorist attacks are a way of shaking public opinion. Witness the bomb attack on the Sheraton Heliopolis Hotel in Cairo on 17 March 1990 that left 19 people dead.' The editorial of this special number on Egypt, however, sung the praises of 'the irreplaceable force of the sacred'. But only as long as the sacred is of the good pharaonic type, needed by the editorial writer to maximise the condemnation of the vile political ambitions of intolerant Islam.

When, on his return from Khartoum, a special correspondent sent by a large press agency concluded in May 1992 that the leadership of Omar al-Bashir and Hassan Turabi's regime in Sudan was perhaps less corrupt than that of its predecessors, his readers were never informed, for his despatch was twice amputated of such an incongruity. If one of this journalist's colleagues failed to uncover any sign of the thousands of Iranians that his magazine has asked him to track down in Sudan, his editor would abstain from printing conclusions of such low commercial value and any other article (which would be inevitably more nuanced) about the country to which he has been sent in search of 'news'. The hint of a comment on the economic situation, written for a research centre, will also be twisted beyond recognition before it reaches its destination. Confessional divisions will be portrayed as the sole cause of the political divisions in Sudan, and there will be no hesitation in implicating Omar al-Bashir's regime in international terrorism.[13]

Why is it that our political observers, so cautious when it comes to the electoral victory of the FIS, are so astonishingly short-sighted when Zein al-Abidine Ben Ali or Hosni Mubarak are elected by overwhelming majorities? If the subject is the repressive methods of the Tunisian[14] or the Egyptian head of state,[15] what possesses our media barons to adopt a system of information that even the Soviet Union (thanks to *perestroika*) managed to abolish?

It would be better to provide an explanation for, rather than to simply condemn, the difficulty that the West has in assessing the changes in the Arab world. Those who work at the heart of the academic scene are quick to draw attention to the gulf between the scholars, who 'know', and the journalists, who do not. This distinction not only presupposes a compartmentalisation which, thankfully, is far from straightforward, but also tends to mask a far more alarming reality. There is a profound differential of awareness that equally affects all levels of the relationship between the Western north and the Muslim south of the Mediterranean which is not confined to the media network. Beyond the specific constraints of televised information, the inability of the mass media to abandon sensationalism reveals the structural fragility of its own – and that of politicians and academics – capacity as a mediator between north and south. In the 1980s, if one takes account of the essential criteria of a command of the language, there were no more French political scientists capable of speaking Arabic than the already minimal number of diplomats. This tiny number of diplomats who could deal with written Arab sources was surely not much higher than the number of journalists, which was about the same as the number of businessmen or bankers, and so on.

As we know, the price that the West is today paying is simply the flip-side of its colonial policy. Between 1960 and 1980 France, buoyed up by the success of its policy of acculturation of the Arab elite and solely preoccupied with the economic dimension of relations between north and south, allowed the number of potential readers of the cultural reality in the Arab south of the Mediterranean to decline to the point of marginality. As a result, at the moment when this region of the world was expressing the need to reconnect with the mythical attributes of its pre-colonial culture, the vast majority of its interpreters in the West, who did not have a command of its language, tended to perceive this simple desire of the south to become once more (symbolically) distinct as aggression.

The political gossip market in France greeted the Islamist discourse with the same dangerous unanimity as the nationalist discourse before it. Today, the small number of those who shook the colonialist front in the 1950s and 1960s is remarkably less visible – all the more so because those who were politically and intellectually receptive in the face of the nationalist upsurge during the Algerian war have too often lived with the conviction that, because they had been on the right side of history once, they had definitively identified the elites born in this period as the only legitimate actors.

The political right has found in the Islamist spectre a confirmation of some of its old prejudices towards Islam, the Third World and Arabs. The Left is in principal more inclined to accept the emergence of the 'other', yet it too has made the most spectacular mistake: although it is capable of recognising Arabs, it loses its bearings and ability to be rational when dealing with Muslims. Its anticlericalism focuses on the religious content of a phenomenon. Once the left has retreated behind its supercilious (should one say fundamentalist?) attachment to the symbols of its 'secularism', it becomes incapable of admitting that the universalism of republican thought might be challenged in part or in whole, and that someone might one day dare to write a piece of history in a vocabulary that is not its own.

Since it is, above all, the rupture with Western political terminology that fuels the Islamist recipe, the potential for misunderstanding is enormous. Whoever tries to curb this misunderstanding often faces the fundamentalism of both north and south: they prefer to exploit rather than to restraint it.

Causes and effects

The course, the volume and the impact of a river on its environment depend entirely on the relief of the terrain that it runs through. Would we dare draw definitive conclusions about the nature of the water based on the level of noise as it flowed through rapids? What can be said about social scientists who base their perception of a complex phenomenon on such flimsy deductions? Trends that can be observed in the social environment or the political situation are often put forward as providing the key to an understanding of the Islamist movement. But there is often confusion between conjuncture and structure, essence and circumstance, cause and effect.

The cause of this methodological slip is the gap between the apparent unity of Islamic rhetoric and the extreme diversity of their followers. For example, on the question of the existence of an absolute being of celestial origin, the answer given by the sacred texts will in practice depend on the individual who reads them and the attitude of the political environment towards them. The misunderstanding is exacerbated by the fact that these religious references are either self-proclaimed (from within) or are just as well rapidly considered as intangible and immaterial (from without). But the apparent unity of the Islamic references has never prevented a multi-dimensional reading: Islam is, above all, what a majority of Muslims say it is. In reality, it is therefore Islamist individuals who have created Islamism, rather than the other way round. It is the characteristics rather than the emblematic slogans of the Islamists that define their methods of political expression. These characteristics are extremely diverse and, as a result of development policies, they are affected by a constant dynamic of change.

The resurgence of certain parts of Islamic culture means that there is not just one but an infinite variety of political attitudes and ways of being Islamist. When one artificially removes the whirlpools of the Islamist river from the context which triggered them, one deprives oneself of the ability to understand that, a few kilometres downstream, or a few years on, in another social climate or political conjuncture, the same river might well be used for irrigation or transport, or that the same movement might well be integrated, and indeed modernised. Depending on the nature of the social environment that it affects, on the political forces that have adopted Islamism, but also how regimes react to it, the Islamist upsurge is expressed on a multitude of levels, employing many extremely different courses of action, which should not be seen as unique or eternal.

The violent rhetoric of the Egyptian Sayyed Qutb, who while in prison witnessed the elimination of most of his companions – under torture – before he himself was hanged after a show trial, was largely the result of the hostility of the state, led by Nasser, towards him. This hostility hardened his analyses to the extent that he refused to speak to his torturers, then to the regime that supported them and finally separated himself from practically everyone else. The fact that before the repression, the associations of the Muslim Brotherhood, of which he was a member, had completely different views, is overlooked, and today the alpha and omega of Islamist thought is persistently seen in terms of what was in reality mostly a reactive posture, circumscribed in time and space.

During the 1990s the fact that political openness has been replaced by repression throughout the Arab world is a major contributory factor to the radicalisation of the Islamist movements. The violence of the FIS, which is more than mere 'Islamist violence', is above all a reaction to the ruthless attempts by the Algerian military to cling to power, and of the short-sightedness of the West which helped them to do so. The confessional violence that regularly erupts on the banks of the River Nile should not be used to build a universal, intangible model of Islamism any more than the ruptures of the bloody war of succession in Algeria. It would be a grave mistake to forget that the bottle-smashers (of alcohol) of the Gama'a Islamiyya are above all the product of the social environment and political conjecture of the semi-rural region of upper Egypt in the 1970s and 1980s, where they were born and from which, thanks to the carelessness of some political analysts, they have never, metaphorically, managed to emerge. There is absolutely no reason to interpret their terms of reference, their modes of expression or behaviour as functioning within the framework of the Quran – which is universally applicable and geographically unconstrained. They are products of a context, not of a universal Islamist principle.

Victims of growth?

The secondary origins of the Islamist upsurge have too often been portrayed as the essence of the phenomenon. Are the Islamists really a mere product of the crumbling of Arab economies? Are they not the 'rejected of the development process', the product of the combination of inflation and unemployment which characterises Middle Eastern economies?

It is certainly not inconceivable – far from it – that the frustrated issue of identity came to the fore sooner in the de-structured universe inhabited by those who have endured the disturbing effects of modern-isation before experiencing integration. The 'mal-modernised' and the 'mal-urbanised' ranks of the middle classes were thrown into a world far removed from that into which they were socialised, were given television before they were guaranteed a say in at least a part of its output, and so on.

The unrest caused by the policies of structural adjustment and privatisation – to which the Arab economies committed themselves for several years in order to gain or maintain favour with the International Monetary Fund (IMF) and the World Bank – the fall in the purchasing power of most of the population that resulted, the structural limitations of public policies (notably infrastructure, housing, health, education and employment), the aggravation caused by administrative negligence, and finally the demographic explosion that sabotages any real progress, have all combined to keep millions of suburban dwellers from Cairo to Casablanca on the brink of the 'Fourth World', while the millions who are their rural counterparts are left to live in a pre-modern state. This loss of social status, not simply a question of economics, which has resulted from the crisis in the rentier state, fuels the emergence of the demand for an identity: who am I, if I am not given the right to exist by working?

The Islamist upsurge also mobilises against elite social groups which have little power. But when clientelism is a strong trait in a regime, and when, moreover, there is a rentier economy, the further away from power you stand, the less access you have to the benefits it distributes. It is therefore true to say that a difference of social status separates the anti-Islamist elite in power (who are sometimes rashly labelled as secularists) from the (Islamist) opposition who challenge them, and that poverty may radicalise this movement.

It is therefore undeniable that there is an economic dimension to the conflict between the secularists and the Islamists, or rather, for some at least, between those in power and those who are not in power. But it is dangerous for an analysis to place too much emphasis on a conjunctural split, linking the emergence of the Islamist generation to the decline of Arab economies in order to comprehend a process that is essentially a question of identity. The economic reading therefore supports the falsehood that, because one is poor, one is not only in opposition but also an Islamist, and would become not only law-abiding but also secular if one was not so poor.

The robust social and professional health of entire sections of the Islamist movement – particularly of the Muslim Brotherhood in Egypt and Jordan, which are strongly represented in the liberal professions, and also of the technocratic wing of the FIS – and the number of its leaders who stand as members of parliament, underlines the limitations of this equation. It would also be incorrect to think that the political struggles between regimes and oppositions in the Arab world today (that is secularism versus Islamism) are purely ideological. In fact, the ruling *nomenklatura* are increasingly concerned with protecting their privileges rather than any ideology. By using forecasters of social trends who discourse on the television, and intermediary *'ulama*, the regimes themselves do not hesitate to exploit religion, and do so in a fashion which is not necessarily any more modernist or liberal than their Islamist opponents.

The economic view of the Islamist surge is similar to the error made by those of the French who were convinced that the Constantine Plan, launched in 1958 by General de Gaulle, could weaken the nationalist upsurge in Algeria. This error remains a pillar of the rhetoric of the Arab regimes and, more troubling, it is shared by the vast majority of international observers who hope that booming Arab economies will cast off the Islamist millstone.

The refusal by all these regimes to recognise the profoundly endogenous character of the Islamist upsurge has meant that, together with their allies, they have systematically and readily intervened in the affairs of their neighbours. Algeria, for example, has for a long time wanted to believe that Sadat had his hand in the initial Islamist unrest. Was it not Sadat who, having released members of the Muslim Brotherhood from the prisons in which Nasser had locked them away, unwisely flooded the Arab labour market, allowing some of those men to contaminate an Algerian university that had sought to import the majority of its teachers once the Arab-speaking departments of its universities were created?[16]

In Egypt, moreover, if it was not the confrontation between the Muslims and the Copts that produced Islamism, then it must have been migration to Saudi Arabia, whose petrodollars allowed it to impose the Wahhabi model and where Egyptian teachers first grew accustomed to that deplorable habit of wearing the *hijab*.[17] Pakistan also exported the ideas of the founding father of Islamism, Abu'l-Ala al-Mawdudi[18] with his armies of Tablighis;[19] Lebanon's neighbour Iran imposed Hizbullah on it. Palestine, moreover, is not so far from contaminated Lebanon. Tunisia is paying the price for sharing a border with Algeria, which did not put a stop to the activities of the FIS early enough. What does it matter if the vast majority of Islamists supported Riyadh's Iraqi enemy, conclusively proving the limits of Saudi authority over the Islamists? What does it matter if the corrupt regime of the guardians of the Islamic holy places are on the blacklist of many Islamist movements? Saudi Arabia, with its well-known financial influence, is seen as the 'conductor' of the world Islamist 'orchestra', a role that the Saudi princes have probably dreamed of, but which today has no relationship to reality.

The other great sorcerers of Islamism would be those heads of state, few in number because it would be playing with fire, who committed the culpable error of not immediately fighting evil. Supported by historical revelations, the Arab left constantly reminds us that the Islamist phenomenon came about because of the negligence of these unflinching presidents who were busy trying to stamp out Marxism. Bourguiba and Sadat were responsible for having encouraged the Islamists to oppose their left-wing opposition, which to a certain degree is absolutely correct, and are in this way made responsible for the entire Islamist dynamic, which is wholly inaccurate.

To see in the process of re-Islamisation only the negative effects of what some regard as an error of political conduct, and others see as an economic crisis, a repressive conjuncture or foreign manipulation (by the Saudis or the Iranians and also, for the less scrupulous, by the US), is to overlook the essential ingredients (the plurality, the ambivalence, the historicity and the dynamics) of a political movement. All the interpretative keys needed to decipher a complex logic are missing. There is in all this a risk of courting a double impasse: a methodological impasse for those who provide analysis and a political impasse for those who feed decision-making.

The Islamist formula, as the author will attempt to show, is both more sophisticated and rather more balanced.

CHAPTER TWO

From Nationalism to Islamism

You cannot be seriously nationalist if you are not completely open to Islam. For Islam is the very identity of this nation.

Adel Hussein

One is born an Islamist, or one becomes an Islamist. The transition or return from secularism to 'religious' thought, as related by those who have experienced it, is sometimes a better indication than analytical discourse of the determinations that feed the Islamist dynamic, which, from one individual to another, are both different and comparable. It is here that we can see the divisions as well as the agreements and disagreements with other ideologies.

But confusion must be avoided: neither the Egyptians Adel Hussein and Tareq al-Bishri, nor even the Tunisian Rached Ghannouchi are representative of the majority of groups who have never abandoned the Islamic reference. But perhaps it is this relative marginality that makes their path more revealing. Whereas the demarcation of power is masked by the discourse of the 'lifelong' Islamists, which is sometimes obscured by traditionalism, but which is often less rigorous in its representation of the Western secularism it defines itself against, the path of the 'converts', even if it is not the path of the majority of the actors on the scene, tends on the contrary to explain them.

When in 1980 Bishri launched a spectacular re-reading of the system of references which until then had structured his thinking in the introduction to the third edition of his work *The Political Movement in Egypt*, the echo of this flight from secular nationalism was hardly noticed beyond Egyptian intellectual circles.[1] For Bishri over the past few years 'the fight is no longer defined as a conflict between "progress" and "reaction", but between "the endogenous" and the "exogenous", "the inherited" and "the imported", the Arab–Muslim legacy and Western influences'.[2] Re-examined more than a decade later, the itinerary through which the Egyptian writer-jurist, vice-president of the State Council, came to gradually refute his secular culture in favour of that of his former political enemy, the Muslim Brotherhood organisation, is a particularly good example of how a large number of Arab intellectuals came to adopt Islamist themes rather than those of secular nationalism.

The itinerary of Rached Ghannouchi, the leader of the Tunisian Renaissance Party (hizb al-Nahda, formerly the MTI), consists for its part of a first marked moment of 'Tunisianism', then a phase of transition (from secular Arabism to Islamism) closer to the 'universal' process of the formation of an Islamist intellectual.[3] At the beginning came the shock of the secularisation and the linguistic Gallicisation determinedly imposed by Habib Bourguiba immediately after national independence. In Tunisia, as elsewhere, these policies were adopted even though they clashed strongly with the cultural codes of the majority of the population, including the elite. This process has its parallels in the rest of the Arab world, but in Tunisia, where the linguistic dimension of identity is more particularly explicit and more advanced, it is marked by a greater degree of specificity. It is this which, since independence, has fuelled what Ghannouchi refers to as this 'army of Bourguiba's victims'. There is no strict equivalent in the Algerian situation – where, during the colonial period, the linguistic deculturation of the elite was much more complete, nor in the Arab East – where linguistic deculturation was much less marked – nor even in Morocco, where independence did not seem to divide regime and popular religious culture.

The mechanism of disconnection from the semantics of secular nationalism, gradually associated with Western symbolism, and of recon-ciliation with religious culture, perceived as alone capable of satisfying the demand for identity, mark out the paths close to the Islamist 'constant', at the very least for all those (that is to say nearly everyone in the Maghreb and a very large number in the Mashreq) political militants of this generation who once belonged to a universe other than that of religious thought.

The path of Hussein, presently the Secretary of the Egyptian Labour Party, who was imprisoned for nearly 11 years as a communist militant, is similar to that of Bishri. But his itinerary is more explicitly political than intellectual. The brother of the founder of the Young Egypt Party, one of the first expressions of Egyptian nationalism (apart from the Muslim Brotherhood) to promote Muslim values, he made a long detour through Marxism before rejoining a trajectory already perceptible in the politics of his elder brother. It was to be, notably, the 'ideological dependence' on the Soviet Union induced by membership of the communist world which would shake the Marxist certainties of a militant nationalist.

There are others besides Hussein, Ghannouchi and Bishri in the Islamist movement. But they undoubtedly help to understand the contours of its most determining ingredient: identity.

Tareq al-Bishri: From the 'popular' to the 'endogenous'[4]

I was born in 1933. My political and cultural awareness was formed towards the end of the Second World War, between the ages of twelve and twenty. I first became interested in politics when I was a student at university. Egyptians were absorbed in the question of national independence. Everyone's dream was to see the country liberated. What are the elements of independence? What does it consist of? I believe that, from this point of view, the Egyptian national movement went through many stages. At first it sought only political independence and wanted Egyptian soil to be free of foreign occupation. This is why the nationalist movement grew in Egypt from the turn of the twentieth century until the end of the First World War.

To this initial vision, the movement later added the idea of *economic* independence and began to demand independent economic development without which political decision-making could not be free. It is during this period that the Islamist movement began to challenge the nationalist movement. The Islamist movement was based on *legitimate foundations*. In the 1930s and 1940s, this contradiction was witnessed in the struggle between the Muslim Brothers and the Wafd. The Islamist movement added a third dimension to the independence movement: it invited society to return to the values that had previously dominated it and to Islam as a source of legitimacy and social regulation. After the emergence of the secular nationalist movement, this is what the Islamist movement represented.

The reason why there were no Muslim Brothers during the period of Mustafa Kamal before the First World War is because the nationalism of Mustafa Kamal was expressed in the language of Islam and not the language of secularism. After the war, the liberation movement began to adopt Western references. It came to be an incarnation of the values of modernity, which it regarded as the basis for the construction of societies and the ultimate reference for their way of life.

At first, I belonged to the nationalist movement. Political and economic independence was the priority until the defeat in 1967. This defeat was extremely significant, and remains so to this today. It forced us to reconsider the very foundations of our system of thought and all our presuppositions. After this catastrophe, everything had to be re-examined. One of the many essential questions that had to be addressed was the role of religion as a central element in the social system, of its development, and of its internal cohesion. I slowly came to realise that the Islamist movement was in fact continuing the political and economic independence movement on the cultural level. I didn't think so until 1967. It was 1967 and what ensued that made me look at things differently.

I wrote about this intellectual journey in my book, *The Political Movement in Egypt*. The first edition did not have a preface. The book was the product of a secular and nationalist review of social and political forces, of the country's future and of the situation of the time. Then, in the second edition, I took my new experience into account, that is to say the link between religion and the social question and the manner in which I had slowly adopted this vision. I had realised that Islam was an essential ingredient. If the future of the country demanded it, it was Islam which would make us capable of sacrifices; it was by relying on Islam that we would be able to have a future at the expense of the present, whatever the sacrifices that were necessary in order to overcome the obstacles of the moment, whatever, at first, the number of hindrances to this economic and social renaissance. I do not think that humankind is capable of rising to the challenges of history without a psychological underpinning which enables it to accept self-renunciation in favour of the motherland, renunciation of the demands of the present in favour of the future. In the nineteenth century, all the nationalist movements were based on Islam. I began to understand the language that they used to deal with the realities that they were living. I began to understand how they managed to convince people to reduce their material desires to build a better future [...].

Gradually, I began to reconsider the vocabulary of political discourse and that of thought itself in its intervention in reality. I began to reconsider the relation of religious thought to reality. I found that there was a link with the question of national belonging and that it, on the whole, had something to do with Muslim religious thought to which it was linked. Gradually, I also took account of a particular aspect of the constitution of various social institutions. To me, society seemed to be made up of institutions, themselves subdivided into sub-units sheltering individual activity and organising the mass of humanity in their bosom. I realised that the cement of these different entities, which make up the institutional fabric of society, was religious thought. It became apparent, for example, that the evolution of certain professional strata coincided with that of the Sufi movement and with the social institutions implanted in the popular neighbourhoods. This configuration gave society a sort of decentralisation and permitted individuals to belong to the primary micro-societies within which they were living, while inscribing them in an increasingly wide network of belonging. When religious membership was attacked, it was this network of institutions that was attacked and annihilated rather than improved. The social fabric was ripped to shreds. I think it is very difficult to build a society with isolated individuals. The individual must necessarily enter a network of increasingly large communities. Without this interweaving of intermediary social groupings, he can in no way enter into a relationship with the state. The loss of primordial attachments has thus affected all higher attachments. It has affected the capacity of the state itself to manage people's affairs as well as the ability of the individual to belong to the general entity.

I then realised that it was necessary to review everything, that Muslim thought could allow us to form institutions at all levels of activity and human interaction. These were the lessons of the 1967 crisis: defeat forced us to question everything. The result was that throughout the 1970s, during which I wrote my book *The Muslims and the Copts*, I experienced serious difficulties in making rapid progress. I began to publish a series of studies in *Majallat al-Katib*, from 1971 to 1974. The initial idea was to write three or four studies on the question, but the more I pursued my investigations, the more I wrote. I decided to finish, and stopped writing completely from 1974. I then became interested in a whole range of matters without managing to shake off the subject that was preoccupying my thoughts.

From 1977 to 1979, the idea of a return to narrow Egyptianism resurfaced. I personally had faith in Arabism. And, in my discussions outside intellectual circles, the fundamental argument that linked the Egyptian man to Arabism was Islam. No other evidence was taken seriously. I remember that I concluded a symposium in Beirut with the words, 'coming from Cairo, I can say that nothing protects the Arabism of an Egyptian better than Islam.' At that moment, I truly felt something very profound, which had a considerable impact and in which could be found the answers to many questions that man was asking.

Rached Ghannouchi: From Arabism to Islamism[5]

15 June 1966. On that night, I took the final decision to pass from the world of Arab nationalism and Nasserism to Islam.

It is not easy to put a finger on the precise path from one intellectual and ideological universe to another, and all that that implies in the transformation of human relations.

In many respects, this change, especially in its initial phase, was the equivalent for me of passing from one world into another. From one thought, one ideology, one system of relations, one itinerary, to another world, new ideas, new values and new relations. It was a brutal rebirth.

For my part, I can certainly describe the context of the events that took place, but it is not easy for me to reconstruct the exact chain of facts, to distance myself from them so that I can see them as if they were a film. The most important events occur within the soul, in a way that may even be subconscious. How did all that happen? How did I come to this change? All I know is that it happened at a moment that I can identify precisely: the night of 15 June 1966.

That night I made my final decision to move from the universe of Arab nationalism and Nasserism to that of Islam. This discovery constituted a kind of seismic shock for me. I realised I was not a Muslim. I discovered I was a stranger to Islam.

The 'army of Bourguiba's victims'...

I nevertheless had a very religious upbringing. My father was one of those who had learnt the whole of the Quran. He prayed with his family and spread incense around the house, as very religious people do. He was not a professional in religion, he was a simple peasant, but he taught the Quran to everyone in the village [...].

Afterwards, I received a religious education at Zeitouna University. But this education did not help at all in giving my conscience roots in the value of Islam and its capacity to organise existence. In order for you to understand this properly I should add that, with the return of Bourguiba from exile, Tunisia entered upon a period of change.

In reality, Bourguiba's victory was more a victory over Arabic and Islamic civilisation in Tunisia than a victory over the French occupiers. Bourguiba came as a conqueror, and like the foreign invaders he took power. Then he began targeting religious institutions, the institutions that were the very life of Tunisia. At this time, everything revolved around the University of Zeitouna: traditional craftsmanship, Tunisian literature, and all thought. In a sense, all of Tunisia was produced at the Zeitouna. So this brutal blow against these institutions constituted a blow against the social, economic and cultural structure of the whole of Tunisia. For those who had been raised in an Arab and Muslim culture – the majority of Tunisian intellectuals who came out of the educational institutions affiliated to the Zeitouna – recognised the link between Arabism and Islam. They added weight to the importance of Arabic language and literature, the roots of Arab-Islamic belonging in Tunisia, which breathed into the spirit of resistance to foreign invasion [...] and served as a kind of shield for it against Europe.

The attack on religious institutions was one of the first decisions taken after independence. My generation thus felt excluded, alienated and ostracised. We constituted an Arab–Islamic base and the country was in the process of Westernisation: administration, culture, the university, education, the arts, and literature were all Westernising. People wondered if they were really living in their own country. It was necessary, as Bourguiba used to say, 'to do everything to catch up with the march of civilisation,' to integrate oneself, to blend in with the Western environment. All they asked of this generation was that it abandon its identity and beliefs in order to merge with the new world into which Bourguiba was throwing Tunisia. Even those who had studied at the Zeitouna, sensing that there was no longer a future for Arab–Islamic culture, started to send their children to the Lycée Carnot, or to Sadiqi or one of the foreign institutions.

This stirred up unrest among the graduates of these institutions, as well as inferiority complexes and feelings of alienation. There was nothing left for them to do except withdraw and to regroup and to try to control their rancour at this occupation. Although no longer a foreign occupation (by the French), it was still an occupation (by the 'Tunisian sons of France'), and it was more brutal than that of the French. They were at least openly declared as such in front of us […].

For the generation reared on Arab–Islamic culture, which studied at the Zeitouna and the traditional institutions, Tunisia's Westernisation was a violent experience. This generation had been repressed. It was the victim of violence. But this generation represented the majority. At independence, there were about 25,000 to 27,000 people attending institutions affiliated to the Zeitouna. There were between 4,500 and 5,000 studying at the secondary schools created under the French occupation. So it was the majority who felt marginalised by the minority. Secularism or Westernisation did not in any way represent a popular movement. It was an effective minority, which had been able to marginalise the majority because it could understand the West and understand foreigners and communicate with the new international order. The majority did not have that knowledge, so it was intellectually marginalised. It was the same for this entire social economic substratum which depended more or less directly on the Zeitouna, on the traditional crafts sector which surrounded the Zeitouna, and also on the sector of the *waqfs* and the property of the *habous* which represented an important part of landed property. About a quarter of the agricultural land in Tunisia was attached to the *waqfs* and in particular to the Zeitouna […].

So, by striking at the Zeitouna, or the economic institutions that financed it, they were destroying society. The generation that attended these institutions was like a defeated army. All that was left for it was to melt into the new army. But to do that it had to crawl out of its own skin. Either it could withdraw, and close in on itself, or it could resist, or go into exile. Many of my generation were attracted to the East. If the new international order which Bourguiba represented in Tunisia, and its representatives, drew their legitimacy from the West, those who rejected the violence of this forced change turned towards the East, towards the sources of Islamic and Arabic thought, where they sought support. Besides, there had just been several upheavals in the East, notably the *coup d'état*, which afterwards became known as the revolution, of Gamal Abdel

Nasser. This revolution exalted Arabist ideas, Arab unity and resistance to the international order. The Zeitounians consequently had a special vocation to be Nasserists, they were Nasserists 'by nature.'

In Nasserism they found the moral support they were seeking without seeing the secular dimension or the fact that it was another expression of nationalism: in the Maghreb, the distinction between Islam and Arabism had never been made. The Zeitouna preached an Arabic Islam or a Muslim Arabism without distinction. In North Africa, Islamisation and Arabisation were equal. All the foreign aggression in Tunisia was simultaneously aimed at Arabism and Islam, as it was elsewhere in Algeria. The sense of Arab belonging was even more entrenched in religion since there are no religious minorities in the Maghreb, and since the region was not Arab before it became Muslim. North Africa encountered Arabism at the same time as Islam. So Arabism had no other cultural identity except the Muslim one. The regions of the Arab East were Arabised before becoming Muslim. There were Arab tribes who were Christian and remained so, and others who converted to Islam. In the Arab East, Arabism, on the whole, was perceived as predating Islam. It was sometimes feared that using the Islamic reference would lead to a kind of segregation. In North Africa, however, the absence of minorities meant that the problem never arose.

I have already said that, in this context, life weighed heavily on me. I felt profoundly alienated. I often went to the gardens outside my village and spent many hours reading the news and novels. The radio? Yes, I listened to Sawt al-'Arab, especially the radio stations of the Mashreq. I read Naguib Mahfouz and Tawfiq al-Hakim. After graduating from the Zeitouna, I stayed on for a year and a half as a teacher, but it wasn't for me. I was filled with this feeling of alienation (*ightirab*) my generation felt. We felt a strong nostalgia for the sources of Islam and the Arabism of the Mashreq. So in 1964, I left for Egypt.

... In search of lost Arabism

The discovery of Egypt? My point of view did not really change. Of course, what had led me to reject Bourguibism, Egyptian literature, the songs of Umm Kalthoum, Abdelwahab and Farid al-Atrash, or Radio Egypt and the speeches of Nasser, disappeared when I arrived in Cairo. At first I had enormous difficulties in enrolling in the university. There were about forty people from North Africa, and we were not part of an official group. We only met each other here. We came by land, across Libya. Everyone was searching for them-selves [...] The government of Bourguiba hated Tunisian students going to universities in the Mashreq. They were afraid that they would be influenced by Nasserist, Ba'thist or Arabist 'madness'. A few official groups had nevertheless been sent to Syria, but our group was not that lucky. It had been chased out. All escapees from the Zeitouna, we came from the ranks of the army of those

defeated by Bourguiba in search of a new army to join, and to do this we had
come to the real intellectual and spiritual centres.

Strictly speaking, it was not a political decision. It was the result of a
confused feeling of alienation, the search for a better life, to be a part of the
great centres of belonging. It was a sort of return to authenticity [...] As the
Tunisian University had adopted French, the graduates from the Zeitouna had
no other choice but to enter the faculty of theology in Tunis. I took courses
there for a while, but I wanted to learn science and [for Arabic speakers] that
was not possible at the university. So, the rest of the Zeitounians went to the
Mashreq, and especially to Cairo, Syria and Iraq. Most obtained diplomas in
science, mathematics, polytechnics and medicine.

In Egypt, I lived in Agouza, with some friends from my village who were
studying there. We spent two or three months trying to enrol in the University
of Cairo. The administrative routine, the bureaucracy ... We even staged a
demonstration in front of Nasser's house to demand our rights to enrol in
Egypt, and after intense pressure, we succeeded. I chose the faculty of agri-
culture. I planned to spend my life improving conditions for the peasants in my
village, whose methods were very backward. Farming was hard notably because
of the lack of water. I had to help my father. I even had to interrupt my studies
at the Zeitouna. But that only lasted four months.

Egyptian society is very difficult for me to talk about since I was never truly
integrated. I did not have a chance to integrate. I spent most of my time trying
to settle in, trying to enrol in the university, to take the steps to enter the
university. The only place I visited was Alexandria. At this period, I had not
found in Egypt what I was looking for. I thought I would find enthusiastic
Egyptians all mobilised behind Nasser. But I found a people who were more
involved with their daily life. The mobilisation, the songs, the discourse of the
radio - it was a façade, a media enthusiasm on command which did not respond
to the realities on the street.

In any case, this stage was over very quickly. Egypt and Tunisia broke off
diplomatic relations. Cairo had supported Saleh Ben Youssef in his conflict
with Bourguiba. Bourguiba had appealed to the French army and Ben Youssef
to Nasser. That was one of the reasons for Bourguiba's violent bitterness
towards Nasser and Arab nationalists and the entire Mashreq and Arabism.
One of the reasons at least. The important point is that, when bilateral
relations were restored, the Tunisian embassy in Egypt came looking for us to
tell us that we were no longer welcome in Egypt. And it pressured the Egyptian
administration to have us thrown out of the university. After all our efforts to
enrol, we were barred in one fell swoop. The embassy asked us to return home,
as one part of our group did. The victorious army of Bourguiba even followed
the escapees, those who fled. And it managed to get us expelled from Egypt.
We either had to accept capture, return home or flee somewhere else. So I left
for Syria. I almost went to Albania. How did I live? I had taken some money

from Tunisia. I had worked as a teacher and had saved around 500 Tunisian *dinars* that I took with me and spent bit by bit. In Egypt, I made do with plates of *fuul* and *ta'miyya* in order to spend as little as possible.

From Arabism to Islamism

In Syria on the other hand we had no problem enrolling. The university was independent of the state. A little later the minister of education gave us grants. All the Tunisian students received one. It wasn't much but it was enough. Damascus is not a big city like Cairo. A foreigner could find himself there more easily and could integrate more easily into the environment. Living costs were low then. Those who had been sent by the Tunisian minister received a comfortable grant. When Bourguiba made his famous journey to the Mashreq after the reconciliation, we went to meet him in Beirut and he agreed to award a grant to everyone, which he announced during the famous speech at Ariha. Unfortunately, as in this famous speech he had called for the recognition of Israel and for the respect of the division of 1948, Arab public opinion, especially Syrian, rebelled. There was a riot, the Tunisian embassy was burnt down, relations between Syria and Tunisia were again broken and the grants were suspended. An emissary came to ask us to leave this country whose regime was hostile to Tunisia, and to return home. Some did, the majority refused.

What was the political climate among the Tunisian students? Apart from a few Bourguibians who had kept in touch with the embassy, there was of course a quasi-consensus against the regime. We were all victims of Bourguiba's war against Islam and Arabism. The liberal period had not yet finished. Socialism and Ba'thism had not yet destroyed Syrian society. It was in fact the beginning of the Ba'thist experience and economic liberalism still produced prosperity in the country. The university still enjoyed cultural and political freedom. All the political currents were represented and there was still dialogue and political and intellectual debate. We began to take part. The great debate of the period ranged the Ba'thists against the Nasserists. Egypt and Syria had not yet separated. The principal preoccupation and central theme of the Nasserists was the restoration of the unitary state. Given my Nasserist background, which I had acquired in Tunisia, I easily integrated myself into this current.

There was no real difference between the Ba'thists and the Nasserists. The discovery that the Nasserists and Ba'thists were arguing for poor and futile reasons and the intellectual progress that allowed me to study philosophy were two of the reasons for my late metamorphosis. Philosophy led me to question everything, including the effective content of words: what exactly is 'Arabism'? What does 'unity' or 'socialism' mean? The atmosphere of permanent political debate meant that our slogans were charged with more than their content.

The debate took place on two levels, between the Nasserists and Ba'thists and also between members of the Tunisian community. The Tunisian group was divided between the minority who remained Bourguibist and the majority, which was split between Ba'thism and Nasserism. The debate between these two groups was very intense. Most of the debates took place in the League of Tunisian Students. There were elections, confrontations: a complete political life. And each party prepared an electoral campaign, proposing their programme. The Nasserists were in the majority. The Bourguibists only had a marginal role and there was not a single Tunisian Islamist in the League. As far as I can remember, out of a group of 150 students, only one or two performed prayers. That was in 1965. Prayer did not figure in philosophical or general political discussions. The struggle concerned one's attitude to the Tunisian regime and it was not just between Tunisians. It equally opposed all representations of Arab nationalism on one side and the Islamists on the other. The Islamists at the Syrian university had a large mosque which held a Friday sermon and they could count among their ranks several famous personalities, official or not; those with the most magnetic personality were of course 'unofficial'. At that time in Syria, they were either Muslim Brothers or members of the Islamic Liberation Party. They were the teachers at the university, the great teachers of the Shari'a faculty. So the dialogue took place between these two currents. What did it deal with? The foundation of the debate was almost always political. We debated the attitude to adopt towards different regimes and to the Palestinian question.

The discourse of the Muslim Brothers at the time concentrated essentially on the condemnation of Arab nationalism, because it was secular. They blamed secularism for the loss of Palestine, for political, moral and economic corruption. In opposition, the discourse of the Nasserists or the Ba'thists against the Muslim Brothers accused them of being a reactionary current tied to colonialism, to the Americans. This kind of progressivism was tied to Eastern Europe and so it called the Muslim Brothers Americans, valets of America, supposedly anti-progressive, reactionaries, etc...

Saudi Arabia was not a player at this time. It still had no part in the religious struggle, which only came after the oil revolution, when it found it could print religious books with its point of view and affirm its presence in Islamic circles. At this time, the great ideological references were Egypt, Syria, Pakistan and Abu'l Ala al-Mawdudi.

The Islamic Liberation Party concentrated on the question of the return to the caliphate. At first, it was only a minority. It was a *salafi* [fundamentalist] current that demanded the return to the sources of religion. Its sheikh, Nasser Al-Din al-Albani, was a man of great importance and is still considered today in the Muslim world as a great orator. Today he must be eighty years old and he lives in Jordan. The name of Said Ramadan al-Buti must be added to the list of leading figures in the field of religious thinking.

At this time, some Nasserists began to doubt the premises of Arab nationalism, which they accused of having a non-Arab content, of only being formally Arab. As one of the ingredients of the debate consisted of accusing Arab nationalism of having a Western, non-Islamic content, minimising and criticising Western civilisation was naturally a part of the argument. It is in this context that all the works which gave credit to the Islamist position took their value: Islamic civilisation was showing all the symptoms of the diseases that affected Western civilisation. Modernisation had not only given us Western science and technology, but also its maladies.

One of the most widely read books was *L'Homme, cet inconnu* written by Alexis Carrel, a doctor. The book was perhaps not well known in France, but it was at the centre of the literature of the Islamists at that time. Sayyed Qutb himself often used it to criticise Western civilisation and to show the misfortunes of Western man, the degradation of the family and social relationships, or the international relations it has initiated. There was also Spengler's book and Toynbee's writings as well as *The Fall of Civilisation*, written by an Englishman whose name I can't remember, and many others.

Another factor that prepared me to accept the criticism of Arab nationalism as being more Western than Islamic was my trip to Europe. Having studied philosophy in Damascus, from January to June 1965, I left Syria with a group of friends for Europe, Turkey, Bulgaria, Yugoslavia, Austria, Germany, France, etc. I worked to earn some money so that I could move on. I finally came back to Syria in January of the following year. Most of the time I stayed in youth hostels. There I could talk to all sorts of people. I returned to Syria with the impression that Western youth was living in a sort of confusion. That undoubtedly prepared me to admit the criticism of Western civilisation [which contained in it the arguments of the adversaries of Arab nationalism]. This trip and the attitude of the young Europeans I met in the youth hostels made it more acceptable.

The Islamist discourse derived its strength from its very simple résumé of the West and by relativising many distinctions which for others were essential. The debate between capitalism and socialism, West and East, no longer meant much. At the end of the day, there was still only one West. For a young person, the very fact of breaking intellectual categories constituted a revolutionary act. He discovered that men live in injustice and that many of the usual ways of distinguishing between things, and political trends, were in the last instance impossible to make and therefore fraudulent. This discourse told the different groups ranged in conflict, the Nasserists, the Ba'thists or the liberals: 'You are all in the same boat. Your references are European and not nationalist, and in the last instance, on an intellectual level, you are nothing but the agents of this West.' And that was also a revolution, because the Nasserists at the time considered themselves the representatives of a grandiose revolution.

The Ba'thists and the Nasserists fought each other over formal, futile questions. We told them: 'Deep down, you are just agents of Western civilisation.

You have no authenticity and this is why you have always failed. And you will fail in the struggle against Israel. You will fail.'

And in fact, when the war of 1967 broke out, while I was in Damascus, the young Ba'thists were convinced that they were going to spend the summer on the beaches of Tel Aviv. It was an absolute certainty. They had faith in Ba'thism and their faith was unshakeable. The Islamist discourse, on the contrary, said the opposite, that defeat was inevitable because an ideology such as Nasserism could never bring victory. The Islamist discourse was significantly bolstered by the defeat.

My intellectual mutation to Islamism had already been completed. The most important moment, the key factor for me was a sort of internal explosion. It made me realise that our belief in Arabism was in conflict with Islam, and that I had been fooled for a long time; I had believed in an Arabism for which I was prepared to die but which was in fact opposed to the Islam which had nourished me and of which I was proud. This discovery was difficult for me. I started to experience a feeling of tension with my previous Nasserist culture. I had risen from being an ordinary member to a position where I was responsible for a cell of seven or eight people, meeting in private. I initiated a debate on the relation between Arabism and religion. The members of the cell did not manage to convince me. They then asked the party the same question. They regularly sent someone to talk to me. In the end, I agreed to stay in the party on the condition that faith in God was considered as a condition of membership, even for Christians. They made the excuse that there were Christians among them and I told them, 'Even Christians believe in God, so why not make faith one of the elements of joining the party?' They said: 'We are a party that does not make a relationship between religion and politics,' 'Religion belongs to God and the country belongs to everyone', etc...

When our discussions reached that point, I was convinced that I had been mistaken for too long and that the years of enthusiasm and struggle were founded on an illusion. I felt like someone who had turned their back on his family, his education, his civilisation and who realised that he had unconsciously been a prisoner for a long time, believing that he was free when he was living in a prison and in obscurity. It was as if my life had been turned completely upside down. I remember the night of 15 June. I didn't sleep a wink. I was very agitated. Just before dawn, I decided to start praying. I said a prayer. But I was not able to remember the details of it since I had forgotten the religious culture of my childhood. My religious culture had become a theoretical rather than a practical, operative, or active culture. I then began to re-educate myself in Islamic culture, to read and compile a bibliography of writings on Islam. The available Islamic books at the heart of the Islamist current were written by Sayyed Qutb and Mohammed Qutb, Abu'l-Ala al-Mawdudi, Mohammed Iqbal, Malek Bennabi and a number of classical writings by Abul Hamed al-Ghazali and Ibn Taymiyya. I began to tour the religious schools in Damascus. I became acquainted with the school of the *hadiths* [the sayings of the prophet Mohammed], of the *fiqh* [Islamic jurisprudence], of different Islamic groups. I listened to everybody. I wanted to know what was in this religious universe which I had been communicating with from a distance without being truly integrated.

Adel Hussein: Communism, anti-imperialism and Islam[6]

My brother Ahmed Hussein was the first person to influence my character profoundly. I was a member of Misr al-Fatat (Young Egypt). I was very young at the time, perhaps fourteen years old. But this is where I started. My brother's party then changed its name to the Socialist Party. This was at the end of 1949, but his activity only really started in 1950, when the Wafd party came to power.[7] I was an active member of this socialist party at the beginning of the 1950s. At the University of Cairo, I was head of the Socialist Youth. Then, after the revolution in 1952, I defected to the communist movement. I was one of the opponents of the revolution of 1952. I began to show my opposition within the Socialist Party and then in 1953, I went over to the Communist Party.

Such was my relationship with Ahmed Hussein at the beginning of the 1950s. After that, as you know, political parties, including the Socialist Party were forbidden. My Marxist tendencies distanced me from my brother, both ideologically and politically. He believed, while I evidently did not. We therefore had a completely contradictory view of the 1952 revolution. The most serious debates only took place after I had been released from prison in 1964. After this difficult period, coming out from a very bitter experience, I began to distance myself from Marxism. It was only then that I began to have serious discussions with Ahmed Hussein. He was no longer a lawyer, as he had retired and devoted himself to reading and writing. Therefore, he had all the time in the world to have these long ideological debates which profoundly influenced my new political career.

Today, after everything that has happened, I think that these conversations in fact led me to continue the work of Ahmed Hussein in the political and Islamic struggle in Egypt. In effect, I think that Misr al-Fatat was in itself the continuation of what we called the tendency of the nationalist party of Mustafa Kamal, who was the leader of the Egyptian nationalist movement at the end of the nineteenth century. The idea of Mustafa Kamal and his followers, and then of his successor Mohammed Farid was, through the idea of nationalist party, to create an organisation which recognised Egypt's identity and also its proximity to other Arab and Islamic countries. It was a cocktail of nationalism against foreign occupation but, at the same time, it was a call to inscribe this struggle in the framework of Islamic values. When the Young Egypt Party was established in the 1930s, I think that it represented a kind of comeback, a new layer of youth of Mustafa Kamal's nationalist party, created by very young people who had only just left university.

At the very beginning, the two key personnel were Ahmed Hussein and Fathi Hiwan. Fathi Hiwan disagreed with Ahmed Hussein on many points and left to rejoin the old nationalist party, which at the very least showed that there was still a link between the representation of the old nationalist party and the new generation represented by Misr al-Fatat. Even when Ahmed Hussein changed the name to the Socialist Party, he was very clear that his vision of socialism was very 'specific' and very distinct from the Western (Marxist) vision.[8] He was at pains to differentiate himself from the Marxist reading on several points. To him the concept of communism implied a dependence on the Soviet Union. His Socialist Party was very nationalistic, fighting for total independence and some sort of reconciliation with the other Arab countries. One of the points in his party's manifesto in the 1950s was: 'We are fighting for the United Arab States, encompassing all Arab countries from Morocco to the Gulf.' His struggle for economic, political and military independence, his relationship with the other Arab countries, his strong belief in social justice were very clear and were all shaped within the framework of Islamic values.

I believe that what we now represent in the Labour Party is a 1990s version. Of course, we are not just repeating what Ahmed Hussein did in the 1950s, but the general ideological and spiritual framework remains the same. We advocate Arab unity, social justice, an effective independence, but this is all expressed in the framework of Islamist ideology. Undoubtedly, our interpretation of Arab unity and social justice was probably very different to that of Ahmed Hussein. Details vary, either because circumstances are different or because there are new variables today, or again because we have discovered that certain concepts he supported in the 1950s have been proved wrong. Because circumstances have changed, or in order to correct any errors, we have not made a carbon copy of Young Egypt in the 1950s. But the general framework is the same. In this sense, I consider myself to be the continuation of Ahmed Hussein's work. We went our separate ways during this period because I was taken with Marxism, and particularly the classic communism of the 1950s. Of course, my views on religion differed from his, as did my views on nationalism, internationalism, Arab unity (including the Palestinian question), as well as on the economy. In fact, I thought that I was much more revolutionary than he was. I opposed all private property, an opinion that the Socialist Party did not share at the time. Of course, since then I have realised that they were right and I was wrong. My difference, our differences, were primarily due to my Marxist beliefs.

I think that my experience was very similar to Tareq al-Bishri. Our paths have run parallel. We became friends in 1964, when I left prison. Intellectually, we evolved in the same direction. We have always exchanged our points of view and discussed them. The book *The Political Movement*, even in its first edition, represented for us both a transitional period in our evolution. We both had a Marxist background and we had both been influenced by Nasserism. We both became supporters of this radical nationalist tendency and it was because we had become radical nationalists that we were able to understand and appreciate Ahmed Hussein's Socialist Party. In his book, Tareq al-Bishri was very positive about the experience of Ahmed Hussein in the 1950s.

We were partisans of radical social reform, which was certainly in line with Marxist thinking, but the difference between our spiritual state in the 1960s and our creed in the 1950s was that we were fully aware of the need to link these objectives of justice and social reform to nationalist objectives. At the time, we looked to China, which had a superficial relation to Marxism. There was no relationship between what Mao was trying to do in China and what Marx had said. We thought that it was simply a radical nationalist revolution trying to transform China into a new independent state. They discovered that the role of the state was vital in planning development. What looked like socialism was only the nationalist search for rapid development. We understood that Nasser's relationship with the Arabs completely coincided with the objective of a strategy of independence. We started to look at everything which was spread from Egypt throughout the region in the light of radical nationalism. In this light, when we were examining recent history, as Tareq Al-Bishri had done in even the first edition of his book, in the light of nationalism and in the name of transformation and societal reform in a nationalist framework, we were quite close to what Ahmed Hussein represented and we thought that the 1952 revolution was truly the continuation of what Ahmed Hussein was saying at the time.

From communism to Nasserism

We were both reconciled with Nasser in 1955. From 1952 to 1955, I was in the opposite camp. Why? Perhaps primarily because Nasser put us in prison! He was very dictatorial in his methods. Torture had been introduced in prisons. All these very negative aspects of Nasserism were extremely worrying. Even if we were heading in the right direction, people were wondering: what good will come of such a dictator? I think this is what happened to Saddam Hussein in 1990; we ourselves tried to drum up support for the Iraqi people, but many opposed us for the sole reason that they saw nothing good in him. People thought that you couldn't trust Nasser, that he could not express our aspirations. Even if it was shown that he had his positive side, many did not want to accept him easily.

During the first few years of the revolution, not only was there the dictatorial aspect but there was still no benefit of hindsight. Nasser was relatively passive, people even suspected him of being incapable of doing anything positive. Apart from the agrarian reform, which ran from 1952 to 1955, he hadn't done anything that suggested that this indeed was a revolution and not just a coup d'état, or that there was a real change in social relations. When he began to oppose Britain's decision to withdraw from the Suez Canal area, the tone of the negotiations was a lot different to Farouq's day. He had done nothing to show that we had entered a new phase of our development that would justify our revaluation of him. On the one hand he dictated, but on the other hand he did nothing to justify this dictatorship. This is why we initially opposed him.

At the time our reasoning was still rather simplistic. For example, we thought that because 'Marx or Engels had said nothing about the armed forces being likely to do anything positive, there should be no hesitation in fighting a military regime, because they are bound to get up to no good.' Our reasoning was superficial. On closer inspection, it is true that we saw nothing serious in it and that is probably the real reason for our reservations. When Nasser began to oppose the Baghdad pact and went to Bandung, when he sent the army into Yemen, we began to reconsider, moving from the opposition to the supporter's camp. This change, in which I played an important role, affected all sectors of the communist movement from late 1955 to early 1956. I was one of the first people to understand nationalism according to Gamal Abdel Nasser. We understood and greatly appreciated his brand of radical nationalism. It began in 1956 and it took shape throughout the 1960s. This was our line of thinking and this is how our analysis differed from the analysis at the start of the revolution. This reappraisal of the Nasserist attitude to nationalism was the prerequisite of our reappraisal of recent history. You could say that Tareq al-Bishri and I had very similar ideas about this.

When we realised this, however, we had not yet reached the end of our evolution. We supported the Socialist Party. We were partisans of social justice. But at the same time we both wanted to pursue this objective within the framework of nationalism, while retaining our Marxist influence. This is why we were so critical of the Muslim Brothers while we appreciated Young Egypt. To this day I remember how Tareq and I would want to say to Ahmed Hussein during our discussions: 'You're very hard on the Muslim Brothers. They're not as dark as you think. Of course I don't agree with them, except on this point. You should have another look at it.' That's what we used to do.

At the time, we criticised the Muslim Brothers from both a philosophical and a political angle. We supported Nasser while the majority of Muslim Brothers opposed him. To us, they were just reactionaries opposed to progress. They seemed stupid and weak-willed to us, which was not necessarily incorrect. They were given the opportunity to explain their anti-Nasserist violence at debates and discussions. They said they had been tortured by the regime. Nevertheless, we thought that resistance to foreign pressure justified putting internal problems on the back burner. That's why we went from being totally anti-Nasserist to almost fully supporting him. We thought that the persistent refusal of the Muslim Brothers to fully support Nasser was strange and very unproductive.

Nowadays, the Muslim Brothers have changed, as we ourselves have. Not just me, but nationalists in general. I see it clearly when I look back now: we were all underdeveloped. Maybe the Muslim Brothers weren't very intelligent, but the Nasserists could hardly be called brilliant. Each was as mediocre as the other, which is why they could not initiate a serious dialogue or do anything constructive. Even Tareq al-Bishri, one of the most brilliant and most open-minded intellectuals of the time, could not make at that time this transition that he made later from Marxism to nationalism and then to Islamism. In the 1960s, even Tareq couldn't comprehend the Islamic tendency, and he showed only bitterness towards it. Even he lacked objectivity on this topic, although he was undoubtedly one of the most astute and most flexible intellectuals. So what could be expected of others? The Muslim Brothers, it is true, were unable to question themselves and evolve. It is true that they could not integrate the changes constructively. And so they completely withdrew into themselves. Resistance was their priority. It was a question of survival, of resisting all external pressures, of reading the Quran and so on. I don't think that their long spell in prison really helped them intellectually, because they only ever read the Quran.

Then, in the 1960s, we understood the positive side of Young Egypt or the Socialist Party, but we were not yet advanced enough to be able understand the Muslim Brothers. I personally believed in a sort of radical nationalism with a hint of Nasserism, which was reflected in my contacts, who included communists as well as Nasserists. Before joining the Labour Party, I began influencing Nasserists and I tried to persuade them into an Islamic nationalist movement. I always said that it was a new version of Nasserism. Of course, the complete integration of Islam involves a very profound transformation.

This step was taken at the beginning of the 1980s by a group of Nasserists. I began to wonder: if I support Arab nationalism, if I feel tied to these people in many ways, that must mean that we share a common culture, and this culture should be infinitely more respected than it is at the moment. Nasser stressed integration and economic independence. Of course, these things are important, but not as important as cultural independence and this is where we began to differ. This is when everything started to happen for me. The more I studied, the more I discovered the sources of Islamic reference, and the more I realised that it was true and that it was a real force. I then began to influence the traditional nationalist movement by saying to them: 'You cannot be seriously nationalist if you are not completely open to Islam. For Islam is the very identity of this nation. So if you really support this nation's identity, if you are really proud of your nationality, you cannot do it seriously if at the same time you do not appreciate what Islam represents. Islam created this Arab nation; that's a historical fact. You cannot respect this Arab nation if you neglect, ignore or doubt the history of its transformation, the history of its creation. Be logical: you must look at the bigger picture.

This is how I began to convince others. I took part in hundreds of discussions, dialogues, seminars and meetings, academic or otherwise. I also wrote studies on the question, which had a sizeable impact on Nasserism, but which I felt were still a bit hesitant. My proposals were perhaps appreciated, but they were not accepted, at least not with enthusiasm. I then decided to directly enter political action by joining the Labour Party, which was affiliated to the Socialist Party (thanks to Ibrahim Shukri and Dr Helmi Murad). I thought that, together, we three could transform the Labour Party into a true successor to the Socialist Party, and I think we succeeded.

What separates us today from the Nasserists? We are all convinced of the necessity of finding common ground. The psychological barrier that stops us from doing so has disappeared and that is a very important step. Today people are perfectly capable of making agreements, of engaging in communal action, etc. In fact, the differences have diminished. Even if the Nasserists are always secular and religion is never their priority, at least it is not at the bottom of their list as it used to be. Nasserists are not always as critical of Nasserist history as they should be, of the way in which they have conducted themselves towards opponents, or of their vision of the public sector. They'd have to criticise a whole host of things, which they refuse and they are not ready to do, because this is their system of belief. It is their faith.

There are also a number of differences with the Muslim Brothers. Some have been very dogmatic. But that is not the issue, we do not support a single party system. People are bound to differ. The important thing, more important than these differences, is that we can have something in common and that something is Islam.

CHAPTER THREE

From the Secular Break to the Reconstruction of Identity

In Algeria, Egypt and elsewhere in the Arab Mediterranean, those Islamist currents that are on the front pages of our newspapers have sprung from a double historical logic. As a force of opposition they are a natural outcome of the regimes' repression. But the FIS in Algeria did not just emerge because its predecessor, the FLN, had disbanded. The weaknesses or errors of Sadat, Bourguiba or their successors cannot explain the Egyptian Muslim Brotherhood or hizb al-Nahda. By looking at the Islamist upsurge simply as a result of the failure of the regimes in power we prevent ourselves from understanding the secret of its capacity to mobilise and why, even when confined to the Arab world, this Islamist phenomenon strikes fear into Western hearts.

Why are the Islamists alone exploiting the economic or political failure of Arab regimes? Why are there no 'left-wing', 'secular' or 'liberal' currents that encourage people into the polling stations? And why, for the politicians of the southern shores of the Mediterranean, is there practically no chance of winning an election unless the letter I (for Islam) is included in the abbreviation of your party?

From imposed to imported secularism

In Cairo, Algiers, Amman and Sanaa, the political enemy has for a number of years been defined as the 'secularist'. How has one of the most cherished values of Western culture assumed a negative connotation among so many of its closest neighbours? How has history distorted our 'good' into their 'evil'? What do the merchants of doom mean by 'secularism', whose abolition they demand? In order to understand how such an important value has become so negative, we must re-examine the logic of its propagation in the countries where it is so passionately rejected.

When in the north people speak of 'secularism', they mean the capacity of French revolutionary society to put an end to the power of the Church, which is welcomed as the emergence of a politics that has finally been freed from 'arbitrary religious law', and which guarantees new rights and liberties for the individual and minorities. For others, however, the same vocabulary is interpreted differently, as the foul stench of retreat. For the Islamists who fight it, secularism has never really guaranteed rights or new liberties – partly, of course, because its arrival coincided with the triumph of Western armies, but more importantly because in their sometimes simplistic, but not necessarily unfounded, logic it has at best served to guarantee the rights of the foreigners who imported it, or of non-Muslim minorities, Christians or Jews, whose support helped the foreigners to establish their domination. The Trojan horse of secularism is seen, above all, as the most pernicious of the West's ideological weapons, which, at the peak of the colonial adventure, gave legality and respectability to the business of eradicating the normative Muslim system. It was secularism that spawned the idea that the inherited normative capital of nearly 14 centuries of civilisation was suddenly no longer the right way to run the whole society. It was secularism that strongly believed in regulating the sphere of personal status (marriages, inheritances etc) and more than this, the relationship of society to its external environment or to its non-Muslim components.

The fact that in the reality of Muslim history, which by definition is more complicated than the political ideologies would allow, the supremacy of Islamic law has regularly been contested by tribal custom, changes nothing. For all those who today hold it in contempt, secularism is blackened for the part it played in the downfall of the hegemony of the symbolic Muslim system. It expresses, be it sometimes through the voice of part of its own elite, a form of defiance of Islamic civilisation, in some way acknowledging the inability of this civilisation to produce the rules necessary for its regulation and its reproduction. When the dissolution of the caliphate in 1924 eliminated the institutional expression of Muslim unity, it was in the name of 'the secularism of the state' and the irresistible principal of 'the equality of all before the law' that the survivors of the great defeat of the *umma* (Muslim community) witnessed the rapid disappearance of their indigenous legal institutions. The dissolution, the marginalisation, the 'domestication', or, more broadly speaking, the 'folk-lorisation' of institutions (Islamic universities, *shari'a* courts, *waqf* religious foundations) and of the norms and rules proceeding from the Muslim system will reveal this decay little by little. The 'modernists' have irreversibly gained the upper hand over the 'reformists'[1] and modernisation is inscribed, not from within the symbolic system of Islam but against it or, at best, without it. Paradoxically, the blows aimed, in the name of secularisation, at the social networks linked to different forms of religious practice, far from encouraging 'modernisation', have perhaps brought about its downfall. For Bishri, 'modernising' secular violence has severed the ties between the individual and the public forum by destroying the complex mechanism of infra-state micro-associations.

Of course, the categories of Muslim culture have not disappeared from the subconscious, individual or collective memories any more than they have from the political discourse of the regimes. In the Arab world people have maintained, by all evidence, their Muslim character. But as the internal logic of the colonial culture unfolded, the framework of reference and meaning that came from Muslim culture was being insensitively divested of its former authority. Excluded from public places, it preserved its right to exist only in strictly 'cultural' religious and private spaces (for example weddings or inheritances). Thus excluded for the most part from the system of representation, the claim of Muslim culture to universality is inexorably disappearing. Even if they go unnoticed for a while, such wounds rip apart the fabric of identity. It is against this background that Islamism would eventually develop.

The political ideologies that helped the Arabs to find their feet in the twentieth century have, in one way or another, reconciled themselves with the intrusive presence of the foreign invader. In one form or another, they all take account of the demand for identity, and, even if they use categories devised in the West, they all express the need to maintain a cautionary distance from it. It was the 'secular' nationalism of the first generation that demonstrated against the last remnants of the Ottoman Empire, then against France, Britain and Italy, the will of populations, now regrouped into more-or-less finished 'nations', to obtain or to regain their legal identity in the international arena. There is nevertheless no doubt that, from the discourse of Emir Abdelkader[2] to the calls of the *mujahidin* of the FLN and the role of the *'ulama* in the national movement, there are many examples in Algerian history that highlight the permanence and centrality of the Islamic reference in the resistance to colonisation. According to Tareq Ramadan, grandson of Hassan al-Banna, the founder of the Muslim Brotherhood, the Islamists have been denied the credit they deserve for their participation in the national movements by the combined hostility of the colonial powers and the secular elites.

The case of the Turk Sa'id al-Nursi (between 1922 and 1924) is by itself telling. Nursi's discourse was both nationalist and Islamist and was initially adopted by Atatürk; but, as secularisation began, it was discarded. Recent accounts from the first president of the Algerian republic, Ahmed Ben Bella, suggest that the French went out of their way to separate the nationalists that they considered too 'religious'. The precocious British vision of the 'danger represented by the Brothers' provides a comparable illustration. Hassan al-Banna's Muslim Brothers was one of the spearheads of the nationalist movement. But they were ousted by the combined action of Britain and the so-called secular elites. And Banna was himself assassinated in 1949 with the known complicity of the British, if not on their initiative.[3]

The fact that the nationalists assimilated certain categories of Western political thought did not preclude their political ascendancy. At the heart of national struggles, the so-called accultured elite not only stood its ground, but also succeeded in assuming leading positions in the national movement. By turning the weapons of the foreign masters against them, the nationalism of the first generation succeeded in achieving its objective: 'independence'. The issue of the secular divide was, however, far from being resolved.

Ambiguous 'modernisation'

Once the first stage of independence – often limited by the maintenance of military bases (Bizerte in Tunisia, Mers el-Kebir in Algeria, Wheelus Field in Libya, the Suez Canal area in Egypt etc) – was realised, economic resources had to be brought under national control. Between the 1950s and the 1970s, this was achieved by 'nationalising' oil wells, agricultural land and other means of production and infrastructure such as the Suez Canal. Even though the terminology of Muslim culture had not disappeared from political discourse, it was the Marxist ideology of 'anti-imperialism' and 'development' which helped in the fight against the interests of former colonial powers and the US, which tried to take their place. It was from the exploitation of this fight, now economic and not just political, that the regimes (as well as the first generation of their opponents) essentially drew their legitimacy. For them it was not a question of turning towards the past but, on the contrary, towards the future, towards 'progress'.

Yet notions of progress and modernisation were at that time expressed entirely in the language of Western culture. Paradoxically, immediately after political independence, the culture of the coloniser enjoyed a new success. The distancing from the former empires, the construction of national states and the expression of their first policies of development was effected through the use of, not the rejection of, semantic categories of the West. Modernisation was written in French or in English more often than in Arabic. Mass education meant that 20 years after independence there were 10 times more French speakers in the Maghreb, instilled with Western philosophy, than there had been during colonial times.[4] Under Nasser, more books were translated from Western languages than during the entire colonial period. Nationalist elites of the first generation were unconcerned with healing the rupture in popular identity caused by the marginalisation of the institutional, legal, linguistic, architectural and artistic codes in which Islam played a central role, and which were 'folklorised' by powerful European challengers. Indeed, far from healing the wound, post-colonial modernisation deepened it: to a far greater extent than was the case before independence, it seemed that modernity could only arrive by jettisoning institutions deemed as too 'religious', or 'pre-modern' and thus potentially 'anti-modern', even if they were part of the fabric of social identity. More explicitly than in the colonial era, modernisation was synonymous with 'de-Islamisation'.

It was not before, but well after, independence that the prestigious Zeitouna University was closed. The nationalist Habib Bourguiba was not afraid to sacrifice 12 centuries of local university tradition, something that even the colonisers would not have dared to do. The Tunisian Aziz Krichen remarks:

> Here we touch on what is certainly the most extraordinary result of colonial domination [...] The historical irony is that the bilingual and bi-cultured urban elites that colonialism wanted to co-opt were now heading the fight for independence. But the real irony lies in the second point. This modern intelligentsia has successfully fought the political domination of France, but it has quite evidently ensured that French language and culture have continued to dominate. The bilingual elite was proclaimed, and announced itself to be a successful hybrid, a harmonious synthesis of opposing cultures. In reality, it was spiritually enslaved by Western values. It internalised its own inferiority and the superiority of others.[5]

Mohammed Mzali refers to this as the 'cultural break-in' of Tunisia under Bourguiba.[6] In the same vein, Rachid Ben Aïssa opines that Algeria has been 'ideologically raped':

> For twenty years the state has overshadowed Islam. For twenty years there has been no Islamic higher education. In the West, universities offer all manner of academic qualifications in Islamic theology and *usul al-fiqh*. In independent

Algeria, there has not been a single example of Islamic education, and when one was finally established, it was a police institution.[7]

By stressing that it is not a problem of discussing *in absolu* these unilateral policies, Aziz Krichen points to the 'spiritual earthquake' of the first 20 years of independence and the 'infernal dialectic of destruction without rebuilding' unleashed by a political elite 'lacking the ideological attributes of its domination'.[8]

For a decade or two nothing was to trouble this modernisation, as the state, confident of its new efficiency, had no problem in papering over the cracks that began to appear. But the wealth that came with the discovery of oil and economic independence could not forever hide the shortcomings of these 'nationalist illusions'. Irresistibly, demographic pressure, the downside of development, and the pangs of recession, revealed the limitations of the first industrialisation plans and a future that was anything but assured. The promises of modernity produced not triumphant results, but are rather to be found in hesitant graphs and stagnant figures, in the 'bread riots' or other events in Casablanca, Constantine or Algiers, where a succession of urban disturbances linked to a fall in spending-power broke out.

With the emergence of the Baader Meinhof gang, unemployment and inflation, and the far right and the 'cultural retreat' of May 1968, the West had become vulnerable and was no longer sure of what it should do. It was no longer the source that it had long been of ideological certainties, whether Marxist or liberal. The credibility of the humanitarian or democratic principles it claimed to be universal suffered in addition from the blatant inconsistency of its actions, which fluctuated quite openly with its immediate interests. Unwittingly, the West was on the verge of digging the grave of its culture's universalism. It was in this context that the south began to feel once more that it was necessary to 'speak with another voice'.

The elements of the identity reconstruction

When Omar Abd al-Rahman, the leader of the Egyptian Islamist movement, imprisoned in the US, denounced these 'seventy years without the *shari'a*',[9] which he unequivocally blamed for all the ills of his community, it appeared that he was trying to reconcile a profane norm with the demands of divine law which he valued above all else. But if the impact of this appeal was so clearly surpassed by the radical Islamist fringe, if much of the Arab world is today calling in unison for the same 'application of the *shari'a*', and if the Islamist upsurge has become, despite all the repression, the focus for rebuilding the entire political scene in the region, it is because it has raised the stakes beyond the 'return of the sacred' to encompass the restoration of a symbolic order in its totality. The 'law of God' is here primarily endogenous rather than celestial. Of course there are certain 'religious factions' whose re-acquaintance with the system of representation has been less than smooth. But there are also ways of dressing or decorating a home, speech or thought patterns, philosophical, literary or political references – in fact all those ingredients that constitute an identity – that the intrusion of Westernisation has discredited, which are no longer folkloric and whose attraction and credibility are inexorably being rediscovered.

The upsurge, from the Iranian revolution to the assassination of President Sadat and the double electoral victory for the FIS (on 12 June 1990 and 26 December 1991), is as indicative of rupture as it is of continuity. However real the various catalysts may be (especially the economic), however diverse its political expressions, it is essentially in the old dynamic of decolonisation that Islamism has taken root.

At first political, then economic, the distancing of the former coloniser through the rhetoric of oppositional Islam becomes ideological, symbolic and more broadly cultural, on the terrain where the shock of colonisation has been most traumatic. In addition to its own language, local culture and history endow the dynamic of independence with something that has been missing for a long time: the precious attributes of a sort of ideological 'autonomy' which perfects it, the right of those who propagate it to regain universality, without denouncing the structural elements of their 'specificity'. Even if this chronology responds more to the demands of the didactic than of a manifestly less linear history, it is primarily the reaction to the cultural impact of the colonial irruption that today has ignited the Islamist 'third stage' of the 'rocket of de-colonisation'.

When discussing the 'rejection' of the West we should not speak in its language nor use its terminology. As for the intruder, who 30 years after independence has managed to maintain cultural superiority, what better way to highlight the distance than by rejecting its references and returning to a system of codes and symbols which is ostensibly foreign to it? From Qadhafi and his 'third way' to the Non-Aligned Movement, the search for a double distancing from the 'Westernising experience' in the East, as in the West, is certainly not new.[10] But the first manifestations of the quest for identity were tarnished by their recourse to Western concepts, whether nationalist, socialist or liberal. The specificity of the Islamist discourse and a great deal of its effectiveness is conversely due to its recourse to a set of references that are free from outside influence.

To the 'political man' who appropriates it, the Islamist rhetoric, however, allows a beneficial reconciliation with the categories (real or mythical, it is not important) of the culture he lives intuitively.[11] By adopting a vocabulary or a terminology based on local references, this intuitive culture returns to its former universalist claim, and restores the precious symbolic continuity interrupted by the irruption of Western categories. The Islamist rhetoric has caught the public imagination, whereas the hegemonic representations fabricated by other social systems have had the most destabilising effect. It is helping to close the traumatic chapter of colonisation and this is undoubtedly the secret of its formidable ability to mobilise. In order to survive the pitfalls of globalisation, it allows its followers a precious and reassuring feeling of belonging.

State-approved Islam or anti-state Islamism?

The functions of the Islamist discourse have not been confined to acting as an outlet for individual or collective identity. The ideology is just as much a 'language of protest'. The critical re-reading of the Western legacy has therefore expressed its defiance of those governing, and the dynamic of identity often confirms a banal dynamic of opposition. The very principle of the glorification of a divine authority amputates the presumed authority of whosoever claims this, in equal and opposite measure – whoever he may be – because his own power can only ever reside in the temporal. Evoking the absolute character of divine sovereignty underlines the limits of its terrestrial competition. For those who believe that only God can claim to be 'the greatest', the reticence that greeted the claim of the first president of independent Tunisia to promote himself as the 'supreme warrior' (al-mujahid al-akbar) was a very early indication of this possible conflict of legitimacy.

The Islamist discourse, while it has undoubtedly served resistance movements and the opponents of government well, has also served its turn for those in power. From the Egypt of Azhar to the Morocco of the 'Commander of the Faithful', the first generation of pro-independence elites always managed to ensure that the Islamist wind did not just fill the sails of its opponents. In truth, not all of them showed the same aptitude for entering or remaining in this 'gold mine' of legitimacy. Depending on whether the monarchies were returning to the symbols of the pre-colonial regime or whether the secular republics were disposing of the old structures, the regimes have either exaggerated or restricted the modernising rupture of independence. Depending on their proximity to religious values, they have either, at least in part, addressed the demand for identity or they have left it to their opponents. The monarchies of Morocco, Jordan, Saudi Arabia and the United Arab Emirates, whose legitimacy is naturally founded on traditional ground, are more widely thought of as guardians of religious values than the republican leaders of North Africa, Egypt, Iraq and Sudan or particularly of the former Marxist South Yemen. Unsurprisingly, this has affected the components of the Islamist movement in different ways. In order to resist the rise of the secular ideologies – whether Nasserist or Ba'thist – in power in most neighbouring states, the Hashemite kingdom of Jordan relied upon the support of members of the very Muslim Brotherhood organisation that Egypt imprisoned in their thousands.[12] The Moroccan throne, for its part, had no hesitation in reinforcing, and sometimes even recreating, the associative Muslim network at a time when, in Algeria, Egypt and Tunisia, it was discreetly but efficiently all but wiped from the political scene.[13]

Other parameters, it is true, render this political fact relative. If it is correct that, in a very underhand manner, some secular regimes have encouraged political Islam (although such strategies did not in themselves produce it, nor can they account for what is happening today), they have also deliberately encouraged non-oppositional religious mobilisation. Having taken care to reduce their powers considerably, the secular states have maintained the institutions of official Islam and even given them a facelift. In Algeria and Tunisia, a long time after Morocco, councils of *'ulama*, charged with adding religious caution to public policies, were hastily set up. After it had been largely shorn of its prerogatives, the help of the University of al-Azhar and the Mufti of the Republic of Egypt was solicited in order to endow the regime of Nasser and his successors with religious legitimacy.[14] And besides the institutions of official Islam, the regimes have used the traditional Islam of popular religiosity, the brotherhoods and the spiritual teachers (considered as 'non-oppositional'), to 'reap political benefit from re-Islamisation'.

However, the slice of the 'Islamist cake' that supports the rulers seems to be gradually shrinking in favour of their opponents. There are several reasons for this evolution. The first is the extreme fatigue of all Arab regimes, a logical outcome of their excessive longevity. Their system of mobilisation – however sophisticated and no matter how hard they try to renew it – following a universal law, is less effective day-by-day. Conversely, the Islamist rhetoric, free from all compromise with power, can efficiently exploit the utopian dimension inherent in all oppositional discourse.

Secondly, those in power in the secular republics of the Maghreb, Egypt or the Fertile Crescent have all been associated more or less directly with the enforced secularisation that followed independence. All are implicated in the sometimes authoritarian marginalisation of the institutions of traditional culture (the domestication of the Islamic University of al-Azhar, the closure of the Zeitouna, the dissolution of the 'religious' tribunals in Tunis etc), which at one time appeared to be the only way to modernise. The elites in power are therefore noticeably less credible when they demand the re-evaluation of religious references that they have more or less directly discredited. History, which has been cruel, has portrayed the Westernised nationalist intelligentsia of the first generation as close to the coloniser and therefore, even on the nationalist terrain which made it an elite, as less credible than its noisy Islamist successors. The sound of 'Praise be to God' rising from the mosques reflects not only a rejection of the West, but also of elites which are 'secular', (which, according to Islamist logic, means hostility to the endogenous normative and symbolic system) and, should the claim fit, corrupt and despotic, accused of prolonging the domination of the West.

The situation is hardly any better for the secular opponents of these regimes. They have escaped the ignominy brought about by the failure of development policies and accusations of corruption. And they do not have a history of repression to excuse themselves. But however courageous their fight may sometimes have been, the Arab left has rarely acquired any real ideological distance from the secular regimes it has been fighting.[15] Where this has been the case, as in the conservative monarchies, its symbolic capital has borne the full brunt of the communist collapse. In all cases, today the left is as discredited as the regimes that it has fought.

Throughout the region, the distance between this secularist opposition and those in power is shrinking noticeably. In Tunisia, Algeria and Egypt, when it comes to 'choosing which side you are on', embattled regimes often find it better to lean on those very forces that the Islamist upsurge has marginalised, which they find can face the Islamists more effectively than those who are in power. These 'objective convergences' have often taken the form of a more-or-less-declared alliance. A prime example is the Algerian Rassemblement Pour la Culture et la Démocratie (RCD), which is likely to have been born of the goodwill of the government rather than the pressure of democratic and liberal forces. This was also the case with the old Trotskyist oppositionist Mohammed Boudiaf, who suddenly offered his services to those he had fought all his life. The same is true of the heir to the Algerian Communist Party, the former Socialist Vanguard Party (today called Ettahadi, 'the Challenge'), which has defended the same 'eradicating' line as the Algerian generals whose absolutism it at one time challenged. Similarly, the Mouvement Tunisien des Démocrates Socialistes has gradually renounced the fight against the authoritarianism of Bourguiba's successors and has preferred, without shame, to rally round the regime with weapons and supplies. Or again the Egyptian National Union (al-Tagammu' al-Watani) led by Khaled Muhieddin, which in 1991 refused to be associated with the boycott of obviously rigged elections, preferring to forage around in doubtful ballot boxes for seats they knew would be out of their reach in a fair contest.

There are of course some notable exceptions to this rule. In Algeria, the Workers Party of the Trotskyist Louisa Hanoune, which has always been extremely vocal in its opposition to Islamism, refused to ignore the demands of electoral logic, and as a result earned the abiding recognition of its adversaries in the FIS. The Socialist Forces Front (FFS), although more reticent, has never gone so far as to categorically dismiss the electoral results. Mohammed Mzali and Ahmed Ben Salah, former Tunisian ministers who defected to the opposition in exile, both chose, without entering their ranks, to make contact and co-ordinate their action with the Islamists of hizb al-Nahda.[16]

The growing inability of the regimes to reap the rewards of re-Islamisation originates in a contradiction: the credibility of the Islamist rhetoric is incompatible with the allegiances that economic difficulties and US pressure force the Arab regimes to adopt. The Islamism of those who have to bow down to the arbitrary commands of US foreign policy thus inexorably loses its most precious ingredients: nationalism and identity. The collapse of the Islamic legitimacy of the Saudi guardians of the holy places of Islam immediately after the 1990 alliance with the US against Iraq and the resulting emergence of a powerful Islamist opposition to the monarchy in Riyad is one of the best recent examples. Another is the growing difficulty the Egyptian institutions of Islam encounter in their attempts to preserve their credibility without departing from their support for a regime which signed the Camp David Agreements and was a member of the US coalition against Iraq. The inability of the Palestine Liberation Organisation (PLO) to capture the same dividends as its opponents, who saw more *istislam* (submission or capitulation) than *salam* (peace) in the Oslo Agreements, underlines the same unavoidable contradiction. From one end of the Arab world to the other, the normalisation of relations with Israel has thus irresistibly transferred the monopoly of access to nationalist dividends to those who oppose it – essentially the Islamists.

Islamism 'from above' or Islamism 'from below'?

The fruitful distinction made by Jean-François Bayart between politics 'from above' and 'from below' is well-known and must not be ignored.[17] But we should concentrate less on the difference between a revolutionary Islamisation from above and a social Islamisation from below than on the chronological instrumentalisation of this distinction proposed by Gilles Kepel and Olivier Roy, and focus on the strength of their long-established explanation for this, rather than its description.[18] What is happening in the Arab world today? There has long been one unique answer for those preoccupied with the unrest in the Mediterranean:

> the Islamist movements, which for a long time opted for a 'revolutionary Islamisation from above', have changed their strategy and have recently followed a policy of a 'social re-Islamisation' from below'. What is really meant by this 'profound transformation' that the Islamist movements are alleged to have experienced 'during the 1980s', and 'the revolutionary political model, which aims to seize power through violent action by means of a strategy of re-Islamisation of the whole of society from below?'[19]

Such a transformation presupposes, firstly, that the Islamist currents had very monolithic modes of action. Secondly, it implies that during the 1970s there was a clear predominance of revolutionary plans, while during the 1980s it was social action plans that held sway. Thirdly, it supposes that the truly revolutionary part of the movement in the 1970s effectively changed its point of view in the 1980s. However, none of these three assertions holds, either for the Arab East or for the Maghreb.

The hypothesis of an initial revolutionary tendency that towards the end of the 1980s reappeared from below supposes that the movements of re-Islamisation from above of the 1960s and 1970s appeared from nowhere, and that no religious or social mobilisation had previously occurred in the area. But before engaging in bold revolutionary political action, a large majority of the leaders of the 'revolutionary' Islamist movements in Egypt, the Maghreb or elsewhere in the Arab world, had only religious or social ambitions, whether they were Tablighis, Sufis or members of any other non-revolutionary (yet not strictly apolitical) movement.[20] The pacific proselytising of the Tablighis even seemed to be one of the precursors of 'revolutionary' Islamism. 'We were influenced by the simplicity of the Tablighis', explains Ahmida Enneifer, one of the founders of the Tunisian current, 'by their way of living which had completely disappeared in Tunisia'. The Moroccan Islamist leader, Abdessalam Yassine, remembers that 'it was exactly the same' in his country: 'It was the Tablighis, not the

Muslim Brothers, who came first'. Even in Egypt, there were associations that were tolerated because they were supposedly apolitical, such as Gami'a Shar'iyya or Ansar al-Sunna, whose mosques avoided control by the Ministry of Waqfs, and who acted as a focus for revolutionary mobilisation.[21]

In Egypt, the Muslim Brotherhood could not possibly be identified as a group that only endorsed re-Islamisation from above, unless the intention is to completely distort the reading of its first references. It would be necessary to wait until the maturation of the thought of Sayyed Qutb and then be prepared to accept that his single shadow covers every other wing of the Islamic movement, to make the reality of the 1960s and 1970s submit to the proposed 'up then down' model.[22]

The vast majority of the current has never really accepted revolutionary modes of action. Indeed, except for those who ignore a large part of reality and substitute official *communiqués* or the tabloid press of the Arab left for observation, large parts of the Islamist current, including the most 'active', have never been party to the strategy of re-Islamisation from above.[23] Since then, it is evident that their educational ambitions cannot be interpreted as the result of any sort of 'change of strategy'. When this has been the case, educational preoccupations have always remained intact.

The majority of those labelled as 'revolutionaries' in the 1970s were in fact much more inclined to action from below. Apart from the small Egyptian organisation Tanzim al-Jihad (in the limited sense of the term, that is referring to a much smaller and less influential group than the media hype around the name would imply), the practices of social Islamisation have remained at the forefront of the preoccupations of all the groups that are considered revolutionary since they began to react to the violence of the state. In Egypt, the doctrine of the Muslim Brotherhood is unquestionably linked to social and educational action. The Gama'a Islamiyya can itself no longer be associated solely with re-Islamisation from above. Even if it is classed as a 'revolutionary' group (as it is accurate to do after the pact with M.A.Farag's group at the end of the 1970s), the supposed turning-point at the beginning of the 1980s only takes a very small part of the reality into account. Even when the idea of a revolutionary prolonging of pietistic and social action emerges, it is indistinguishable from the educational practices of Islamisation from below.

This ambivalence reduces considerably the scale of the distinction between the two ingredients of the same mobilisation. It has absolutely nothing to do with a simple methodological nuance. To say that the Islamist currents have 'changed their plan of action' contributes to allowing the paradigm of violence to explain a much more complex phenomenon, and therefore often supports the official representation introduced by the regimes to impose their oppressive options.

Where the separation of from below or from above is justified, as it is for Tanzim al-Jihad, the distinction, for once functional, is nevertheless not really convincing. Here again we see that the events and activities of the 1980s contain a fair few surprises – and not just in Egypt. If the doctrine and practices of the minority – which during the 1970s was deemed to be 'revolutionary' and nothing else – are examined, it is clear that in the 1980s it did not in fact change course at all, and once again the claimed 'profound transformation' has absolutely no grounds in reality.

Of course, the activist groups, who at the end of the 1970s pooled their resources to attempt the assassination of Anwar al-Sadat, have made it appear that they have adopted a more discreet strategy following their failure. But the fact that the 1980s saw fewer revolutionary manifestations is not due to any 'fundamental change' among the groups in question. Tanzim al-Jihad activists, who whilst in prison (some were imprisoned until 1984, others for a lot longer), weighed up the contradictions and risks of action from above, injected some realism into the organisation's strategy and appeared to temper its action. In reality, the only reason for this was their consciousness of the failure of 1981. Primarily, Tanzim al-Jihad had to rebuild the networks that had been wiped out by the repression. It had, in particular, learnt lessons from the imbalance between the apparent success of the Sadat affair and its complete inability to prolong that success politically. Without the extremely hazardous alliance that had allowed the achievement of the suicide operation at the grandstand, no-one wanted to risk their necks again.[24] The assassination of Sadat has in fact established in the West an inflated image of Tanzim al-Jihad's potential, as its former leaders willingly admit.[25] When, rightly or wrongly, such an alliance was deemed more favourable, particularly to counter the increasingly repressive violence, the members of the group identified as Tali'at al-Fath went back to their old methods of revolutionary struggle in 1993 by attacking the summit of the state apparatus.[26]

This particular organisation never really questioned its modes of operation in 1980 or afterwards, and did not seriously consider changing any of its first tactics. The Tanzim al-Jihad militants have always believed that in order to seize power and impose an Islamisation from above it is necessary to secretly invest in the army, in their eyes the only credible instrument of revolutionary action. The Jihadians have not reverted to any sort of educational Islamisation from below, which they mistrust even when it is authoritarian. They stigmatise the 'bottle-smashers' and 'video-burners' of the Gama'a Islamiyya and the 'compromise' of the 'traitors', as both they and the Gama'a Islamiyya perceive the excessively legalist Muslim Brotherhood.

One of the reasons for the split between the jailed leader of the Gama'a Islamiyya, Omar Abd al-Rahman, and his Tanzim al-Jihad counterpart, Abboud Zummer (the Commander of Military Information implicated in the assassination of Sadat, and the only one of the accused to escape the death penalty), is precisely the option defended by Zummer: namely, to engage in clandestine action and avoid the open proselytising advocated by the Gama'a Islamiyya.[27]

The proposed chronological dichotomy of the 1970s and 1980s also prevents us from taking into account the fact that several groups entered the political arena during the 1980s. In 1982, the Lebanese Hizbullah entered politics fully armed, in reaction to the Israeli invasion of Lebanon. In 1987, the birth of Hamas added firepower to the arsenal of the Muslim Brotherhood's contribution to the Palestinian resistance.

Even if it means accepting the notion of a chronological break, it is however vital to underline the primacy of the social and educational manifestations of the dynamic of this re-Islamisation process which developed in the societies of the former colonial periphery of the West. But this chronological dichotomy can interfere with our understanding of the later phases of the Islamist upsurge. It was clearly the success, not the failure, of these first forms of proselytising which alarmed the regimes or their foreign defenders sufficiently to justify the first repressive measures (of which the assassination of the founder of the Muslim Brotherhood was one example) that inspired the 'Qutbist' radicalisation and its various Jihadian incarnations. This is, therefore, at odds with the original chronology, which mistakenly overlooks a series of essential causalities.

Instead, the author proposes that there has been an almost constant coexistence of revolutionary and social modes of action. Not only have the troublesome movements of re-Islamisation from above failed to die out in the 1980s, but it would also seem that it is only in the eyes of outsiders that they are accorded precedence, even an autonomous presence in the process of re-Islamisation. This has happened notably in the West, where their emergence has been highlighted in the media. The recognition of the social dimensions, which is more difficult to observe, did not occur until later, and only to a limited extent.

There is no less contempt for the representation of re-Islamisation from below than there is for the representation of revolutionary action – this is undoubtedly the crux of the matter. It is commendable that Sister Emmanuelle, a French nun, can invest a fortune in an Egyptian humanitarian aid network without troubling the Western conscience. But similar social and educational movements, which generate admiration when they are a result of Western, Christian initiative, suggest the ominous tip of a totalitarian iceberg if the shape of the female teacher's hairstyle or the cut of the doctor's beard is different. The 'fundamentalists' no longer assassinate, they 'infiltrate' – a no less worrying action.

Yet, like any sort of reactive movement, or any political movement, the Islamist upsurge is not without its limitations or its contradictions, as we shall see.

CHAPTER FOUR

From one Islamism to Another: Islamism Between Reaction and Action

The limitations of Islamist rhetoric are governed by the historically specific situation in which it is located and the combination of advantages that its political exploitation offers. The phase of the 'reintroduction of Islam' cannot go on indefinitely. Those who today profit from it will soon have to find new sources of legitimacy, as their 'secular' nationalist predecessors did.

This fatigue, sometimes seen in Tehran, is by no means the rule in the Arab world. Even in the case of Khomeini's successors, whose difficulties have been gleefully highlighted, the reality is more that of a political team which is in the process of wearing itself out than of the exhaustion of the political principle of rupture with Western symbols (which was a factor in their seizure of power). The Islamist challengers of the FLN in Algeria, however critical of the party's regime, have never questioned its opposition to colonialism. In the same way, if the group that came to power in 1979 in Iran were to be defeated, there is almost no chance, with all due respect to those who predict 'the end of the Islamist dream', that they would have to witness the founding act of Khomeinism condemned. Despite their importance, these changes are no more than the internal adjustments of a new system and certainly do not constitute a revolution.

The most telling limitation of Islamist rhetoric is not to be found in its denunciation of Western cultural hegemony. There seems to be a relative consensus among the actors that acknowledges the reality of colonial deculturation and the need to remedy it. From Tunis to Cairo, regimes prefer to profit from re-Islamisation rather than contest its legitimacy. A good proportion of 'anti-Islamist' forces oppose the Islamist current on clientelist and circumstantial, rather than ideological grounds. We have already seen how the conflict between the regimes and their opposition has little to do with ideology (Islamism versus secularism), as is often thought.

Therefore, the ambiguities, contradictions and dangers of part of the Islamist rhetoric lie less in the diagnosis than in the cure, less in its 'principle of functioning' than in certain characteristics. They are to be found not so much in the distancing from Western culture as in the ways of rebuilding 'authenticity', namely in the choice and the reading of the 'local' or 'authentic' references that Islamist rhetoric wants to substitute for the existing 'imported' ones in order to forestall the 'cultural schizophrenia' of the societies concerned.

The *shari'a* and nothing but the *shari'a*?

The hardcore of the Islamist discourse believe that the alternative to 'cultural dependence' is the restoration of 'divine sovereignty' and the rehabilitation of the normative order which arises from it. An Islamic state is therefore a state whose leaders respect a fundamental demand: namely to govern 'with what God has revealed' to mankind – divine law, the *shari'a*. Not surprisingly, all Islamist political programmes make this claim, together with the restoration of the *dawla islamiyya* (the Islamic state). In the literalist version of Islamist rhetoric, the restoration of 'divine sovereignty' and the ensuing imposition of the *shari'a* will fully satisfy the normative needs of society.[1] However, if there is unanimity over principles, there are substantial variations in the interpretation of the notion of *shari'a* and the concrete conditions needed to impose it. It is in this space left for interpretation that the main misunderstandings are likely to occur. Yet it is amid this same space of tension and negotiation, in this unofficial political area, that the principal dynamics of difference and evolution also emerge.

Even if it is represented as celestial, the 'law of God' has always been interpreted by mortals. Apart from a limited number of explicit commandments, it requires interpretation by jurists (*fuqaha'*), who are necessarily complicit with the environment that solicits their knowledge. If the techniques of exegesis are catalogued and codified, the philosophical tenure of this perpetual mediation allows for a great deal of initiative. The broadly consensual requirement at the heart of the Islamist upsurge for the 'imposition of the *shari'a*', namely the restoration of the Muslim normative order can, then, be interpreted and expressed in many different ways. The reasons for the diversity of 'Islamist' vision, thought and action are the accepted degree of historically determined contingency in relation to the unvarying core of the dogma, a greater or lesser willingness to adapt this revelation to the immediate situation, a will never to 'read the Quran with the eyes of the dead' (as Roger Garaudy eloquently put it)[2] and, conversely the 'literalism' or 'fundamentalism' of their attitude,

If it is unsurprising that this relation to divine law has proved so divisive amongst the Arab intelligentsia, it does not come as a surprise when the differences of opinion and the internal rethinking process which goes on inside the Islamist movement becomes apparent. Adel Hussein remarks that

> Politically we have aligned ourselves with Omar Abd al-Rahman[3] on many points.[4] On the condemnation of the thousands of arrests and the torture so casually inflicted on members of the Gama'a Islamiyya, on the denunciation of the total freezing of the political system in our country or the iniquity of the Western attitude to the Algerian elections, etc....But Omar Abd al-Rahman is influenced solely by Ibn Taymiyya (14th century), while we look to Ibn Taymiyya but also to each one of his successors. We want to face up to our history, while he tends to cut himself off from it. Our opinion of the shari'a is therefore different. For us, it is a kind of global project that we are responsible for progressively building, while he would tend to see only a catalogue of brutally enforced penal sanctions.

There would be many more examples if we were to discuss democracy, the status of women, the classic penal right or any one of the facets of legal and political modernisation.

A very literalist reading can lead to two possible extremes. At one, is the notion that the shari'a encompasses the whole of fiqh, namely the very detailed translation of the general principles followed for many centuries by generations of Muslim jurists. Muslim tradition constantly attests to the difference between fiqh and the shari'a, the one adaptable and the other eternal. Bishri reminds us that

> The shari'a is the set of norms that the Most High bestows upon his disciples. Its principal sources, the Quran and the sunna, are divine and eternal. Fiqh, on the other hand, is the knowledge of these norms, which govern human behaviour. It is the study of these norms and their definition by inductive or deductive methods. It is imperative that, whilst remaining inside the framework of religion, it [fiqh] adapts to the demands of the time and to human needs. Change does not touch on the source of the norm, only its significance to developing situations and to the diversity of circumstances.[5]

The opposite of the literalist reading points out that the Quran mentions the shari'a only minimally, as a 'path' or a spiritual state of being that must permeate the work of human legislators. For Garaudy, the fact that the

Quran commands respect for the content of the earlier revelations leads to a conclusion that its expressly normative elements cannot be literally applied whenever it contradicts the preceding revelations.[6] Therefore, the 'application of the shari'a' means only that the Muslim legislator must be filled with the spirit of the revelation, that he must keep this corpus of higher principles alive in spirit. He should curb the autonomy of human will without stifling its voice. Even if this minimal vision is not dominant, it nevertheless brings the functions of 'divine law' and the natural rights of the Western system together. It creates a melting pot of precepts beyond human will, which act as a guide rather than a restriction on the free exercise of human will. By setting out the limits, the 'law of God' is an affirmation rather than a denial of the existence of a sphere of autonomy of human will. By marking out the frontiers, it permits a profane sphere in politics to exist.

The more extensive the notion of the shari'a, the more literalist and ahistorical the reading of its juridical corpus, and the more this autonomous sphere of politics and its potential for playing an essential regulatory role will recede. The literalist interpretation of the shari'a, 'this reification of the Muslim from the tenth century',[7] will inevitably heighten the tensions and frictions created by the practices of a fairly broad section of society, such as 'westernised' women or 'democrats', being at odds with a set of norms that has long defied any evolution.[8] For the sole reason that they originated in an alien culture, modernist advances are regarded as illegitimate and those who have internalised such practices are discredited. That 'Islamic' norms need to be resurrected today attests to the fact that the vital contact that every such system must have with the population that it claims to regulate has been lost. Similarly, their 'lack of historicity' means that the rules inherited from a bygone age are as disconnected from the needs of the addressees as the rules they claim to replace. In treating the supposed cultural 'schizophrenia' of the former colonies, the Islamist 'doctor' runs the risk of breeding a new strain. The risk comes from substituting a culture perceived as imported from the West with a culture that, as Zakariya points out, is also entirely imported: not one that has simply travelled over the Mediterranean space, but one that has come through a space–time continuum that separates it as effectively as distance from the needs of the people it must reach in the late twentieth century.

It is quite logical that this literalist relation to the 'divine norm' and historical heritage justifies criticism. Zakariya, whose critique denounces the inability of his compatriots to historicise their relationship with heritage, without doubt touches the heart of the problem.[9] Without falling into an indiscriminate rejection of the heritage on which Muslim civilisation was built, it is necessary, he pleads, to dissociate oneself from old expressions. In order to revive ancestral glories, one must in some way accept the need to 'bury' them. The mystification of a heritage by shielding it from criticism and any dynamic of adaptation, is undoubtedly the most pernicious way of devaluing it. If a builder will not lay a brick on top of another, believing that brick to be perfect, the building will never be finished. This is the contradiction into which some of the Islamists have fallen. Even if it means being buried, the role of the brick is for another to be laid on top of it. In the same way the Islamic *turath* (heritage), particularly its normative expression, can only really be of use to its heirs once it has been removed from its pedestal and 'integrated' into the construction, that is distanced and, if necessary, criticised, in the same way that the artisans of the European Renaissance dared to criticise the Greek heritage. No matter how glorious one's heritage is, pleads Zakariya, one must not ask more of it than it can deliver, especially not the innovations that the present impatiently claims and that – except to confuse the 'ritual' (the *'ibadat*) and the norms of life in society (*mu'amalat*) – no sacred rule has ever forbidden.

The fact remains that the autarkic temptation that lies in wait for the less demanding Islamist ideologues produces, here and there, incantatory demands for a literalist imposition of the *shari'a*. The Islamist rhetoric, in this ideological field, has all the traits of a conquering and satisfied ethnocentrism, which is no better than the one it denounces.

This fundamentalism gives reason to those who want to equate re-Islamisation solely with regression and reaction. It is definitely the most serious obstacle to the dynamic of civilisational renaissance that it hopes to promote in the Muslim world. Present in the traditional sectors of society, it forms the basis of the fears of those who reject such a strictly reactionary logic. In fact, such a 'backward step' cannot take place without the support of a logic that is dictatorial. This is one of the lessons learnt from the Iranian experience, whose most radical phase ended with the death of its principal architect. Because it did not measure the ambiguities and the insurmountable limitations of such a position, the fundamentalist section of the Islamist current has rapidly seen its ability to mobilise evaporate. Only in this hypothesis would the Islamist upsurge find itself confined to the role of a tribune, as described by Rémy Leveau, and the bastions where secular ideologies are today, in search of a second wind, could take back the initiative.[10] But withdrawal fixed solely on a reactionary imitation of the Islamic golden age is far from being the only possible outcome for the Islamic movement. The more so because the ways for Islamists to interpret doctrine are not only multiple, but also changing.

Paths of diversification

In terms of analysis, any declaration by an Islamist leader or theorist only makes sense if the idea of a constant ability to evolve is retained. After that, it is less the discourse of an Islamist at a given moment which makes sense than the verification that this discourse not only varies from one place or one individual to another but also from one era to another. The multitude of Islamist attitudes, from which self-criticism is never absent, are evolving as much in accordance with their actors' own evolution as in accordance with economic and political changes in their environment, be it local or international, repressive or liberal, integrating or ostracising. Therefore, only the major trends which appear among these powerful dynamics can facilitate a conceptualisation and a perspective of 'Islamism'. In politics, observers should not see Islam as a source of tangible and directly usable formulae that the actors either accept as Islamists or reject as secularists. This viewpoint should, it is sometimes forgotten, be clearly segregated from the beliefs of the actors. More realistically, we should refer to Islam as an endless supply of legitimacy. The diversified – even contradictory – answers, whose meanings can and do evolve over time, given by the sacred text to those engaged in political combat should therefore not be referred to as 'absolutes' of divine origin – a mistake made by too many observers. The future of the Arab world cannot be sought simply in the *suras* of the Quran or in the history of Muslim thought. Such responses are simply the reflection of the personality of these actors and of the context that generates their demands.

The reasons for the existence of a multitude of 'solutions' that can, if necessary, legitimise religion are the diversity of the social and educational backgrounds and the conscious and unconscious political expectations of religious practitioners. The reactionary sector of the Islamist rhetoric ensures that its users are careful to state their ideological position vis-à-vis the options offered by the West or the Arab regimes that it denounces. This is an initial type of interaction. But the political behaviour of the Arab or Western environment also has a direct impact on the Islamist itineraries and their forms of expression. Through direct contact with the Western environment, the candidates for expatriation often experience an 'intellectual openness', as well as a tactical hardening: the Islamist leaders forced by the oppression of their governments into exile in Europe have gained a sort of spiritual openness, but direct experience might equally fuel their rejection of the Western model.

We get the 'Islamists that we deserve': the political behaviour of Islamists is partially determined by the political behaviour of their local and international counterparts. Firstly, leaders can be influential, depending on whether they know how to manipulate the language of repression. Secondly, the environment in the West can be influential, depending on whether the humanist and democratic references that it claims to promote are given a measure of credibility by accepting that the 'undemocratic' practices of its political allies should be confronted (for example, by denouncing the widespread torture and the election-rigging of its 'democratic' Arab allies), or on the contrary, whether its attitude to these practices fluctuates wildly according to its interests.

Here we might refer to the real influence of those economic determinants that often monopolise analysis to the point of falsifying it. The rhetoric of the students of the Arab diaspora in the US is not the same as that of their predecessors in the technical institutes of Assyut, or of people living in the suburbs of Algiers who are excluded from the educational, economic and political systems.

Should the fundamentalist sector of the Islamist upsurge allow a true representation of the process of re-Islamisation as a whole? Definitely yes if one wishes to support a political fight, as those analysts of the Islamist currents who are also its adversaries are often doing.[11] Certainly not if one wants to avoid controversy and remain analytical. The reactionary component of the Islamist recipe is not the only one. The fact that the literalists and the fundamentalists appear condemned to grow and evolve means that no-one should dare to predict if and how Islamism, generally and specifically, will ever adapt or play itself out in terms that we would call 'modern' – meant as a term to denote a core of universal values.[12] However, many of the West's political strategists believe that Islamism has definitely turned its back on democracy, human and women's rights and on progress – in short on the values of modernity. Are they really correct?

Sufism to the rescue of Islam?

The author has often been accused of only discussing the 'evil', 'radical' Islam, where there is a 'good Islam', which is 'healthy' and 'popular'. Why bother with a phenomenon that only concerns '3 or 4 per cent of Egyptian society', when 'there are six million Sufis'? Since every religion has its own fundamentalists, why concentrate on Islamism?

Admittedly, this accusation was made several months before the Algerian municipal elections in June 1990 and before the foregone conclusions of their results were shattered. The rhetoric of 'good' Sufism, which is popular and therefore in the majority, 'endogenous' and therefore 'authentic', 'apolitical' and therefore 'moderate', has not, however, been abandoned by the regimes that receive little support from religion, or by all those who hope to see a providential 'third force' emerge from the Arab political scene.[13]

In 1990 and 1991, a number of analysts tried to pretend that the old guard of the Algerian Zawiyas, who had been erased from national history because of their alleged collaboration with the colonial authorities, would save the country from the growing threat of the FIS. From a Sufist perspective, the Islamists are regularly described as 'foreign', excluding themselves from a 'political system based on Sunni principles', which is itself a continuation of 'Ottoman influence'.[14] The fact that the brotherhoods would often ignore national boundaries is often conveniently forgotten, so that a 'good', 'endogenous' Sufism is promoted, as opposed to an imported Islamism. For Algeria, the picture of 'good' Maliki Sufis, and 'good' North Africans threatened by the bearded Wahhabis from faraway Arabia, is passed off as scientific observation. This type of political skulduggery is not always condemned. The author of a study on the (good) 'religion of the people' was happy to note that 'if such an amount of information and facts about the Algerian Zawiyas had been made available to the general public over a period of not more than three months (May to July 1991), it was only really due to the "democratic wind" that was beginning to sweep the country'.[15] The Zawiyas' programme seemed, unsurprisingly, to consist of 'pledging allegiance to the President of the Republic' and 'confronting anyone who, in the name of Wahhabism, of Shiism, or of any other imported rite, has attempted and is attempting to tamper with the Maliki rite, held in common by most of our population'.

The differences and the disagreements that face the two socially, intellectually and politically distinct types of mobilisation should obviously not be ignored. The development of the brotherhoods, particularly the Marabout Brotherhood, is seen by the Islamists as a kind of traditionalism, whose doctrine and politics are suspect.

Rached Ghannouchi explains that the Islamist message

has come up against internal barriers, because of the traditionalist image of inherited Islam ... I mean the spiritualist teachings of latter day cults that have no relation to Islam, such as Sufism, the dervish movement, visits to ancestral tombs, the *hadra* [prayer ceremony, including ritual religious dances] of Sufi meetings, the cult of the saints, etc.[16]

Since 1954, when he wrote his *Vocation de l'Islam*, Malek Bennabi has argued that this vision of the cult of the saints, a long-term fascination of Orientalism, is simply an expression of the disarray of profoundly destructured societies. The narrative begins with the integrated man, who continually adapts his efforts to his ideal and his needs and achieves in society the role of both actor and witness. It ends with the disintegrated man, with no centre of gravity, an individual living in a fractured society which offers no moral or material basis for his existence. Therefore, the escape into Maraboutism or into any other nirvana is just a subjective form of a social 'every man for himself'.[17]

The following description, given by a member of the Gama'a Islamiyya in upper Egypt of its entry into politics, provides a good example of the context in which Islamism and Sufism – which was at the time synonymous with traditionalism – became different, including attitudes towards the use of violence.[18]

When we returned to Cairo, we were up against several adversaries. The Sufis primarily, but also families. The Sufis were a powerful enemy due to their doctrine as well as to their intense activity. The other enemy was family traditions. Families were also formidable opponents. But they were not without honour, and would not hesitate to protect you from your enemies, which is no small matter.

The struggle continued against the Sufis and families, who shared the same position, which differed from ours. How did it differ? Well, for example, in the Sa'id people usually greet each other by saying 'Hello, how are you? What are you doing?' etc. But we say 'May peace be with you!' Saying 'May peace be with you' in the morning or evening sounded very strange to the locals. Once he had heard this a few times, my great-uncle went to see my father and said to him, 'If your son says that to me once more, I'll swing for him. That kid is always doing something strange, he prays differently, he fasts every Tuesday and Thursday,' etc. Really our practices were foreign, as were our way of praying and our doctrinal choice. The people in the Sa'id are Malikis. The Gama'a Islamiyya rejects ritual differences and promotes harmony for all. We were subjected to violent attacks, as if we were the disciples of a new religion, which was no longer Islam. Having a beard was also a contentious issue. At the time, there wasn't really any repression. That came later. It was a purely a religious question. When the war with the Sufis began, the police initially did nothing. They only stepped in when they saw that we were about to win. The Sufis acted as spies.

We were arguing with the Sufis over beliefs. We completely dominated them. We exposed them in front of the young in all the precincts. They came to fear admitting their doctrine in public. At that point, the young people rejected the Sufis. We gained control of all the mosques. Our preachers were in such demand that they had to be booked in advance and we still could not meet the demand.

Adel Hussein, General Secretary of the Egyptian Labour Party, says that

> The relation between the Islamist and the Sufi movements has in fact varied from country to country…In Afghanistan, Sufism has played a major role. Even if the Saudi position was very critical, the Muslim Brothers have always maintained good relations with the Sufi currents of the resistance. In Sudan, to this day, the traditional brotherhoods have yet to identify with the modern Islamist movement, even if they have always maintained contact. It is the same in Egypt. It can honestly be said that the relationship between the Sufis and the new modern Islamist movement involves a great deal of discord. This is surely a matter of two parallel movements, not just one. Since Hassan al-Banna, even if he himself was aware of it and tried to react and unify the different movements, it is well known that, in practice, the Muslim Brothers have always been an urban movement of the middle classes, leaving the countryside and the poor urban districts to the Sufis. At the moment I do not think that the relationship is strong enough for a real unification. I do not know exactly how the situation is in Tunisia or Morocco, but in Egypt we are seeing a contradiction that we have yet to overcome. Ideologically, the Sufi interpretation of Islam is much more simplistic and primitive than the Sunni interpretation. For many Sunnis, it is not Islam at all. As a Muslim intellectual I believe that our interpretation of Islam, in the modern sector, or in the cities and right at the heart of the Islamic movement, is more authentic than the Sufi's. This is where there are ideological differences.
>
> This is reflected on a political level. Maybe because of their marginal position in society, or their relative intellectual poverty, the Sufis have mostly been exploited by the Egyptian authorities, as they were by the British before them.[19] They have therefore lost their original role as both religious and political opponents. Their attitude is the logical consequence of the declining impact of their doctrine and their social marginality. This is what separates us.

The fact that the clientelism inherent in the brotherhoods sometimes provokes both ideological and 'corporatist' resistance to the Islamist movement tends to suggest an image, which is reassuring for some, of a sort of antipathy between Islamism and Sufism, which could be considered as a major analytic key. Michel Chodkiewicz, an expert on Sufism, prefers to play down such facile oppositions, stressing the importance of the 'grey areas' and the 'transition' between the two different movements.[20]

The fact that the Islamist current is largely – in Sudan almost exclusively – made up of former brotherhood members shows how the brotherhoods are able to end up in other types of movement. Hassan al-Banna was the first example; others include Hassan Turabi and nearly all the members of the Muslim Brotherhood in Sudan, Abdessalam Yassine, the Islamist leader in Morocco, and Leith Shubeilat, his Jordanian counterpart.

In Sudan the internal conflicts inside the two main brotherhoods, the Khatmiyya and the Ansar, have forced their members to align themselves outside their primordial group, which has led them into the arena of modern politics. The reading proposed by the Egyptian political scientist Abd al-Gamal Gawad to understand the connection between the Sudanese Islamic Front and the main brotherhoods can undoubtedly be applied outside Sudan:

> In spite of its success, the Islamic Front was still limited to the modern sectors of society. To transform itself into a mass movement, and to open itself to other social categories, it had to adopt another approach to the situation in Sudan and, more particularly, to traditional Islam. The Islamists began to speak with another language when they were allied with the former President Numairi. On this new base, co-operation with the tribes and the brotherhoods, traditional as they were, was accepted as long as they agreed to support the Islamist movement. Moreover, the popular Islam of the brotherhoods was no longer denounced as a heresy. The Islamic Front realised that to become a mass movement in a tribal society, the target of their recruitment drives was not the individual, as in such a society there is no such thing as an individual outside the modernised sector. Therefore, it had to address groups. This realisation allowed the Islamist movement to come out from its modern, urban stronghold and extend itself to the rural and least modernised areas.[21]

There are many examples of this kind of shift elsewhere in the Arab world. Throughout the region, the behaviour of Islamists at the heart of the rural Sufi territory, once scarred by the authoritarianism and mistrust of modernisation that fuelled their resistance, has experienced a remarkable evolution.

The long history of the brotherhoods demonstrates that their important political quality is undoubtedly their infinite adaptability, which they have always shown.[22] The ability to mobilise and form alliances must remain, and analysts must ensure that they are not blinkered by the notion of the 'good Islam' of the Sufis, which could, no matter how little they encourage it, 'save' the Arab world from the 'Islamist peril'.

The return of God or the return of the south?

At the heart of our difficulty in keeping up with the Islamic resurgence lies the notion that, no more than a simple mystic 'irritant', it is both condemnable, in the name of the stubborn rejection of any fundamentalism, and spreading throughout the world. Muslims are certainly not alone in looking to the heavens for the solutions that materialism denies them. Jews and Christians have both done the same. There is a temptation to see a universal phenomenon as an 'act of divine revenge'[23] or of revenge by 'God's defenders'.[24] But are the successors of Khomeini, Rabbi Kahane or Monsignor Lefebvre fighting the same battle? It is doubtful. One can only analyse the role that individuals or groups demand of religion by recognising the individual historical dynamics of each of the environments concerned. Knowing that the individual or collective imagination is without doubt the primary determiner of religious behaviour, how far can the comparison of the behaviour of these three revealed religions be pushed? Stimulating as it may be, an analogical reading might in fact overshadow the specificity of the Islamist movement and the reasons for its particular size, as well as the foreseeable path of its evolution.

It is the return of the forgotten sons of the south, rather than a 'return of God', that has unquestionably been the most outstanding dynamic of the late twentieth century. The south is certainly not just Muslim – far from it. The north, on the other hand, is almost exclusively Judeo-Christian. By force of circumstance, the vocabulary of Judeo-Christian culture has been used to express – if not to found – the marginalisation from which the Muslim component of the 'Third World' is presently trying to emerge. A central element of the cultural identity of the Judeo-Christian north is its relationship with the south, where the many consequences of the colonial period are at the forefront of the individual and collective political conscience. There is as much a rejuvenation of the Christian and Jewish faiths in the north as there is a re-Islamisation in the south; consequently, a purely analogical reading would eliminate the dynamic which opposes the expression of this supposed 'act of Divine revenge' in the north and south, instead of making it the axis of analysis.

The distorting effect of such a reading would be that much more pronounced because there is no conclusive proof of a 'return to religious values' in the north. Patrick Michel points out that

> If we are not competent to establish the validity of the figure of the revival of Islam... it is, on the other hand, clear to us that in Central Eastern Europe there has never been a religious revival. Consequently, it is the responsibility of regional specialists, to validate or invalidate the idea of a religious revival at work in the countries or areas that they study, but the idea of a 'global' religious revival, which would articulate the processes of re-Christianisation, re-Judaisation, re-Islamisation, etc. should be dismissed.[25]

It is therefore all-the-more important to state the limitations of a possible comparison. In the south, as in the north, certain types of religious resurgence in the political system highlight the 'moral decay' of society and question the values and categories that have dominated the century. But this is as far as the comparison goes. If, over the past few decades, mosques have seen increasing attendance numbers, it is certainly because that is where the word of God is spoken, but also because the language used in them is that of the only movement to have resisted the cultural pressure of the north. In this case, the apparent return to religious values is driven less by the resurgence of the sacred within a secular universe than by the rehabilitation of the references, notably political, of a local culture which is now looking beyond the colonial period to reclaim its former universality.

If certain European churches are also experiencing growing popularity, it is because entering them is an expression of distancing oneself – particularly in the old centres of communism – from once-dominant material values. But these values, the product of a purely local history, cannot possibly be perceived as 'imported'. Consequently, their rejection demonstrates a crisis of an altogether different character. Furthermore, the impact of the post-colonial arrangement in the south, and the importance of the migratory dynamic that it has triggered, must be taken into account. If there is a return to Christianity, for example in France today, it is because the protective shield provided by a notion of 'national' has been pierced – particularly in areas that have experienced a wave of migration from the south. Certain exhausted identities are retreating or preparing to withdraw into religious strongholds to retain their national identities, a sanctuary from the rise of the south.

What is the Islamic version of this return to religious values? The fact that the culture perceived as endogenous is a religious culture has, without doubt, lent weight to the language of spirituality used to condemn the 'materialist' north. But the propensity of both north and south to employ religious vocabulary should not mask the profound differences between the dynamics that are producing this apparent act of Divine revenge. The north and south may well have met at the crossroads of politics and religion, but it should not be forgotten that they are heading in opposite directions.

The north has, here and there, become reacquainted with religious practice, whose regression had once cleared the way for the idea of secularism; the south has, however, withdrawn less from the values that inspired only a very small cultured elite, and more from a language, foreign to its real culture, used to express these values. The diffusion of this language has coincided in modern history with the marginalisation of its symbolic heritage.[26] The act of Divine revenge which seems to be happening in the Muslim south, does not prejudice the relation being built up with certain types of secularism, that Islam could easily readopt, for both religious and profane lifestyles exist in Muslim culture.[27]

The ultimate paradox is that if at the end of the 1970s, the human and civilisational substratum of Islam really produced this radical and literalist fringe whose image obscures the present Islamist reality, it will, over the coming decades, have to learn to abandon its backward fundamentalist phase in tune with economic and cultural development and political openness. On the other hand, the ideological and sociological pressure that Islam exerts on Western civilisation and religions (as simplistic as these generalisations that omit so many minorities usually are) tends to favour the development of the same fundamentalist offshoots that Islam has largely begun to control. It is a rediscovery of identity for those in the south, whose worries are now abating, and a crisis of identity for those in the north, among whom doubt is rising. This is far from a uniform act of Divine revenge.

CHAPTER FIVE

Revolutionary Violence and Unofficial Violence

Before 1991, the methods of the Irish Republican Army (IRA) or Action Directe had not reached the shores of the Mediterranean. In North Africa, more so than in Egypt, political assassination and blind terrorism were anything but the norm. However, the examples of this phenomenon had already laid the blame at the door of the violent elements of the Islamist upsurge. The dramatic exacerbation of the situation, first in Egypt, then in Algeria in the 1980s, has in some way confirmed this exaggeration *a posteriori*, which has led many observers to say 'I told you so'.

The paradigm of Islamist violence, against the state, minorities, 'deviants' such as Christians, women and intellectuals, and, for good measure, 'against the peace' with Israel, is so firmly entrenched that there seems to be no other explanation for it. Can this truly be justified?

To answer this question, we must first point to a distinction. Depending on whether its objective is to ensure that the obligations of religious law are respected by the state or by the individual, the violence associated with the Islamist upsurge falls into two distinct categories. Revolutionary or vertical violence is a riposte against the action or legitimacy of those in government. Private or horizontal violence is perpetrated against people who are not political adversaries, those who are accused only of contravening a religious norm that the Islamists insist should be enforced by any means necessary. It will be shown that there is nothing specifically Islamist about vertical violence, and that neither its frequency nor its nature should lead to the construction of an 'Islamist model' at odds with the practices of any other ideological group. It will also be shown that horizontal violence is not a feature of the Islamist movement as a whole, but of just one of its expressions, and that it is linked to the political culture and the socio-economic and educational environment of a section of its membership. Whether it is revolutionary or private, confessional or social, Islamist violence – undeniable as its manifestations are – can in no way be considered as a key factor in the reading of the dynamic of re-Islamisation.

Fighting the infidel prince

Even before it engulfed the margins of the urban sub-proletariat (as is the case in present-day Algeria), the diverse social substrata of the Islamist movement already included those who regarded the use of political violence as 'legitimate'. Before some of their number formally recognised the demands of democratic procedures, many Islamist movements had at one time or another considered taking up an armed struggle against the state and its representatives as a legitimate, not to say inevitable, course of action. Before their predictions were spectacularly confirmed by the annulment of the Algerian elections in December 1991, the members of the current immortalised by the assassination of Sadat were convinced that the only way to bring an end to the regimes that developed after independence was through an armed struggle. Their most important reference was the doctrine of the Damascene theologian Ibn Taymiyya (1262–1328), one of the first to theorise the need to overthrow governments that do not respect the divine law. More recently, the evidence suggests that the principal radical factions of the Muslim Brotherhood have their ideological roots in the thought of Sayyed Qutb.

Armed groups of various sizes, influence and durability have developed on the surface and on the periphery of the vast movement for the return of Islam. In Egypt they date back to the 1940s, while in North Africa they appeared much later. In Egypt, the radical expression of the process of re-Islamisation has given birth to many organisations, such as the underground Shabab Muhammed, the organisation that killed Sadat, and the 'Special Wing' of the Muslim Brotherhood, created at the beginning of the 1940s and dissolved 20 years later. Such organisations have used the complex notion of jihad as an emblem and a reference. On one hand, they have aimed their violence against their political competitors. The prime example of these confrontations is the war fought between the Marxists and the Islamists, notably on university campuses, at the beginning of the 1970s. But the primary target of Islamic revolutionary violence has always been those in power and their system of government, which in general is seen as the product of the evil (batil) that good (haqq) must fight.[1]

In view of the fact that the triumph of this good is highly dependent on the state apparatus, this category of actors is no longer satisfied with the public lessons of morality given by the pacifist preachers of the Tablighis, or with the gradualism of the Muslim Brotherhood (which started to participate in the institutional game in 1958),[2] or even with the limited confrontations of the wrong-righting students of the Gama'a Islamiyya in upper Egypt. They have sought to arm themselves in order to fight the state and those that they identify as its ideological or political allies, particularly because they do not recognise the rules of electoral procedure. The archetype of the armed struggle is the Tanzim al-Jihad organisation. In the strictest sense, Tanzim al-Jihad, born in Egypt in 1973, has only manifested itself a few times.[3] The first was in 1974, with an abortive attempt to take control of the Military Academy; this was followed by the Sadat affair, when, after they had joined with two other groups, they became to all intents and purposes a national force, even if only one of its segments was truly mobilised. During the 1980s the organisation, which was slowly recovering from its dismantling in 1981, was completely dormant.[4]

There was no equivalent in North Africa to the armed groups that sprung up in the 1940s in Egypt until the birth of the Mustapha Bouyali's *maquis* in Algeria in 1982.[5] In September 1987, the aborted attempt by military sympathisers of Rached Ghannouchi's MTI to depose Bourguiba confirms the reality, if not the size, of the Islamist presence in the very sectors of the state system that are supposed to limit its development.[6] From 1992, the desertions, the passive or active complicity with the Islamists of members of the Algerian armed forces and the repeated purges of the armies in Algeria and Tunisia illustrate the fact that the selection process devised in the military academies 20 years earlier could not insulate the army from the Islamist surge.[7] They also illustrate the fact that, faced with sealed ballot boxes, at least a part of the Islamist militants feel they have a right to use violence in order to seize power.

Demanding good and forbidding evil

In the name of the commandment to demand good and forbid evil or, more precisely, in the name of a literalist interpretation of this Quranic principle, a part of the Islamist movement has not renounced the idea of using force to reform individuals (and not just the state).[8] This is the most emblematic form of Islamist violence. Of course, the Islamists are not alone in resorting to violence in order to impose on individuals a set of norms that is more cultural than political. Throughout the voluntary modernist period in the Muslim world, the states themselves did not shy away from attacking symbols of cultural or religious membership. The Nasserists publicly cut off beards, the supporters of Reza Shah in Iran tore off *chadors*, the partisans of Ataturk hung the defenders of the *fez* (the traditional headwear) and, more recently, the wearing of the *hijab* in the workplace, in schools or even on the street has been banned – all bear witness to this fact.

Yet if Islamist violence is perpetrated in this sphere, it does so without any state mediation and without then modernist blessing. When they act as members of a religious police enforcing the *nahi 'an al-munkar bi'l-yad* (the severe punishment for breaches of the religious code), the Islamist activists consider that they are, in their logic, compensating for the passivity of the state. The Gama'a Islamiyya militants in upper Egypt provide a classic illustration of this type of behaviour, which has never been a marked feature of the Muslim Brotherhood. In March 1978 Mohammed Abdessalam Farag,[9] the ideologue from Cairo behind the Sadat assassination, met with the 'Sa'idi'[10] Karem Zohdi, a member of the Consultative Assembly (*majlis al-shura*) of the up-and-coming Gama'a Islamiyya, and found that a common sense of purpose united their methods and their destinies. Zohdi gave Farag some words of advice and a long staff that was supposed to symbolise them:[11] we must 'stop the spread of evil' by all means. That was the preferred mode of action for the members of the Gama'a Islamiyya and their specificity.

The most frequent targets of the ban on evil were drinking establishments and their customers, people who openly flouted the fast, distributors of video cassettes and publications that were deemed immoral, couples thought to be illegitimate and reputable secular ideologues who, in the uncompromising terminology of the Gama'a Islamiyya, were atheists. The members of the Sufi brotherhoods, who themselves practised popular forms of religiosity, such as the cult of the dead and ceremonies held in cemeteries, and who were judged to be opposed to Islamic orthodoxy, have also been long-term victims of this type of violence. In Algeria, this sort of moralistic violence has sometimes degenerated into execution: for example, the son of a widow accused by some of the population of lacking moral standards died in an arson attack on his apartment;[12] and a number of women who ran their families without men were deprived of their homes.

Therefore, it is clear that the Islamist rhetoric is capable of initiating an exegesis of the doctrine responsible for totalitarian or fascistic behaviour. There is no doubt that it is important to keep one's eyes open and not underestimate the danger of such potential radicalisation. But the fact that this needs to be taken into consideration is not enough to build a realistic appreciation of the present situation, much less the possible outcome of the meeting between Islam and politics in the Arab world. The unnuanced image of an anti-Copt, misogynist, anti-intellectual, anti-peace Islamist is far from the reality of a much more ambivalent movement.

The role of state violence

Both the Italian Communist Party and the Red Brigade have long criticised the capitalist system, but when it comes to appreciating the nature of the political dynamics of the contemporary West they are fortunately seldom confused with each other. In the same way, the Ku Klux Klan is rarely taken for the Republican Party. Even when their terms of reference appear to be identical, it is advisable to avoid equating, in space or time, the frame of reference and the political methods of Sadat's assassins or the video-burners with the totality of the Islamist tendency. By denying itself the means to determine the origin of this violence and failing to take into account its environment and its specificity, outsiders often do not notice that it is less the product of a component part of the Islamist political landscape than of the system as a whole. Outsiders have too often tended to lump any sort of social or simply political violence together with the list of Islamist acts of violence.

Unless the actions of the IRA demonstrate a congenital link between Catholicism and terrorism, it is necessary to point out that Islamist violence is not so much the result of the ideological references of those who promote it as of their personal itinerary and their political and economic environment. No serious historian would dare suggest that the Muslim religion had as a whole produced significantly more political violence than any other religious or materialist dogma, and no recent historian has done so up till the time of writing. There has been no credible proposal of a structural link between the emergence of the Islamist current and revolutionary violence. From the 1950s to the 1980s, many left-wing groups shared this belief and adopted the methods that it implied. In fact, violence seems to be one of the few products of Arab politics that has been shared democratically.

Revolutionary violence is more than the concoction of a particularly totalitarian ideology with unscrupulous, power-hungry candidates; it is the relatively predictable, if not natural, result of the behaviour of the governmental and international environment. It should be remembered that the methods of political opposition are to a large extent determined by the methods of those in power. Throughout this century, the Arab regimes have had nothing more than the opposition that they deserved: people brought up with their political culture and educated in their political ways. Since the Arab countries became independent, there has not been a single example of a transfer of power that has not involved an armed struggle. To this day, no head of state in the Arab world has shown the foresight that the African leader Senghor demonstrated when he relinquished power. It is difficult to show that, in such a restrictive atmosphere, the Islamists have deployed more violence than others.

When it has not cynically taken the initiative, the state has provided the lead in matters of violence more often than not may be credited. A close inspection of the chronology of the rise of Islamic violence reveals that regimes which have little popular support have frequently understood the benefits to be gained from the existence of a 'fundamentalist pest'. Whenever this most useful weapon has failed to appear, measures designed to help its radicalisation have been taken. The assassinations of left-wing militants linked to the Moroccan movement Chebiba Islamiyya in the 1960s undoubtedly owe a great deal to this strategy. There is plenty to say about the judicial repression of the Islamist, explains J. F. Clément, if only because most Islamist movements have been infiltrated by General Intelligence agents. Benjelloun's assassination by the Na'nmani organisation, for example, took place in front of a General Intelligence inspector.[13] From this point of view, Algeria's political situation at the time of the explosion at the airport in 1992 was very similar to Egypt's at the time of the explosion at the café in Tahrir Square several months later. The multiple shadows of this event have never lifted.

The last acts of repression carried out by the Bourguibists were totally illegal. The repression resorted to by Bourguiba's successor, Ben Ali, and then his counterparts in Algiers, was hardly any better.[14] The repressive methods deployed by the regime in 1987 must consequently be analysed with the same precision as the attempted armed uprising prepared by the MTI immediately after the deposition of the supreme commander. The fire at the militia headquarters of the governing party, the RCD, in the spring of 1991 must not be isolated from the context of the 6000 summary arrests made when Bourguiba, unnerved by the April 1989 election results, realised that there was no other way to save his throne. The excessively repressive measures that he deliberately implemented immediately after the Gulf War – for example, the violence triggered by the refusal of the Algerian regime to be judged in the polling stations – should be remembered. The violence that these practices generate, which is just as deplorable, must be seen in the same light as the violence, silently supported by Arab and Western opinion, against the members of the FIS in Algeria or the Gama'a Islamiyya in Egypt, whose debilitated activists enter the judge's chambers blindfolded, not always knowing to whom they must repeat the confessions extracted under torture.

Of course, each of these currents inevitably has a fringe that is prone to take direct action, and the recourse to violence is an integral part of certain strategies. However, more often than not, the path to violence is the conclusion of the pacifist proselytising first encountered in the mosques. As we have seen with Generals Nasser, Nizar, Ben Ali and Mubarak and Colonel Qadhafi, the armed forces in power have been the first to resort to a repression that is disproportionate to the actions blamed on their opponents. In Tripoli, Casablanca and Tunis, the slightest mis-demeanour, such as membership of an outlawed group, has been punished with severe custodial sentences, which have begun the vicious circle of radicalisation.

Furthermore, the methods of the North African states bear no relation to the methods of Hafiz al-Asad in Syria or of King Fahd of Saudi Arabia: with the technical support of the pride of the French gendarmerie, several thousand people were killed during the quashing of an uprising in Mecca in 1979. They were gassed, drowned and electrocuted beneath the large mosques of the sacred city. Without protest from the West, 1800 people were sentenced to death and executed. The suffering of the Syrian town of Hama remains unparalleled: in 1982, at the end of a week-long bombardment by aeroplanes and tanks, more than 15,000 people had perished. The good conscience of the world media has never thought that it should weigh these deaths on the same scales as the victims of 'terrorism' that the good secularist Asad was supposed to be fighting.

Without doubt, the universal claim of the monotheist religions hides a totalitarian potential which, in Islam, is only exacerbated because there the barrier of secularisation is refuted– at least in theory. But from the Catholic inquisition to the Stalinist gulags, the role of world history is to show that it is the way in which dogmas of all types are appropriated, the depth of social traditions and the violence of political unrest, rather than their intrinsic content, that determine the level of violence which they can deploy. From this point of view, the most important lesson of the second Gulf War concerned the relativity of the categories devised by the West to prioritise its political solidarities in the Arab world. The violence perpetrated by the Iraqi 'secular ally' has shown that the behaviour of political actors is not solely dependent on their ideological references. Nor does the degree to which a regime is determined to avoid political violence, within or outside its borders, bear any relationship to its anti-fundamentalist rhetoric.

The first lesson that a proper interpretation of the political reality of the Arab world reveals is that, as real as it can be, confirmation of 'Islamic violence' can blind us to the existence of another violence – namely that of regimes which, rather than accepting election results, prefer to repress their challengers and ban them from the legitimate political scene in order to survive. The Islamists therefore have no choice but to resort to the violence that they are supposed to monopolise.

This reality will be covered in the following chapters, concentrating on the cases of Egypt, Algeria and Palestine. But first, it is important to illustrate a particular dimension of Islamist violence in Egypt, which concerns the Copt minority.

CHAPTER SIX

Egypt: 'Anti-Copt Islamism'

The record of confessional violence, especially in upper Egypt, must be handled with more care than other acts of denominational violence. This is because it involves behavioural patterns whose limits are not always easy to define and because a section of the media has distorted the image to a large extent. The clashes between members of different denominational groups (continued or not by a part of their clientele) have consistently been the acts of Islamist violence most focused upon by the media, but their coverage has, by the same token, been the worst.

In order to mark out the vast area of this debate, it will be useful to be reminded of a few historical indicators. In Egypt, the Copts have been in contact with Islam since the seventh century.[1] For more than 12 centuries their place in the national fabric was almost exclusively defined through the categories of Islamic law.[2] For the next one-and-a-half centuries, however, with the emergence of the secular principle, it was expressed in juridical categories established – or influenced – by Western political thought. There is no question that, from the time this area con-verted to Islam, Christianity has been in a state of gradual demographic decline.[3] Yet if the primary objective of the imposition of the normative Muslim system and the often-condemned *dhimmi*s was to wipe out any minority opposed to Islam, 12 centuries of Muslim domination would have been more than enough time: Spanish Christianity managed to achieve this in respect of Muslims and Jews. There is no doubt that the status of *dhimmi*s (minorities, such as Christians or Jews, protected by Islamic law) that was in place until the fall of the Ottoman Empire was clearly in need of a strong *ijtihad* (the personal interpretation of the sources of Islam, as opposed to *taqlid*, blindly following them). But its present denunciation, the starting-point for any anti-Islamist argument,[4] only makes sense if it is compared to the legal status given by the West to its own confessional minorities over the centuries, and then to the unbending exclusion of these minorities from the secular protection that followed. In any case, the way confessional minorities have played out their roles within cultures, religions or dominant political forces still, undoubtedly, leaves a lot to be desired.

From social violence to confessional violence

In late-twentieth-century Egypt, and particularly in the semi-rural regions of the Sa'id, social actors are more likely to settle their differences with a gun than in front of a judge. Denominational confrontation often results from the extension of purely local conflicts to confessional ones, a system of vendetta which has been operating in this region for quite some time.[5]

However, some of these confrontations cannot be explained by mere 'Sa'idi' violence. Some collective mobilisations are indeed religious. Rumours, often linked to alleged moral violations (prostitution or the rape of young Muslim women), have for several reasons mobilised crowds much larger than the activist groups. Members of the Gama'a Islamiyya regularly attack traders who they believe to be in breach of the religious order or merely 'provoking' Muslim sensibilities.[6] Since the beginning of the 1970s, a section of the activist movement has been mobilised by the fantasy that the Christians were amassing weapons in their churches to forcibly re-impose Christianity on Egypt with the help of the West. Even if the organisation often lays the blame for the confessional violence at the door of the state – which was trying to exploit it – the members of the Gama'a Islamiyya have no qualms about this dimension of their political engagement, even if for some it belongs in the past.[7] 'There is no point denying that, at the beginning of the 1970s, we were preparing ourselves for an armed struggle in the desert', recalls the lawyer Muntazir al-Zayate. 'Our goal was to resist a possible attack by the Christians, who we really believed were stockpiling weapons in their churches.'[8] Some of his former colleagues have not really changed their opinion. One of the former Gama'a Islamiyya leaders explains that

> In 1980 the director of security in Minya told us that he had it on good authority that the monastery at Donka, close to Assyut, could only be taken by air and with heavy losses. It is built onto a mountainside and protected at the front by natural features. Inside, there was a cache of arms that had come directly from the United States. All this happened under the personal supervision of Mrs. Carter. 'We know,' the officer told us, 'but we can't go in.' We then asked

him, 'Can we go into a mosque?' 'Yes,' he replied. 'What about a church?' No, we don't have the right. He also told us that some young Christians were going to train, via Greece and Canada, with the Maronites in Lebanon.

To this day, the incidents of social violence take place against a backdrop of a barely concealed anti-Christian backlash that is mainly limited to the activist movement of the Gama'a Islamiyya. When disputes between neighbours give them the chance, they are ready to whip individual conflicts into an orgy of partially confessional violence.

My enemy's friend, or the minority syndrome

For the most literalist section of the Islamist movement, Christianity is seen as an obstacle to the ambition of restoring the symbolic and normative monopoly of Islam. It is easy to suspect the Christians of 'toeing the line' of regimes which profess to reject all religious parties, and of supporting this foreign foil directly, by the presence of foreign missions, or indirectly by interposed communities of immigrants.[9] These ambitions are fed by the reality of the Western cultural and linguistic influence on at least a part of the Christian community, including the Copts, the highly selective interest of the Western media in the Christian communities of the East, the confusing manner in which they highlight the Islamist phenomenon and confessional tensions, and the open proselytising of some Catholic and Protestant foreign missions. Some study centres led by Anglo-Saxon Protestants are therefore regularly accused of 'spreading the Christian word in the heart of a Muslim country'.[10]

To some Islamists, Christians (including the Copts), no matter how Egyptian they are,[11] are part of another *umma*. Through tourists, business-men and missionaries, their relationship with the West has been developed more and often seems more at ease than that of the Muslims. In 1994, many foreign companies in Cairo continued to recruit Copts almost exclusively – indeed in some cases the hiring of Muslims was forbidden. Few Western embassies have resisted the temptation to develop their cultural policy in Egypt through the Christian minority alone. The colleges, universities and other institutions that benefit this community receive much greater support than their size merit. This is a symbolic imbalance that is not necessarily compensated for by the huge investment in the Muslim institutions by the Saudis.

There are other rhetorics of exclusion, mainly economic, that are linked to the over-representation of Christians in certain professional areas, such as medicine and pharmacy. In the 1950s, more than 80 percent of graduates in these subjects were Christian. If Christian communities throughout the East – Maronites, Catholics, Protestants and Copts – are today entering a period of political turbulence, it is partly because they are feeling the repercussions of the economic, political and ideological benefits that were so unevenly distributed during the long years of European hegemony in this region.

As elsewhere, this explanation is not a justification. But when the matter is looked at from the Islamist point of view, the principle of secularism that has managed to restrict the Muslim normative system to the sphere of personal status, and therefore deprived it of its hegemony in society, has been imposed, whatever its real objectives, in the name of the 'defence of confessional minorities'. As Laurent and Annie Chabry note,

> the defence of Christian minorities was simply an excuse for the powers to intervene. This intervention aspired to achieve equality by using a general regime of inequality that it intended to preserve. When pushing reform and modernisation, it had no motive other than to undermine and destroy the Empire.[12]

The European victors have clearly interfered with the economic and political foundation of the Christian elites. They have done so in Lebanon by allowing a confessional political system to emerge that is in stark contradiction to the supposed universality of its secular vision. Moreover, they have done so by favouring Christian educational establishments, by extracting a part of the Coptic community from the national fabric, whether or not it has been converted to Catholicism or Protestantism, so that it becomes the country's economic elite within the framework of a system that has very quickly shown the limits of its social preoccupations. Again Laurent and Annie Chabry stress that it is the cultural element of confessional pluralism, rather than its structure, that felt the impact of the West. The teaching of the Christian missions and their religious schools widened the distance between the communities. The channels of education instilled a new type of culture among Christians, which was beyond the reach of the majority of Muslims.[13]

Without making it an essential factor,[14] Claude Guyomarch identifies, in the 'epicentre of confessional insurrection' that is Assyut, the part that economic determination plays in the Islamist activists' constant condemnation of Christian 'arrogance'. He writes:

> The higher rate of urbanisation of the Copts and their traditional concentration in certain economic functions suggest that the animosity of many Muslims, and particularly of the poorest, towards Christians is rooted in a past where inequality amongst the denominations was built into the system of social regulation. All the more so because the collective memory has been reprogrammed to include

the memories of colonial domination and the glut of Christian missionaries from the West at the turn of the century. These upheavals led to the emergence of a new urban Coptic bourgeoisie that had grown rich from entry into the world agricultural marketplace. This was totally exploited by the latifundia and their agents in the Assyut region, who were mainly Protestant.[15]

The behaviour of the Christians as a minority gave rise to this type of rhetoric of exclusion.[16] In politics, it has ensured that without exception they have been systematically appeased to prevent them from becoming the opposition.[17] At a time when the regime was facing growing criticism, the stance taken by Pope Shenouda since the end of the confrontation with Sadat in 1981 has shown some of the limitations of the Christian reaction to this. The repression visited on the radical Islamist groups at the time of the confessional incidents, delivered with a violence proportional to the regime's fear of them, appeared to be selective, and the Christians, who had never opposed the 'tyrant', were suspected of having a hand in it.[18] This is one of the foundations of the argument of the militants from Cairo's overcrowded suburbs: 'they [the Christians] know that if there is any confrontation, it is we [the Islamists] who will be repressed. They provoke us.' Alain Roussillon stresses that attacking the Christians 'is a metaphor for the illegitimacy of the government without having to actually attack it, the Copts representing the symbolic incarnation of profane power'.[19] In 1993, the raid on the village of Sanabu was the most violent of the confrontations, leaving 14 people dead. In this case, the role of radical groups has never been established; however, the attack seemed to subscribe to this logic of reprisals against innocent people who had been identified as accessories to the repression.

In terms of Islamist violence against the Christian community, the riots that took place in March 1993 in Qalyubiyya, 30 kilometres north of Cairo, occupy an intermediary position that makes them quite typical. As the result of a complaint by one Copt student, four Muslim secondary school students were accused of distributing cassettes that were judged to be of a nature that would incite a confessional uprising. The Minister of Education decided to expel them, and their teacher was dismissed. Following this, thousands of protestors demanded and obtained the reinstatement of the pupils and the teachers. Although the context of this incident has never really been established, the initial anti-state violence subsequently led to an attack on a Protestant church, part of which was set on fire. As a result, several hundred Islamist sympathisers, real or otherwise, were arrested.

This incident was hugely significant as it mobilised a large part of the population, far greater in number than the activist groups, who have never since been implicated. Initially a form of protest against a state decision, the demonstrations put the Christians in the position of having jointly initiated a repressive measure judged to be excessive and illegal. This gave the regime the excuse to make a wave of arrests, targeting the most radical current of its Islamist opposition and, through the media exploitation of the affair, the Islamist current as a whole.

Confessional violence and political regulation

If we are to understand the ambiguous role of the regime, certain structural aspects of the political scene in Egypt must be considered. Those in power, who are very quick to identify a mere demand for political participation as a confessional uprising, are not as removed from rising tensions as they claim. Despite the lack of credibility of some of the representations put forward by the radical fringe of the Gama'a Islamiyya,[20] it is inescapable that every incident of confessional violence between the communities has been particularly successful in reinforcing, both domestically and internationally, the repressive option of the regime – therefore its one real chance of survival. While Christians do not threaten any country's political stability, the Islamists virtually control the monopoly of effective political opposition. Accordingly, in order to profit from the slightest inter-confessional incident and legitimise the repressive option, there is one course of action that the regime seems to regularly fall back on. The Islamist opposition is denied its right to legality in order to protect the Christian minority, which in its turn appears as the main reason for the regime to ban all legal opposition.

The real question has, therefore, less to do with the reality of inter-confessional violence than with its function in the political game. Is it a natural side-effect of the dynamic of re-Islamisation, which would allow the regime to quash the slightest political expression of this dynamic in the name of the protection of national unity? Or, on the other hand, is it just an analogue form of anti-state violence? If the latter, we should remember the ambiguous attitude of the regime, which, by using the Christians to prolong the repression that ensures its survival, shows that it is perhaps less interested than it claims in the interests of the people it claims to protect.

Tareq al-Bishri says that 'during the 1970s, when the government wanted to introduce legislation to reinforce its powers vis-à-vis the opposition, it claimed that trouble was brewing between the denominations and it drafted a bill, known as the Law of National Unity, that in effect attacked all political opposition'.[21]

In the 1980s, the war against the Islamist current tried to rally its secular adversaries by inciting hatred between the Copts and political Islam in general. Some went as far as to suggest that Islam or Muslims would no longer tolerate the presence of non-Muslims. They went as far as to demand less Islam to guarantee the unity and security of society. This considerably weakened the national framework and each sector of society came to feel that its security and survival were threatened. And not one year has passed without there being the question of another new breach within the community or without the anxiety of one side infecting that of another in a sort of intellectual and political war, where each side only feels safe deep in their trenches, only daring to poke their head out to assail others or be assailed themselves.

The culturalist alternative

The beard of the first man to arrive is short and well-groomed, a characteristic of the Muslim Brotherhood. The second has a long unkempt beard, like the Salafis. But his clothing is black, not white. The two bearded men burst out laughing and embrace in the shadow of the entrance to the old building on the Port-Said Street, the Cairo head-quarters of the (Islamic) Labour Party. One is the leader of this party, the other is one of the Coptic priests responsible for the religion column of the party's newspaper. This un-newsworthy item goes unrecorded by television cameras.

Here, as at other levels of analysis, there seems to be little difference between oppositional Islam, that is reputedly anti-Christian, and institutional Islam, that is supposedly ecumenical. This is partly because confessional tensions – linked, for example, to the rejection of a plan to build new churches – are not limited to Islamic opposition. However, it is especially because the relationship between the surge of oppositional Islam and the Christian population is not confined to confrontation – a point which is often overlooked. For a long time the Islamist opposition has seen the danger of being trapped in the equation: re-Islamisation equals attack on national unity. Away from the marches for unity that are regularly orchestrated by the government and the many seminars or other round tables on national unity, where Christian and Muslim dignitaries pat each other on the back in front of the television cameras, there are more spontaneous and more serious discussions between at least a part of the Islamist movement and a part of the Christian community. The leaders of the Muslim Brotherhood tend to publicise their presence at the public holidays of the Coptic calendar. They are often met by religious leaders and have begun discussions with them at the highest level. It was at these talks that Pope Shenouda revealed his attitude to the question of the application of the *shari'a* – not a rejection in principle, rather a need for much clarification.[22] Some Christians, even if they do not represent the dominant trend in the Coptic Church,[23] are regularly involved in debates organised by the Labour Party. Others are to be found on electoral lists. In 1987, the party of Ibrahim Shukri and Adel Hussein even chose to put a Christian at the top of the list in Assyut. In each edition of the fortnightly publication of *Al-Sha'ab*, the most widely read of the opposition press, there is a dedicated column for a member of the national Church (against the wishes of the Church's hierarchy) to debate a question close to the hearts of the Coptic community; the paper's commentator on Palestine has long been a Christian. Likewise, the supposed revulsion felt by the Coptic community towards political Islam has not prevented the rules of rural clientelism from functioning and the small Coptic village of Bourtubate in upper Egypt from voting overwhelmingly for an Islamist candidate in the municipal elections of 1992.

At the heart of the real or supposed confessional tempest in 1993, it was possible to see members of the Gama'a Islamiyya rubbing shoulders with members of Tanzim al-Jihad, holding a debate with a Lebanese bishop about the history and meaning of Arab Christian nationalism, under the watchful eye of the Muslim Brotherhood and in the presence of representatives of the secular left.[24] From 1993 onwards, there were informal but regular meetings between a small group of Christians and representatives of the Muslim Brotherhood.[25] This ideological activity, which allows the Christian community not to perceive itself as occupying an exclusively antagonistic role in its relations with the Islamist movement, and thereby guaranteeing it some degree of permanence and stability within the Egyptian political system, has been going on for a long time. The formula of the Christian Wafd leader Makram Ubeid ('My home-land is Islam, my religion is Christianity'[26]), who insists that Christians belong to the civilisational universe of Islam, is a good example.

For his part, Adel Hussein urges that

> We need a general ideology, meaning general principles that regulate the entire scene and guide its different components. They are needed so that everything can run peacefully. I think that the general rules and principles of Islam are best suited to this country. It is not a question of forming a single party, but everyone should be united under the symbol of Islam. Why? Because that is our identity. It is the identity of the Muslims but it is also the identity of the Copts. Islam is our heritage, our identity, our soul, whether we are Muslim or Copt. We are all

born of the same history. Whatever the circumstances, Copts have always been part of society. It is only very recently that we have seen Muslim women in towns, particularly in Cairo, wearing different clothing to Christian women. But if you go out of Cairo, to Upper Egypt, you will see that both Muslim and Coptic women wear the same clothing. It represents the common culture, the common tradition. Islam, its values and its lifestyle, are the heritage of everyone living in Egypt, Muslims as well as Christians. You know the famous saying of Makram Ubeid. Well, some of us used to say that Copts were Muslims who go to Church on Sundays. In the classical Coptic language, the word *rab* is used to refer to God in preference to *allah*. *Insha' rab* and not *insha'allah*. In practice, most Copts say *insha'allah* like Muslims. It is very rare that you hear otherwise. There are many other examples. This is why we say that we are facing the future armed with a single culture, whether we are Muslim or Copt, and under this single umbrella, the different political factions should be able to compete in peace.[27]

In Amman in 1989, a section of the Christian community seemed to vote for Leith Shubeilat, a member of the moderate arm of the Islamist current, for him to become an influential member of parliament. Shubeilat confirms

Yes it is true [...] I received Christian votes and I held on to them. I had growing support amongst all the sectors of society, amongst the Christians but also amongst the Left and all sorts of people. Because I knew how to do what the West is completely failing to do today. That is to live by my values, the values of Islam, and to show no discrimination to my own or to others. Why is the West about to fail? It has its own values, some of which are very strong. But its problem is that when it imposes its values, it does so in a racist manner. It keeps them all to itself. Had the West been human, we would have all been Westernised! With the formidable cultural offensive that we endured, we would not have been able to resist. We would have been smitten with the West. But it is difficult to be smitten with someone who does not act like a human being. How on earth do you think there could ever have been any chemistry between us?

Christians and Jews, throughout their history, have benefited from the justice of Islam. That justice protected their churches. They themselves declared that they had been better treated before the Christians came to the Near East. Victor Saad, the Christian Lebanese poet, recognized it: he tells the Christians of today 'You were never persecuted until these Western Christians arrived here...!'

The Christians in this part of the world, in Muslim countries where their religion is respected, are becoming part of this Muslim nation. They are Muslims by nationality and Christians by faith. This was said by Makram Ubeid and also Faris al-Ghouri. You should also read Michel Aflaq. I think I was wrong about Michel Aflaq and his Ba'th. It was he who told the Christians that, as Arabs, you cannot but belong to this Muslim society. You are Muslims. Arab Christians are Muslim by civilisation. It is their culture, their civilisation. They should, they must fight for it.[28]

The existence of this culturalist perspective certainly does not mean that it is presently the dominant perspective and it will not prevent other confessional tensions from emerging. It is primarily the inexorable challenge to the secular principle – at least how the Islamists interpret it in the present climate – and the weakening of the Western presence that are shaking the ideological and political foundations of the Christian communities in the East. Consequently, their future depends on their ability not to get involved with the regimes and the West, who would like to use them to block the path of the Islamist surge. It depends on their ability to maintain the principles founding their political legitimacy in the framework of the ideological and political reconstruction that is today at work in their place of origin. Many of them and many of their Islamist interlocutors have already shown that they are able to meet this challenge.

CHAPTER SEVEN

Egypt: The Spiral of Violence

Each time that it blocks the free circulation of genuine political dynamics in its veins, each time that these channels are clogged to the extent that the flow can no longer be absorbed, a political system plays into the hands of secret organisations and other clandestine groups... When it creates all sorts of legal bodies that have absolutely no bearing on a country's political, social or cultural reality, when it legally conjures up what is not really there while what is really there is not recognised by right, when a political system can tolerate such a dichotomy between what is legal and what is real... that is a genuine schizophrenia that could affect the whole of society.

Tareq al-Bishri[1]

'Skirmishes on the Nile'

Little has been written about the history of the Islamist current's relationship to political violence in Egypt, the homeland of the disciples of Hassan al-Banna, from the first clashes between Nasser and the Muslim Brotherhood to the assassination of Anwar al-Sadat. Of course, Olivier Carré makes a salutary contribution when he stresses that

Nasser and his aides, once he had gained absolute personal power in March 1954, thought it wise to label the Muslim Brothers as congenital terrorists. This meant that they were falsely accused of all political murders that took place between 1945 and 1950 and, under Nasser, held responsible for the plots (which were apparently fabricated by the government) against him in 1954 and 1965, and indeed against Sadat in 1981.[2]

Carré concludes notably that 'despite the advice of the Nasserist A. Imam, there is no doubt about the farce [of the attack] in 1965 [attributed to the Muslim Brotherhood, which signalled a new wave of repression]'. The assassination of Sadat in 1981 did not bring an end to any democratic experiment. It triggered a brutally repressive response from the regime that led to the imprisonment of 1500 members of the political intelligentsia of all tendencies and denominations. Moreover, the revival of political violence at the end of the 1980s suggests an explanation other than the one proposed by the media's scornful approach to 'fundamentalist violence'.

Essentially, the people who are today blamed for the bulk of the violence are a 'delinquent minority', a result of the 'decline in economic conditions' and the 'failure of social policies'. Due to the financial or technical support of certain foreign states, Sudan and Iran in particular, or the culpable tolerance of others such as Pakistan, this minority has rejected 'the democratic option of the regime' and has sought refuge in 'terrorism' in order to 'impose on an unwilling society' a political project based on a 'misguided interpretation of religious references', which therefore threatens in particular the Christian community, and which 'endangers national unity'. This quasi-official version seems to lay the blame for political violence at the door of the radical section of the Islamist opposition. Yet by doing so, it also incriminates, implicitly or explicitly, the legalist part of the current, or practically the entire 'useful' opposition to President Mubarak's regime.

The way in which the most moderate wing of the current, the Labour Party, was treated is a good example of this logic. On 10 October 1992, Adel Hussein published a detailed condemnation of the imbalance between the economic benefits of tourism and its moral and social impact. This happened when a delegation of US travel agents was holding a convention in Cairo. Despite the provocative character of a part of Hussein's rhetoric, the article, published more than two months after the attacks on tourists had begun, was more of an economic than a religious critique of tourism, which he accused of having insufficient benefits for the industrial sector. His often well-founded reservations about the social and moral impact of the tourist industry had long been made, in Egypt and elsewhere, by other political or religious factions, such as the Algerian or Libyan people in the 1970s. Nevertheless, the authorities floated the idea that the leader of the most moderate Islamist group was responsible for the attacks on tourists that were carried out by the radical fringe of its most frustrated members. Even if the reasoning of his accusers collapsed on several points, as the judges were quick to recognise, Hussein was nevertheless handed to a state security court. The foreign press has never redressed the blatant inaccuracies of the accusation, and has even surpassed the propaganda of the regime. The *Le Monde* correspondent explained that

> For the Islamists, the total paralysis of the tourist sector became a strategy designed to overturn the 'impious regime'. For several years, they went to extraordinary lengths. They killed important figures such as the president of the assembly, slit the throats of policemen, gunned down free thinkers and slaughtered dozens of Copts in Upper Egypt. This did not unduly worry the government, who were content to launch a few retaliatory attacks. These attacks were not deemed to be 'very worrying'. It got to the point where they were hardly noticed... But then a former Marxist, who had converted to radical Islamism, had a stroke of genius. He wrote in the weekly paper he edits that tourism is *haram* (contrary to Islam). It was during a summer when tourism was breaking all the records, with hotels 80 per cent full. The *fatwa* [the informal ruling of Islamic jurisprudence] did not fall on deaf ears and, for the first time in the history of modern Egypt, tourists became targets.[3]

The reality is quite different. The 'former Marxist' Adel Hussein does not have the right personality to do this and, no matter how important his status (judging by the wide readership of his party's journal), he had no direct or indirect influence on the Gama'a Islamiyya, who never considered him as one of their own.[4]

Often there are two dangerous shortcomings in the official or media coverage of Egyptian political violence: firstly, the blatant omission of the role of repression, and secondly, the disregard – indeed the negation – of the political dimension of the crisis. Even if none of the 'accelerating' factors (notably limited economic progress and deficiencies in the educational system) can be ignored, the crisis that has swept across Egypt under President Mubarak is primarily political. It feeds on the growing dichotomy between the real political forces and the ability or the will of the institutional system to integrate them. If political expression on the banks of the River Nile is not channelled through the ballot box, it is primarily because these forces are banned from participation in elections. Of course, there is a closed and intolerant side to the Islamist opposition. But its influence is dictated by the regime's policy: by discrediting legalist and participatory attitudes, the regime reinforces and legitimises the dismissive stance of this extremist faction. This places the oppositional dynamic in a dangerous position: the fact that political forces seeking electoral recognition are prevented from becoming legal generates among them a natural tendency to radicalisation. In the face of such preventative repression, this hardline approach has undoubtedly produced a certain degree of counter-violence. The regime, which is in fact more concerned about the millions of votes held by the centre of its opposition than a few bombs planted by its extremist fringe, brandishes this violence to justify the total seizure of the system that allows it to survive – particularly for the benefit of its international backers.

Democracy: Flowers but no fruit

Deprived of the essential dimension of the rotation of power, the political relaxation in the form of the partial liberalisation of the press introduced by Sadat and continued by his successor Hosni Mubarak has been a key factor in the exacerbation of the failings of the parliamentary system. Pluralism has failed to escape the context in which it was reintroduced into Abdel Nasser's partisan autocratic vision of Egypt in 1977. When Anwar al-Sadat confided in some of his aides that 'interlocutors' for the single party in power, in the form of 'political platforms', were needed, it was as much to perfect the liberal image of his regime (notably for the benefit of the West) as to genuinely rewrite the rules of the game. If the single party really did lose its legal monopoly under Sadat, Mubarak has not abandoned in the slightest the privileges on which its predominance was founded. It is true that for the National Democratic Party continued democratisation would be significant: there is no need to conduct an in-depth evaluation of its policies, simply to calculate the extent of the risk that it is taking. When reminded of the universal law of attrition that menaces those who govern 'in the long term', it is more than enough to be convinced that if the many obstacles that currently stand in the way of free elections were removed, the party in power would be defeated. Like many of its Arab counterparts, the Egyptian regime has a limited vocabulary when it comes to discussing democracy, and is becoming increasingly reticent. It has to take two simultaneous yet contradictory steps: to re-establish its legitimacy through political liberalisation without losing control of the balance of power that such openness could redistribute. If this were to ever happen, all forces that are likely to redress the balance to its detriment have been denied access to the system.

This is a fundamental characteristic of Egyptian democracy that is often forgotten. It is not only the radical fringe of the Islamist movement that is ostracised, but also its huge legalist element. In Egypt, a political current can only aspire to parliamentary representation once it has undergone the process of a double selection. Selection by the electorate is by far the easier of the two: first, it must get past the 'all-party tribunal' (made up of five magistrates of the State Council and five public figures), which is much more selective, and which is the only way of gaining legal recognition. On 14 April 1990, new elections were announced because the electoral law, on the basis of which the parliament had been elected in April 1986, was declared unconstitutional. This tribunal recognised three new formations.[5] However, the term 'the test-tube parties', given to them by the newspaper *al-Wafd* summed up the limitations of this 'openness'. Misr al-Fatat,[6] the Democratic Unionist Party (centre right), of which it was said that its seat would never belong to someone from outside its founder's family, and the Green Party of Dr Hassan Ragab (who made a fortune by re-inventing Egyptian papyrus, and who has since resigned), whose media-friendly personality was not enough to ensure credibility, did not have the slightest effect on the elections.

At the same time, the forces that were likely to cause the smallest upset in the parliamentary balance were once more prohibited from integrating into the system. Firstly the Nasserists, who, despite their rapid decline, found their initial demand rejected on the grounds that their programmes '[denied] the principal of democracy and [were] designed to restore the totalitarian regime that had been so ruthless under President Nasser'.[7] Secondly and principally, the Muslim Brotherhood, which had been unable even to resurrect its association, were dissolved by Nasser in 1954. In September 1991, its case was reviewed for the 45th time because of the old ban on political parties with a confessional base.[8] Once again, on 6 February 1993, the administrative court rejected its demand for recognition as a charitable organisation.

The 'recognised parties', or those who on the strength of the alliances tolerated by the authorities have earned the right to take part in the elections, can only enter the political game under strict conditions. It is public knowledge that there is no 'election' for 75 percent of the seats. Only 25 percent are in some way submitted to the hazards of suffrage, a situation which, at the time of the legislative elections in 1990, led the three most important opposition parties to boycott the vote. It is, moreover, estimated that the electoral lists, which have not been available since 1956, account for less than 15 percent of the potential electorate.[9] With the unofficial rate of participation in the legislative elections rarely exceeding 10 percent, it is therefore conceivable that the parliament of March 1991 extended the law of exception – which suspends civil liberties such as the right to go on strike, hold public meetings etc – for three years, then a further two years, then solemnly asked President Mubarak to continue in his post for a third term, represented less than 3 percent of the electorate. This was to happen again at the general election on 4 October 1994, yet again underlining the shortcomings of the system. The huge efforts of the media succeeded in fooling only those who really wanted to be misled. The extent of the perplexity and the cynicism of the political discourse (the newly elected president spoke of how he was 'touched by the unprecedented turnout of the electorate') appeared once again in the harsh light of reality. If we are to believe the official results, the polling stations that were strangely empty and that were briefly troubled by passing demonstrators who were faithfully filmed by national television, saw 15,678,492 people pass through their doors in the space of a few hours. That is 84.16 percent of the electorate, 96.28 percent of whom voted, unsurprisingly, for the president. Under the circumstances, the Western media and press agencies were amazingly silent, except for Reuters, which, three hours after the polling stations had closed, dared to estimate that the actual turnout was less than 5 percent.

The legal parties are not protected from the regime's desire to preserve its absolute monopoly over the 'useful' political scene. On two occasions in 1992, the government tried to take control of Misr al-Fatat, whose newsletter had adopted an oppositional tone that was considered too daring, and the Labour Party, which was legally bound to adopt less hostile policies. In both cases, the decisions of the judiciary were overturned. The day after Mubarak was re-elected for his third term, the Labour Party was subjected to a savage attack: several of its leaders were arrested, accused of insulting the president of the republic and inciting rebellion. Consequently, Adel Hussein was arrested for the second time in January 1995, accused of divulging military secrets and of being a threat to national security.

Where else can the oppositional dynamic express itself, apart from in the institutions whose primary purpose is to channel it? Since 1990, wherever there has been free competition the Islamist opposition has proved significantly more popular than the government or any other opposition party. Faced with these worrying statistics, the regime has tightened its grip on the system and hurled repeated legal offensives at civil groups, which constitute a breeding-ground for politics. In February 1993 it attacked the professional associations, places where the oppositional dynamic could still be expressed quite freely. On 16 February 1993, parliament was requested to adopt a law that would 'guarantee the imposition of democratic liberties', which the Wafd daily newspaper called 'the law of the nationalisation of the trade unions'. According to this law, any trade union that could not count on the support of a minimum of 50 percent of its profession in the first round to elect its leaders, and 30 percent for the second round, would be placed under judicial control. By condemning the poor turnout for the professional elections, the regime has tried to portray itself as the guarantor of trade-union democracy, a title that only the most cursory observers would accord it. At the genuinely free elections, before 1993, the regime wanted to prevent the Islamist tendency – at the time, the Muslim Brotherhood, which was in the majority in the liberal professions – from showing the strength of its position in the socio-professional sector.[10] One of the paradoxes of such legislation is, of course, that it can, if such democratic demands apply to the whole political system, invalidate any election, including a presidential election, if the turnout does not match that of the professional elections. The argument that the Islamist victories were only due to the low turnout is no more applicable here than it is elsewhere: whenever the reinforcement of this participation has occurred, the Islamist vote seems to have remained constant. For example, it stood at more than 60 percent of doctors between 1986 and 1993, while the absolute number of voters rose from 8000 to 22,000.

Other, mainly welfare, associations suffer from an overdose of control. After the earthquake of 12 October 1992 which revealed just how porous the financial channels of state intervention were (channels which had no way of effectively reaching the thousands of victims) the regime preferred to outlaw the fundraising efforts of all associations to avoid competing with the Islamist social network.[11]

The stronghold of the Muslim Brotherhood in the urban middle classes and its legalism make it, in the eyes of the regime, more dangerous than its obstreperous adversaries in the Gama'a Islamiyya, who are heavily represented on university campuses and among the agricultural proletariat of the small villages of the Sa'id. As a result, the organisation was subjected to all sorts of intimidation. The discovery of a research organisation, 'Salsabil', which gathered statistical data about the potential of the Muslim Brotherhood outside the country, and which was accused of being 'involved in a spying mission for Israel', signalled the resumption of its repression in February 1992. On 6 June 1992, for the first time in several years, members of the brotherhood were once again arrested. The accusation that they politically exploited both the earthquake and meetings of support for Bosnia gave rise to more arrests which, at the end of a demonstration on 18 June 1993 organised jointly by six mosques in Cairo and Alexandria, included three of the movement's leaders in Cairo. The campaign was well and truly underway when about twenty of the movement's leaders were arrested in January 1995.

Places of worship were also affected by new restrictions. In April 1993, the minister for the *waqfs* announced his intention of extending the state's control over private mosques over the next two years, which constituted approximately 88 percent of the 170,000 mosques in the country, and ruled that their opening hours should be strictly limited to the hours of prayer. Even the members of the Islamic establishment at the University of al-Azhar, in theory the beneficiaries of these arrangements, objected to this project – a costly affair as it involved paying a salary to thousands of new Imams.[12]

The repressive option

As products of the dysfunctional system, there appears to be a common link between the acts of Islamist violence that followed the gradual intensification of the repression of these currents. In the post-Sadat decade, one of the first steps towards the repressive option took place in the spring of 1986, shortly after Zaki Badr, who stamped his mark on the repression and was its architect, was named as the Minister for the Interior. Shaaban Rashid, a student in Assyut, who was sticking up posters advertising a lecture by Omar Abd al-Rahman, was shot in the head by a member of the secret police.[13] In May 1990, members of the dissident group of Shawqi Sheikh's supporters were gunned down and dumped in an irrigation canal at the oasis of Fayoum. Official figures put the number of dead at 18; others put the total dead at 24. In the same months, seven people suspected of belonging to an armed group in the village of Menqabad, near Assyut, were killed in their sleep. For many, however, the turning-point was the shooting of Dr 'Ala Muhieddin on 9 September 1990 in a street in the Pyramids district. Muhieddin was the national spokesman for the Gama'a Islamiyya, who, a few weeks earlier, had unofficially been ordered by state security to leave Cairo. Continually overlooked by the official media, the assassination of Muhieddin was the trigger for the most high-profile riposte of the armed wing of the Gama'a Islamiyya: the assassination of the President of Parliament, Rifa'at Mahjoub.[14] Against the backdrop of the Algerian elections and the Gulf War, Mahjoub's death signalled an unprecedented escalation of repression. Using the prevention of terrorism as an excuse (or, if necessary, the fight against drug-trafficking), Egypt has continuously renewed its emergency powers, first adopted in 1967, which can be used for the severe restriction of individual and collective political liberties. Nevertheless, in order to reinforce the 'measures to combat armed violence', parliament extended the duration of police custody to six months, and extended application of the death penalty to crimes fitting the somewhat loose category of 'terrorism'. Even possession of material distributed by the Islamist groups was subject to lengthy custodial sentences. During 1992, 9248 people, according to the lowest estimates, were incarcerated – that is an average of 25 per day.[15] Since the beginning of 1994, the number of detainees has exceeded 24,000. Matching accounts, including those of pro-government sources, regularly condemned the widespread torture of detainees, the kidnapping of members of their family, sexual violence, and execution.[16] Emmanuel Sivan, an Israeli Orientalist teaching at the University of Jerusalem, stated that since 1990 the regime had 'even employed marksmen to breed terror. Accordingly, seventy high level fundamentalist agitators were wiped, particularly in the most affected agricultural regions of Upper Egypt.'[17] In May 1992, the Organisation for the Protection of Human Rights in Egypt accused the government of violating international conventions on the treatment of opponents and political prisoners. Two further, particularly revealing, reports were later published on the subject in March and June 1993.[18]

By criticising the reports which he used as a thermometer of political danger, Hassan Alfi, who succeeded Adelhalim Musa as Minister of the Interior in May 1993, and like him was a former governor of Assyut, confirmed the reality of his predecessor's despicable acts – in particular that people had been kidnapped based on the principle of a collective responsibility.[19] For several years, in order to arrest the members of the Gama'a Islamiyya, their wives, sisters and even their mothers were put under pressure. In some cases, if a population refused to inform on suspects, they were punished by embargoes, sometimes by the destruction of their homes and, in at least one case, the destruction of an entire hamlet.

As from 1990, one of the recurrent themes of the clashes was the result of the determination of the authorities to prohibit the representatives of oppositional Islam from holding public prayers, especially during the two annual 'eids (feasts). The diverse tendencies of oppositional Islam heavily outnumbered the representatives of official Islam.[20] Therefore, from 1990 onwards, the regime decided to strictly limit the number of places in which these demonstrations were permitted. It did not hesitate to use water cannons to flood the streets and squares where the alleged opposition were gathered, pumping out water from the sewers. An incident of this kind occurred in Beni Suaif during 'Eid al-Fitr (the end of the month of Ramadan) at the beginning of April 1992, leading to the deaths of four Gama'a Islamiyya members.

Consequently, the outbursts of violence are frequently met by waves of arrests that are often repressive, more often pre-emptive and always brutal. The answer has been 'the harder you hit us, the harder we hit back!' There is a connection between the number of the murders of policemen, which has risen since 1990, and the 'countless' arrests that have ended in the death of the suspect. In the Assyut area, the escalation of confrontations has exacerbated the situation to such an extent that, in the spring of 1992, a curfew was introduced in several localities, the population having clearly sided with the 'terrorists'. More than 2000 troops were deployed to impose the curfew in the town of Dayrut, which was in a state of veritable siege for several months. The end of 1992 saw another escalation of events. On 8 December, hundreds were arrested when 14,000 members of the security forces searched the Imbaba district, in an operation that was accompanied by a relentless press campaign. Such operations were carried out while there was an increase in attacks on the forces of law and order, such as bombs placed under police vehicles and the murder of policemen. In 1993, a series of blind bombings, the assassination of several high-ranking policemen, attempts on the lives of the ministers of information and the interior, an upsurge in the number of arrests and the first legal sanctions all took place.[21] The military court, to which the leaders of some of the attacks were referred, pronounced several dozen death penalties.[22] By 15 August, 15 had already been carried out, an unprecedented figure in the history of the regime.The Mahjoub affair was prejudiced by accounts of systematic torture inflicted on suspects and by a refusal to make allowances for the 'genuine' confessions that had been beaten out of detainees desperate to stop the torture. The state security court, much slower than the military court, which explains why the latter was created, found it preferable, at the risk of releasing some of the culprits, to pass only lenient sentences, so appalled was it by the torture already suffered.

In response to the shock of the Algerian elections in December 1991, the campaign of repression reached new depths, including the extermination of the leaders of the Gama'a Islamiyya; the attacks on tourists represented an 'extreme' expression of this dangerous process.

The attacks against the state, its representatives or its supposed allies, whether they are politicians (for example, President of Parliament Rifa'at Mahjoub, Minister of Information Safwat Sherif, Prime Minister Atif Sidqi, successive ministers of the interior or the head of state) or members of the forces of law and order, have all been claimed by the armed wing of the Gama'a Islamiyya. This group was also responsible for the assassination of the columnist Farag Fodha on 8 June 1992 – a brave defender of secularism whose influence spread from Cairo to Tunis, and a firm believer that, at a time when the repression was already at its height, the Islamist opposition deserved this repression.[23]

The Gama'a Islamiyya has also admitted its involvement in attacks on tourists. During the spring of 1992, a press release threatened a return to this type of action if the systematic repression continued against the movement. In December 1992, For the second time, *Al-Sha'ab* printed a long editorial denouncing such acts, blaming the radicalisation of the core of the movement on the policy of systematically arresting its leaders. Seven militants involved in the first notable incidents of 'strikes against tourism' were sentenced to death, reinforcing this idea. The seven all came from the same small village in upper Egypt,[24] from which they only had to travel a few miles to riddle a coach with bullets.[25] Even if there is a high command in exile, the credibility of the official theory of a conspiracy on a national, and indeed an international scale (from Pakistan, Sudan or Iran), employing teams of experts appointed by a centralised authority, has not really survived intact.

Conversely, the series of 'blind' bombings (at the café in Tahrir square, in the populous district of Shubra, at Ramsis square and on the bridge of the Avenue of the Pyramids) that have claimed several dozen victims, was openly condemned by the Islamist camp, the Gama'a Islamiyya included. In general, the blame was pinned on 'the foreign secret services who wanted to aggravate the political and economic problems faced by Egypt', or even more accurately on the Egyptian Secret Service, which, in order to legitimise the repressive option, was trying to prevent any possible collaboration between the population and the Islamist 'dispensers of justice'. In June 1993, in various crowded districts of the capital, nearly a dozen bombs were disarmed, receiving huge media attention. Unlike all the other bombings, the perpetrators could not be identified with certainty, casting doubt on who had really carried out the bloodiest of the acts of 'Islamist violence' which often limit the analysis of Egyptian political dynamics in the 1990s. Therefore, the bullets of the radical fringe of the Islamist opposition might be confused with those of the police and the shouts of the 'fight against terrorism' might continue to mask the breakdown of the entire political system.

CHAPTER EIGHT

Algeria: Islamism Against the Intellectuals?

Until the 1990s, outbursts of violence in North Africa linked to the rise of Islamism were few and far between. Not that Islamism, like any other political movement, has always refrained from using this fearful practice. But it has hardly promoted violence as its preferred method of action. It was not until the victory of the FIS in the Algerian elections of early 1992, which sparked a fearsome campaign of repression, that the balance was tipped. Nevertheless, the cataloguing of 'Islamic' acts of violence perpetrated on Algerian soil has rarely been informed by the necessary caution and equanimity.

The use of violence by the Islamists, in Algeria as elsewhere, should be neither misunderstood nor underestimated. There is no question that at the start of 1992, the moderates of the FIS took up the armed struggle that the radicals had long been fighting. Of course, the weapons of the Islamists were not pointed solely at those of their compatriots who were themselves armed. They also targeted many of those who were unfamiliar with the direct use of violence. Therefore, it is not the fact that Islamists have used violence which should be discussed, but rather the circumstances that led violence to monopolise practically all political expression of the Islamist current, especially in the media. The most media-friendly analysts have told us how the Islamists had decided to 'brainwash' a country where the people were powerless to stop the confrontation between 'the terrorists' and 'the military'. Is this really what happened? If the country was truly brainwashed, who were the perpetrators and who were the victims?

A three-way split

The Algerian crisis is characterised by a three-way split, similar to the one that is affecting the entire Arab world. The split, is firstly political, resulting from a relatively banal war of succession between a regime which refuses to admit that it has lost its popularity and an opposition which on two occasions has been able to prove its majority support, and therefore has some justification for reacting to the treatment for which has been singled out. Secondly, this political split is to a certain extent compounded by an economic split. The social base of the opposition has benefited less from the educational and socio-professional kickbacks of oil revenues. Thirdly, there is a cultural dimension: the political and economic elites in power, or of the secular opposition, are more at home with the categories of Western culture than with those of Arab-Muslim culture. Paradoxically, it is well-known that the French occupation con-tributed to the marginalisation or discrediting of these religious categories during the first generation of the nationalist elites. This cultural split affected society as a whole less than the individuals who comprised it. The notion of two completely separate camps fails to do justice to the tension which linked them. This twofold wealth of values can be of enormous inspiration, but it can also produce conflict and even schizo-phrenia when one of the sides is frustrated or imposed, or when the free exchange of ideas between the two is blocked.

However, social upheaval and the war of succession conceal a clash of two codes of culture, a case of murderous sibling rivalry between two opposing systems of references. The historian Mohammed Harbi summed up this typically North African reality well by saying:

> One part of Algeria is made up of the former spokesmen and leaders of nationalism, and it is heavily influenced by French culture. This French-speaking political elite has forged the idea of an Algerian nation along the lines of the French nation, without any authentic, historical reference ... Yet underneath this, an alternative Algeria existed, founded on communities, fervent in their religion, that made no bones about their attitude to France.[1]

The FIS was able to capitalise on this three-way split twice: in June 1990 and December 1991. At first, it managed to demonstrate that the worn-out and corrupt regime was no longer wanted, and to give a political voice to the people who had been excluded from the system. It next succeeded in representing the disarray of social groups that had been weakened by the brutal economic measures taken by the state after the oil crisis and the failure of industrialisation 'from above'.[2] Ultimately, it secured the last and the most important of political resources, a 'positive' resource often highlighted by observers, that had eluded the FLN: nationalism. Initially, this resource was used positively, by the very nature of its discourse, culturally and ideologically to prolong the nationalist dynamic that the FLN had once expressed and exploited politically and economically. It was also used negatively, and was condemned on two fronts for its economic privileges and its cultural and political similarity to the France, the former colonial power. This was characterised by the gradual identification of political forces that spoke a different language to the French-speaking elite (which extended as far as France itself) and a particular social elite,

The paradox is that France, its media and its politicians, has played a significant role in steadily undermining the credibility of secular forces. Along with the discourse of the FIS that condemns the 'party from France', the rush to defend the 'democratic camp' has undeniably discredited it while valorising its adversary, allowing it to turn every attack in the French media to its advantage. The ultimate paradox is that the FLN, in its fight against the FIS, has ended up parroting the discourse of the French media, especially on the topic of political violence. Its historical legitimacy, founded on its ability to keep its symbolic distance from the coloniser, has thus begun to disintegrate. Devastating from the time the first attempts at pluralism were made in 1989, this media paradox has since become much worse thanks to the political and media support of the West in general, and of France in particular, given to a regime that resulted from the cancellation of the first round of parliamentary elections in December 1991.

Change the people

In December 1991, when the military realised that the Algerian people had 'voted unwisely', the victims of this electoral insolence thought the only solution was somehow to 'change the people'.[3] On the day after the first ballot, although the FFS had bravely demanded that the elections continue, but the RCD, with nothing to lose, openly welcomed the interruption.[4] It said it was ready to 'paralyse the country' by 'any means necessary'. A 'National Security Council' was established, which the weekly newspaper Algérie–Actualité credited with the support of around 60 associations and, even more imaginatively, by the 'three million members of the UGTA [the General Union of Algerian Workers, whose leadership was close to that of the former communist union, the PAGS]'.

For its part, the FIS agreed to collaborate with President Ben Jedid and called on its activists to be 'moderate' and 'reconciliatory', even if it failed to prevent some of them from steeling their resolve by announcing a government programme that was not a fair reflection of this double-sided preoccupation.[5]

In Algiers, rumours circulated that there was little hope of the elections continuing. On 2 January, 300,000 opponents of the FIS marched to 'preserve democracy', and the creation of 'committees for the defence of republican institutions' was announced. Hossine Aït-Ahmed, the leader of the FFS, spoke briefly and was acclaimed, and everyone began to expect the 'democratic' camp to organise a counter-movement. The number of abstentions (41 percent) led some observers to speculate about a possible counter-majority. In a more pragmatic and more cynical way, others contemplated a second 'jurisdictional' ballot in which the Constitutional Council, flooded with calls for more than 300 results to be declared void – 174 of which were made by the FLN – would agree to deny the FIS its majority.[6]

Behind closed doors there were others who had an even more radical solution. On the evening of 11 January, a short broadcast on national television brought an end to the uncertainty: President Ben Jedid resigned, citing the 'impediments' to the completion of his mission. The High Council of Security was established,[7] and the High State Committee that possessed all the powers granted to the head of state by the constitution.

Once they had confiscated the contents of the ballot boxes, the 'saviours of democracy' announced the dissolution of the party that had had the audacity to gain the majority. At the same time, they began to dispose of the victors of the first ballot and nearly 20,000 of their supporters, by leaving them to rot in concentration camps in the southern Sahara desert. In order to cover up their political vulnerability, they also created imitations of representative assemblies, such as the National Consultative Council, the National Council of Transition and municipal delegations. They substituted those who had been elected in Algeria's first two free elections with 'representatives' they nominated.

Once they had protested through the official channels and appealed unsuccessfully for international solidarity, the Islamists responded by attacking and killing the military and political directors of the strategy of 'eradication'. At first, the growing tide of 'Islamic' violence was aimed at members of the forces of law and order, and then at the authorities nominated by the government in place of the elected assemblies. The Armed Islamic Movement (MIA) started to claim responsibility for the attacks with increasingly regularity.[8]

Even if, as we shall see, it is dangerous to pinpoint the blame, there is another category of political actor to be added to these first victims: not 'journalists', 'intellectuals' or 'poets' per se, but those journalists, intellectuals and poets who, once the ability of the Islamists to disseminate information was completely destroyed, accepted the task of producing an ideological cover-up of the repression. This legitimised the 'eradication' option and the reign of its creators in the eyes of world opinion.[9]

One extremism after another

There were, however, people in the Islamist camp who had supported the used of armed action before the elections were suspended. Throughout the 1980s, Bouyali's Algerian Islamist Movement was the precursor to this tendency that has been present in the FIS since its foundation. From November 1991, armed groups have appeared on the flanks of Abbassi Madani's supporters, who are themselves opposed to an armed struggle. However, this non-violent tendency both survived the initial campaigns of repression and succeeded in gaining the leadership of the FIS at the Batna Congress in July 1991, just after Madani and Benhadj[10] were arrested. As in the congress, only a minority of the FIS took up the armed option, some of its members chose to leave before the legislative elections,[11] and, unsurprisingly, the radical wing of the Islamist movement refused to rejoin the FIS, which it regarded as too peaceful.

After the elections were suspended, the first armed groups, as might be expected, were made up of people who had been involved in the armed struggle for some time and whose political credo was based on their suspicion of the electoral process. They were refugees from Mustapha Bouyali's resistance movement, joined by 'Afghans' (Islamists who had gone to fight the Soviet army in Afghanistan in the early 1980s) and supported by Madani's opponents, whose influence had been diluted at the Batna Congress. The dissolution of the FIS in March 1992 and the intensifying repression was to rally those who wanted to avenge the death of dozens of their comrades and those who simply realised that there was no guarantee that they would survive in the universe of urban legality. From 1993 onwards, the increasing excesses of violence – the assassination of nationals accused of supporting the regime, and of people whose only crime was that they did not belong to the Islamist camp – were claimed by the evolving Armed Islamic Group (AIG). For a long time, the identity of the AIG was to be defined by the rejection of the FIS leadership.[12] Conversely, the armed groups that were loyal to the FIS were to join forces in an Armed Islamic Movement (divided into several regions) that became the Islamic Salvation Army (ISA) in June 1994.[13] The inflated ranks of the *mujahidin* were convinced of the need to claim their victory at any price and, for some, by any means: the political victory that they were denied by the suspension of the electoral process.

From 1993 onwards the threats against foreigners began to be executed, targeting economic collaborators as often as members of religious communities and the surviving remnants of the former French community. The conditions under which this happened must be examined with the utmost caution, however. This episode is essential to the most sombre incidents of the 'second Algerian War'. Often condemned by the FIS and at least once by the AIG,[14] the most gratuitous of the assassinations and the most sordid of the operations and claims of responsibility actually proved to be extremely beneficial to the regime, whose international legitimacy grew in proportion to Western disgust at the barbarism of the methods employed by, or attributed to, its political challengers. This ambiguity has persistently evaded the observer's attention.

The rights of the beardless man

Where violence is concerned, can we fight fire with fire? Can we distinguish between 'good' and 'bad' violence? These questions seem to have preoccupied both media and politicians in the West for a long time.

The advocates of the rhetoric of 'eradication' were quick to monopolise the representation of the Algerian population in the media. Their interpretation of the violence was astonishingly simplistic: democracy in Algeria is threatened by 'terrorism'. Fortunately, it is protected by the army in their barracks, by the (mainly Kabyle) 'democrats' 'from the top of their mountains' and, elsewhere, by 'intellectuals' and by 'women', which is the reason why the fundamentalists are trying to assassinate them.

The reality of the situation was that the secular social movements could not redress the balance of the two successive ballots and had lost their credibility in the eyes of a civil society that was largely foreign to them. The worthless credentials of a small band of specialists in political spin nevertheless afforded them an access to the Western media that was inversely proportional to the reality of their social support in Algeria. Misinformation played havoc with a considerable proportion of the French intelligentsia, and the war of words launched by the Algerian Secret Services enjoyed more than a limited success.

However, the ability of the UGTA to mobilise could not seriously be measured in 1992 by the size of its membership four years earlier, when it was the only trade union in a non-pluralist system. Without casting doubt on the good faith of a majority of members, it turns out that the military authorities persuaded some feminist associations to change their approach in order to profit from Western attitudes to feminism. Any associations that did not toe the regime's line were denied the means of self-expression, while the national press trumpeted the cause of those who supported the policy of eradication. The strategy of at least some of this self-proclaimed 'civil society' has been to co-operate with the military regime to the extent that it has become totally identified with it.

For many months, the protests of Western intellectuals were exclusively devoted to the defence of their colleagues, provided they were not Islamists. However, it was difficult to forget that the electoral campaigns in June 1990 and autumn 1991 had passed off peacefully and that the 'good' intellectuals of the RCD and the former PAGS, and the militant feminists who monopolised the French media, had the opportunity to express themselves without restriction. Herein lies the problem: they could also see that they were virtually incapable of communicating with their own society. In December 1991, one parliamentary candidate, Khalida Messaoudi (who has since been nominated as a deputy by the government), received less than 1 percent of votes cast. The RCD managed less than 3 percent, while the PAGS, which claimed to have the support of the 'three million members of the UGTA', gained even less. Aït-Ahmed's FFS fared better because it could count on ethnic and regional solidarity, especially in the Kabyle area; a solidarity which, in the Balkan conflict, or elsewhere in the world, is usually condemned by democratic standards. To interpret this Kabyle vote as a repudiation of the Islamists or as a particular passion for democracy, would be either naive or extremely cynical.

If we are bound by the terms and spirit of the most common definitions, there is indeed a civil society on Algerian soil. It is even more developed, more active and more autonomous from the state than is generally thought. This civil society is nearly always represented by the powerful Islamist associative network, as will be demonstrated below.

The pitfalls of misinformation

Is it true that in Algeria 'everyone who thinks French' has been 'condemned to die' at the hands of Islamist violence? This has long been the brutal formula used by Bernard-Henri Lévy on prime-time television. However, one crucial element is missing.

During the course of Algeria's torment, a number of intellectuals have been assassinated, many of whom have never wielded a weapon other than a pen. In May 1994, when Rachid Mimouni listed a dozen of them, there had already been many more victims.[15] Several hundred, at the peak of their career or fresh out of university, had been taken by surprise on their doorstep or stolen away in the night, savagely tortured to within an inch of their lives, openly murdered in front of their families or crushed, asphyxiated, electrocuted in the depths of a jail and, predictably, buried out of sight of any television camera.[16] Some had the same convictions as Rachid Mimouni[17] or Rachid Boudjedra.[18] Others in their hundreds, including the 1224 teachers arrested in 1993 who were members or sympathisers of the FIS, thought differently. But they all thought. Some were the prestigious heirs of the secular nationalists of the 1960s or the Marxist opposition parties to which they gave birth. Others followed an Islamist trend that had given Algeria the engineer Malek Bennabi, one of the country's most noted intellects, well before it was condemned to the international pages of Western newspapers.[19] That trend is perhaps less unreceptive of other cultures than our own civilisation has been itself, especially where exercising an arrogant monopoly over modernity is concerned.

However, nearly two years passed before Amnesty International reports and the desire of a small number of journalists and academics to disassociate themselves from the *communiqués* of the Algerian Ministry for Information revealed that the reality was rather more complex.[20] As *Libération* put it, commenting on the Amnesty report of October 1994, claims by armed groups and the state about violence 'should be dismissed out of hand'.[21] The Secretary General of the FLN, who was quicker than most democrats to renounce the eradication option, made official the validity of these initial suspicions by declaring in November 1994 in Rome:

Some countries have the unknown soldier. We have unknown bodies. Bodies which are ignored by all communiqués, but which the people are counting. We have often demanded that independent inquests are held to clear the state of any suspicion that it is responsible for these crimes. Our demands remain unanswered ... international opinion, particularly in some European countries, has been made to think that the violence is solely the result of terrorist activity, which requires a security-based solution. Yet, despite all the changes it has experienced, what is happening in Algeria has little to do with terrorism: it is a resistance movement that has the support of a part of the population.

These declarations may have come too late but they are essential for understanding the chronology and the structure of 'Islamic' violence.

In Algeria, the people who were most in danger were those who thought, whether in Arabic or in French, that they could, contrary to the wishes of a clear majority of the population, hold on to power forever through repression and bloodshed. The violence with which they were progressively confronted is in many respects the very violence they themselves began in some cases, incited in others, or permitted in yet others. When the tidal wave of arrests intensified, making the most barbaric forms of torture commonplace, when the families of the real or suspected Islamist sympathisers found the dismembered bodies of their loved ones, who had been burnt, stabbed and castrated, and when summary executions and mob justice became the norm, the extraordinary selectivity and the blatant bias of the 'eradicatory' press went beyond 'journalism', 'thought' and 'intelligence' to enter the realm of a merciless war where both sides employed the same acts of violence.

Despite the fact that the international observers have slowly adopted the notion of a 'double terrorism', a dangerously misleading dimension still remains. If they both undoubtedly belong to the same family and are both to be condemned with the same ferocity, the two forms of Algerian terrorism make very strange bedfellows. 'Islamic terrorism' is a product of the radicalisation of a powerful popular movement that twice won electoral victory, and that was duly crushed by the boot of repression, and, subject to future investigations, of the possible disruptive influence of some of its elements. The terrorism of the radical wing of the military regime, on the other hand, is nothing more than the retreat, the desperate solution, the last gasp of a regime that has not only lost the support of its core supporters but also of hordes of people in its own ranks.

Consequently the 'explanation' for the violence requires the reintroduction of an essential causal link. The 'two forms of Algerian terrorism' are not twins. One has consciously nurtured the other and has then helped it to develop. As far as the regime is concerned, the radicalisation of the Islamist current is not so much an obstacle as a logical consequence of their actions. More importantly, this radicalisation has become the deliberate objective of its strategy and the focus of its policy of communication with the local and international communities. The idea that there would be no 'Islamic' terrorism without the regime's terrorism would not be so true if the roles were reversed. This is because the military leaders are more afraid of an election that might prove their unpopularity than they are of the violence of indiscriminate bombings that strengthen their position as 'guardians of civil peace'. Therefore, although indiscriminate violence might harm them indirectly, in many ways it is a vital political 'necessity'.[22]

It is the task of historians of Algeria, and their task alone, to tell us exactly who has assassinated whom since February 1992. To do this, they will have to untangle the web of 'Islamic' and repressive violence. They will then have the more difficult task of measuring the impact of crimes that have little to do with politics, that have been compounded by the collapse of the rule of law and the release of thousands of prisoners. They will also have to consider the violence within the two camps, that has long been attributed to the Islamists alone.

Inside the regime, part of the state violence was the intimidation of those seeking a negotiated solution, or those whose faith in eradication had waned. The assassination of Mohammed Boudiaf in June 1992 is a notable example. So too is the assassination of Kasdi Merbah in August 1993; even if 'the AIG duly claimed responsibility' and the names of the suspects, who were killed beforehand, were waved before the press. The assassination of the former prime minister – the man formerly responsible for military security – the leader of the small MAJD Party, which had just held talks with exiled representatives of the FIS, is likely to fall into this category.[23] So too are the deaths of well-known people who were judged to be overly critical, whose death could be exploited, as we shall see, and added to the list of acts of 'violence committed by the FIS'.

The historians will next have to count the persistent provocation that has been the basis for the communication and the rallying call of the armed forces. Hossine Aït-Ahmed, the leader of the FFS, was one of the first to denounce publicly this 'culture of manipulation' that had long been a trait of the Algerian regime and whose role became more important than ever from February 1992 onwards. Since then, another interpretation has emerged to clarify the Algerian divide. Once they had hounded the foreign correspondents, terrorised the special envoys and silenced the local press by arranging the assassination of many dozens of figures from the cultural and religious scenes, the Algerian military authorities appeased Western public opinion to such an extent that they were able to carry out a campaign of repression, without interference or reproach from the international community, that had not been seen since the war against the coloniser.

The radical fringe of the Islamist current, the 'Islamists in soldiers' uniforms', have certainly played an active part in this sordid affair. Undoubtedly prepared to kill 'the other' just because he or she belongs to a different religion or race, the extremist fringe of the movement has taken on the role expected of it: to play the game of 'soldiers disguised as Islamists', the undercover officers – a fatal collaboration.[24]

When dealing with international opinion, the objective of the regime was to make it seem that eradication was the only viable option. The silencing of the press and the systematic and incredibly effective lobbying by the associations and the French media were soon to interrupt the normal flow of information on the shape, spread and logic of the violence. For manipulators on all sides, this task turned out to be remarkably easy. It was enough to pander to an instinctive revulsion towards the Islamist current among the French intelligentsia, who had otherwise been so careful, to become 'incredibly credulous', and for the press to accept and faithfully reproduce the *communiqués* of the Algerian Secret Services. At the mere solicitation of the Algerian military establishment, television channels and radios, together with supposedly 'serious' journalists and former activists, have for a long time been extraordinarily quick to respond, dwelling on the accusatory headlines, the abusive editorials, the vengeful columns, the unanimous 'debates' and the hackneyed stereotypes, such as 'The FIS rots your brain', 'refuses intelligence' and 'culture' and 'condemns thought'. On 29 June 1992, the assassination of Boudiaf by the very people who brought him to power raised irrefutable explanations from all sides, including of course from those who, in good faith, intended to 'defend the rights of men and women against fundamentalism'. One says that 'Boudiaf represented several symbols [...]: a historical hero [...] and man of integrity [...] It was this two-faced symbol that they had to attack.'[25] This is the beginnings of an 'explanation', as it is common knowledge that Islamists find integrity unbearable. The Algerian comm-unications network was quick to aid the refining of this 'analysis'. That Boudiaf was killed in a cultural centre did not happen by chance, as Rachid Boudjedra was to 'explain' to the viewers of TF1: it was because 'the FIS detests thought, intelligence and culture'.[26]

Within the borders of Algeria, this task was obviously harder. The population was by definition better informed and less likely to believe that it is right to avoid the 'Islamist impasse', in which it had made the 'incomprehensible error' of getting lost, at all costs. These words, coming from the north side of the Mediterranean, were simply not enough.

From one terrorism comes another

Despite the period when Boudiaf tried unsuccessfully – or, for a time, appeared to be trying – to alter the situation, the objective was to embrace any position that identified the armed groups with the use of blind violence, so that the FIS would be cut off from its popular base. Two techniques were adopted to achieve this goal. The immeasurable brutality of the repression swelled the ranks of the most extremist part of the Islamist current to an unprecedented level, which unsurprisingly led to counterattacks that were just as ferocious as those meted out by the state. An Islamic knife is no more deadly than an army bullet, but it allows more sensational headlines.[27]

By employing widespread manipulation, the expected effects of this first step have largely been fulfilled. The many accounts suggest that 'the Islamists disguised as soldiers' were usually just soldiers doing their national service. In order to sway the entire population into the 'anti-terrorist' camp, they had to make sure that this brand of terrorism, that produced political dividends, did not just affect the representatives of the regime, but that all categories of society would also suffer at their hands.

By prohibiting any announcement of a loss of power, the official 'information' quickly became limited to reporting civilian casualties, for which only the Islamists were blamed. Behind this smoke-screen, the daily reprisals of the security forces against the families of resistance members were systematically ascribed to the Islamists, and the forms of nocturnal harassment (such as intimidation, robbery and sexual assaults) that were allegedly committed by 'Islamists disguised as soldiers' were inflicted on every sector of society in the name of the armed groups. The regime set up an 'association of the victims of terrorism', which reaped political dividends as long as it organised a few highly publicised marches in its support. Even if it did not lessen the horror of those crimes which can without question be attributed to the Islamists, it is probable that several of the most high-profile assassinations of personalities, chosen for their popularity in diverse areas of national or international opinion, fall into this category of collaboration. So do some of the most unpopular attempts to sabotage the economy, the attacks on the symbols of nationalism (such as the desecration of memorials to the heroes of the war of independence), the arson attacks on schools and public services, the indiscriminate explosions such as the bombing at Algiers airport on 26 August 1992,[28] and other macabre scenes garnished with provocative *communiqués* claiming responsibility.[29]

Men and women have died just so that their assassins could profit from the revulsion felt by the public.[30] Of course, there is no 'absolute' proof yet, but a huge pile of witness accounts and indices are available. Each segment of public opinion was carefully targeted, as were all social, ethnic and socio-cultural movements, in an attempt to guide them from their natural path and use them in the fight against the Islamists. They included women of course, but also students, football fans and followers of raï (North African pop) music, the Berbers, the Islamist moderates etc. Tensions were exploited when they were latent or actual, intensified when they were hardly discernible (in football and music), invented from nothing when they did not exist (in universities, schools and consumers).

Who killed the raï singer Cheb Hasni in Oran? Who exactly torched the hundreds of schools in the Islamist districts in autumn 1994? Who planted bombs in front of Algiers University? Which 'armed groups' inflicted violence on women of all social classes in a drive to 'recruit women for the resistance movement'? Is an Algerian sociologist lying when he confidentially talks about having received, before deciding to leave Algeria, a visit from the emissaries of the Islamist camp to inform him that they did not want to bear the responsibility for his assassination, that they knew the army had planned? Is it true that the (French) mother of another sociologist had to be accompanied to the market by four of her Islamist neighbours, who 'did not want to have to pay the moral price of her assassination by the military security forces'? Is it correct that some French citizens (notably, but not exclusively, two technicians working for an oil company) have died because the army withdrew protection without warning or explanation? Is it true that two French policemen were killed two hours before the official report said they were, namely when the curfew clogged up Algiers' arteries? Is it true that women were sent by the FIS to see the family of Mallek Alloula, another sensationalised victim of 'fundamentalist violence', to assure them that the Islamists were not involved? Is it true that two days before his assassination, the psychiatrist Mahfoud Boucebci, the 'window' of 'fundamentalist brutality', had been guilty of two crimes against the eradicators? Firstly, he had refused to sign the psychiatric evaluation of the suspected assassin of President Boudiaf which concluded that it was the isolated act of a disturbed man. Secondly, he demanded an independent inquiry into the circumstances surrounding the death of the writer Tahir Djaout, because he had not been at all convinced by the confession tortured out of the suspected assassin. Is a Christian monk lying when he says that is more afraid of the military security forces than he is of the Islamists?

Manipulations

The Algerian army had to burn the forests of Kabylia with napalm to drive out the huge numbers of resistance fighters, Berbers as well as Islamists. One of the principal leaders of the moderate wing of the FIS, Mohammed Sa'id, who later became the leader of the AIG, is a Berber, as is Sa'id Mekhloufi, the leader of another armed group, as are countless other Islamist militants. This has not stopped the Western media from portraying Kabylia as impervious to the Islamists, and as 'democratic' as it is 'mountainous'. However, until then the Berber cultural movement, despite its undoubted energy, had been more opposed to the state and the FLN than to its challengers from the FIS. With some degree of success, political manipulation transformed an anti-state movement into an anti-Islamist weapon, going as far as to arm the village militia (and docking the cost from their subsidies), who were destined 'to fight the rebels'. Despite the counter-measures of the Islamist current, this manoeuvre was partially successful.

Not all the victims of 'Islamist barbarity' were killed by the state. In this extremely violent area, the media have manipulated common criminality. There have been sensationalised reports on both sides of the Mediterranean about the settling of scores, not just between criminals and the police, the professional and personal rivalries, and 'political' or simply sexual urges that have been systematically and professionally imputed to the 'FIS terrorists'. 'No, sir,' snapped a gendarme who had just arrived from his native Algeria,

> the FIS is not that important...I can tell you that the FIS had nothing to do with the murder of that doctor the day before yesterday that everyone is talking about. I knew him well; he was alleged to have produced false internment certificates. He's the man you had to see if you wanted to divorce your wife! He had a real scam going. That's why he was killed, no other reason!

Was a young women killed by her fiancé in 1993 'because she was about to leave him'? This did not stop her name from being plastered over the front pages of the world press as a victim 'of the refusal to wear the *hijab*'.[31]

On 1 November 1994, when a bomb exploded at the Mostaghanem cemetery, killing four young scouts who had gone there to celebrate the 40th anniversary of the 'Toussaint rouge' in 1954, the television cameras had been set up there for two days, although there was nothing in particular to justify their presence at one of countless gatherings to commemorate the armed uprising in 1954. This time the outrage, which coincided with President Zeroual's announcement that it was 'impossible to talk with the FIS while they are involved in the violence', and the collapse of the negotiations with the FIS, was fuelled by the almost direct impact. It is a well-rehearsed scenario: the suspect, arrested a few days later after a manhunt, will unfortunately lose his life, and public opinion any chance of verifying the validity of his confession.

A few days after the attack, as the press officers of the RCD bombarded the French airwaves, in one of the rare spaces of freedom left to the press in Algiers, an article appeared that would be classed as 'democratic' or 'feminist' if the terminology had not lost all its credibility, describing the march organised by the 'Association of the Victims of Terrorist Violence'.

> Watching them closely, I noticed that the mothers of those who have disappeared kept their lips sealed. The bits of *milaya* [their long dress] stuck between teeth that are only unclenched to let out a long moan. If they were to open their mouths to shout out the name of their sons, 'they' [the representatives of the regime] might force them to shout out 'Long live the president!'. In spite of the one-sided interpretations, the obligatory merry-go-round of the dominant political code, which wants to drag us from pain to hate, the mumbled words between sobs show that the multitude are no fools ... They were invited to a march in protest against the violence, and they brought with them the photographs of their children to be filmed in a demonstration in support of the president. The portraits of the president were so big that they seemed to cover the photographs of the missing with a shameless veil. It is an unfair fight between pain and manipulation...The people holding a picture of the president look as if they have and always will support him.

'Incidentally', Salima Belkacem concludes, 'the official request for citizens to put a lighted candle in their window on 1 November was soon forgotten. Algiers was not lit up that night. It is easier to manipulate a march than it is to manipulate all the windows of a country.'[32]

CHAPTER NINE

Gaza: The Islamists 'Against Peace'

If, in other parts of the Arab world, Islamists are labelled 'lovers of violence', in Palestine they are the 'adversaries of peace'.

The emergence in 1987 of Hamas, in conjunction with the Intifada, arose from the need of the Palestinian Muslim Brotherhood to find a means of mobilising support more widely than it could through its organisation alone.[1]

The specificity of the situation in Palestine has no relation to the emergence of Hamas, which, as elsewhere, was a reflection of the decline of 'secular' Arab nationalism in favour of the Islamist rhetoric. Palestine's specificity lies simply in the fact that here this classical shift was delayed because the PLO was deprived of a state for much longer than the Arab nationalist movements before independence. The original version of nationalist rhetoric thus preserved in Palestine the ability to mobilise that had elsewhere been lost when confronted with the task of managing a state. The emergence of Hamas can be attributed to the natural political decline of the Palestinian leadership, which has succeeded in benefiting from democratic regeneration only as much as its counterparts in neighbouring regimes.

Essentially, in Gaza as in Nablus, the 'fundamentalists' of Hamas have done nothing more than take over from the *fedayeen* (Arab commandos in resistance to Israel) of the PLO by transforming the nationalist dynamism of the first generation of 'secular' nationalists from a political to a symbolic, cultural force. In the case of Palestine, the 'peace' agreements have, however, given this dynamic a particular significance and scale. The peace talks in Oslo merely served to accelerate the replacement of the *fedayeen* with the *mujahidin*, since to some it seemed that the first generation of Palestinian resistance had failed in its duties.

The impact of the peace agreements

The impact of the Oslo and Cairo Agreements on the internal balance of Palestinian resistance can be represented in terms of the new resources and constraints from which the diverse components of the political landscape have benefited or been deprived. Depending on whether they are for or against the agreements, or whether they have simply accepted or refused the principle of 'peace' or 'autonomy' agreements, the actors in this scene have seen their roles deeply transformed. The principal split has pitted the PLO, which signed the agreement and had a part in implementing it, against the Islamists of Hamas (led by Sheikh Yassin) and Tanzim al-Jihad (led by Fathi Shiqaqi) as well as certain voices within the PLO (notably the Democratic Front for the Liberation of Palestine) which have denounced the principle.

The future of the Palestinian authority, and the capacity of its Islamist opposition to contest its leadership, therefore depends on the balance between the 'winners' and the 'losers'. As we shall see, some of the clear advantages held by the PLO very quickly turned against it. Thanks to the peace agreements, the PLO received dividends of various kinds: from a nationalist point of view, it received the experience of independence, from a clientelist point of view, it had control over public resources, and from a security point of view, it had the use of authorities charged with public order. At first, it was credited with the withdrawal of the occupying army from Gaza and Jericho and with the return of some of the army and police exiled in 1948 and 1967, as well as the release of some of the 9000 political prisoners.

The title of the agreement, 'Gaza-Jericho – A Priority', has also given the PLO hope that it was the first step to a withdrawal from all the occupied territories (except for Jerusalem).[2] Thanks to these 'recaptured' territories, the PLO has earned the right to create or restore a symbolic fiction of state identity in some of the territories claimed since 1967. This has been done by use of flags, army and police uniforms, stamps, 'ministries', a 'parliament', 'embassies' etc. The PLO reinforces its clientelist resources: more than ever, financial resources are injected into the administrative and socio-economic fabric of the territories. In the framework of its powers as the Palestinian Authority (PA), it controls public resources and therefore the whole of Arab or Western state aid. The head of the PA also appoints all civil servants and military personnel permitted in the agreement. While for a long time it has only been one of the political forces fighting for the internal leadership, the PLO has, since the peace agreements, found itself vested with the instruments of public law and order that it has a right to use in order to protect its leadership – the army, police, common law justice, state security court, information services etc.

However, there is a darker side to these positive resources. Having proved incapable of building the legitimacy of the PA and its missions on a broader base than that of its own clientele, the PLO has been faced with overwhelming constraints essentially linked to the incomplete and highly contradictory nature of the transfer of power from which it was to benefit. At the moment that the secular nationalist dynamic was reaping the meagre rewards of 'autonomy', the strengthening position of Hamas was a clear illustration – as elsewhere – of how it could capture the heritage of 'secular' nationalism by prolonging it culturally, but also, in this case, by throwing it once more into the political arena.

This process is not dissimilar to the emergence, followed by a period of rapid growth, of the Hizbullah in Lebanon immediately after the Israeli invasion of Beirut in 1982. The 'fundamentalists' of Hizbullah similarly emerged as a result of the Islamisation of the discourse opposing Israel, but also because they took up the political and military struggle. Following the example of Hizbullah, Hamas has 'rejected' the *status quo* of the Israeli presence on its territory. This is the dimension on which the two groups have insisted in order to build their identity and their system of mobilisation and action.[3]

What peace has been 'compromised' by the first Islamist mobilisations and then the first Islamist attacks? Was it really a peace agreement (*salam*) that Yasser Arafat signed in Oslo or rather, as those who oppose it think, an agreement of capitulation and surrender (*istislam*)? Was it a negotiated victory or just a 'peace of the brave' that all the occupying armies have dreamt of imposing on their adversaries so that they are not forced to admit the legitimacy of their claims? In Washington, did Arafat really save the Palestinians or did he betray them?[4]

Even a cursory glance at the terms of the voluminous agreements of Oslo and Cairo reveals the limits of the concessions made by Israel. Its army has not withdrawn from Gaza, it has been redeployed there. Tel Aviv has given up none of its political or military sovereignty, nor its economic or even its administrative sovereignty, while, more conclusively, foreign policy and the basic tools of communication with neighbouring Egypt were refused.[5] In fact, the autonomous regions remain, through Palestinians, under the most direct control of the Israelis, and stuffed with colonies that they have made no promises or plans not to maintain or even extend. Is it then such a surprise that the 'beneficiaries' of 'peace' have been affected by the conjectural and fleeting nature of the advantages of autonomy? Yasser Arafat is 'in prison in Gaza'; autonomy is like

'American chewing gum; sweet for two minutes and then more and more useless'. Of course, some people will object that 'two types of nationalism have recognised one another'. But how does one deny that, for the camp that was the target of the initial violence, this recognition has a hint of being one-sided? One party, the PLO, had to forgo the constitutive elements of its existence, namely the hope of recapturing the territories given to Israel by the division of Palestine in 1948, while the second made no concession at all on this first 'terrain'.

All Arafat's opponents, not just the Islamists, are entitled to ask 'Who made you the King and how much did you have to pay for your crown?' It is difficult to deny that the price Arafat paid was dropping any claim to borders prior to 1948: he would claim that this was in exchange for peace and autonomy. Some features will soon convince the visitor that the image of 'Indian reserves' or 'bantustans', to which some analysts, hardly suspected of Islamist sympathies, have referred, is not simply a caricature. These include the huge metal gate that gives access, through an imposing barred wall, to a few square kilometres of the overpopulated urban sprawl of Jericho, with lines of Israeli tanks standing on guard only hundreds of metres away, the geographical omnipresence of the 'ideological' settlers throughout the territories and their provocative manners, the queues that remind thousands of workers in Gaza every morning that they cannot leave, even to travel to the other territories captured in 1967, and the huge sense of general humiliation and harassment that each checkpoint represents.

One of the most informed specialists on the occupied territories writes that

> Over a year after it was signed, and just before the [first Islamist] attacks, the agreement of September 1993, the objective expression of the balance of power between Israel and the Palestinians, nearly witnessed the international community's approval of the collapse of one of the parties, the negation of its identity and its rights as a people ... The semi-victory of Oslo was only acquired at the expense of condemning Palestine to death, as Israel left the PLO with no other choice than to abandon its role as guarantor of the unity of the Palestinian people and the institutional safeguarding of its national identity, restricting it from then on to act only within the limits of its nuclear policy. Arafat exercised his authority exclusively on a strip of Gaza that was denied its own airspace, was still about 20 per cent occupied and liable to be broken into three separate enclaves. A hundred kilometres away, but without any access possible overland, because none of the roads that are supposed to guarantee safe passage have been opened, he reigns over small clumps of the West Bank that have been transformed into an assembly camp for prisoners 'liberated' by Israel but still forbidden to enter the occupied territories ... After this, there can be

no ambiguity about the what is happening when we read the headline: 'The enemies of the agreement are the enemies of peace.' When he has to contend with paying the police, ensuring waste collection and strengthening the support of his accomplices, busy chasing money that has been promised but rarely arrives, and pressed into resolving talks with his opposition, Arafat hardly has time to be concerned with the disintegration of the West Bank.[6]

To measure the depth of the gulf separating the Western representation of the 'peace treaty' between the Israelis and the Palestinians and that of the political forces that are directly involved, requires that the distorting effect introduced by the extreme reaction to the Islamisation of the political discourse be dealt with. But it is crucial that such an evaluation recognises the chasm which continues to separate the dominant depictions of the creation of the State of Israel in the Arab world in general, and especially in Palestine, from those of Western public opinion. The West considers that the Jews legitimately saw the 'end of their persecution' in 1948 by 'finally being allowed a homeland', the dominant Arab representation opposed a Europe bowed down by a feeling of responsibility for the Holocaust, and which, once the Second World War had ended, curiously chose to 'wash its dirty laundry on the backs of Arabs'. It may be difficult to persuade those who have not climbed to the top of Mount Nebo to survey the lights of Jerusalem accompanied by one of the people forcibly excluded by the military action in 1948. But even the most moderate elements of the political landscape in Palestine only accept the violence of the Israeli transplant as the result of an international balance of power that is hugely unfavourable to them. At the very most, what has been accepted, at least in the countries of the battlefield, is the end of the state of belligerence, not a real peace.

The PLO soon felt the negative effects of the agreement: the leader of the organisation, who had founded his popularity on his declared ambition to 'liberate Palestine', found himself legitimising, without reservation, the violent foundation of Israel in 1948, and forbidding anyone in his camp from using force to challenge both the division of 1948 and the division that resulted from the 1967 Israeli occupation.

If one pauses to consider the underlying violence that has been stirred up for nearly 30 years by the presence of an occupying army at every crossroad in the West Bank, the irresistible rise of Hamas, the principal movement calling for the 'pursuit of resistance against the occupier' and two left-wing movements led by Christian militants, is hardly surprising.[7] The unequivocal condemnation of the 'Islamic' violence of its militants, found in the analyses of too many commentators, calls for more care in the handling of such a travesty.

CHAPTER TEN

Allah or the People?
Islamists and Democracy

At the time of the legislative elections of 1989, the Egyptian Socialist Labour Party – whose internal balance of power had swung in favour of its Islamic component – opened its doors to candidates from the Muslim Brotherhood; there followed claims that the choice of a slogan had invoked heated debate. A compromise was found based on the dualism of 'God and the people', which the secularists saw as a victory. The Islamists, who agreed to this unifying slogan, contented themselves by the mere addition of 'God is the Greatest!'

Like fire and water?

Was democracy in the Arab world doomed to failure as soon as it saw the light of day? When an election is won, is it likely that Islamists will respect the identity and the rights of 'the vanquished', or on a broader level, those of any minority, including religious minorities, led by a principle, *shura*, which allows for consultation with only those inside the community of believers? Once they have seized power, would the imitators of the Imam of Qom respect the election results if that one could mean their defeat one day? How can the 'sovereignty of God' and the primacy of divine law be accommodated in a place where the primacy of human will holds sway?

The current doubt over whether the Islamists are willing to or capable of respecting democracy has so far stalled any plans to change the leading parties and to reverse the 'fossilisation' of the political classes that has resulted. Behind the smoke-screen that is the 'ban on the establishment of religious parties',[1] it is the presumed 'opposition' of the Islamists 'to democracy' that keeps the main opposition forces on the fringes of the institutional system in Egypt, Morocco and Tunisia. In Algeria[2] there was a supposed return to violence by the FIS to 'sabotage the democratic process that threatened it', followed in December 1991 by 'the danger to democracy if the FIS were to win the elections'; this was enough for the media on both sides of the Mediterranean to justify the army taking control of the first ballot and then imposing its dictatorship.[3]

Essentially, the argument that 'Islamism' and 'democracy' are incompatible takes place on three complementary levels. The incompatibility between unwavering doctrine, 'Islam', and democratic thought is often considered to be the initial structural cause. Is it really possible to be both a democrat and a Muslim? The early indications of the structural incompatibility between Islam and liberal political thought are the obvious inability of classical Muslim thought – particularly the notion of *shura* consultation – to cope with modern forms of opposition and institutionalise political pluralism, the 'secular shortcomings' – the failure to recognise an exclusively political arena – and its corollary, and the affirmation of the primacy of divine law over the will of the people. How can FIS militants be democratic when they subscribe to a doctrine that is not democratic and when words such as 'tolerance', 'human rights' and 'democracy', as *Le Monde* cartoonist Plantu reminds everyone who is tempted to shun such a simple analysis, 'are not in their vocabulary'?[4] Of course this first argument is more digestible for foreign observers than for the Arab regimes, none of which have stopped taunting their opponents with what they know is offensive and proclaiming themselves to be democratic and to respect the laws of Islam.

The notion of incompatibility is further strengthened by the number of Islamists who have steadfastly refused to embrace democracy. If the founders of modern Islamism, Abul 'Ala al-Mawdudi and Hassan al-Banna in particular, were relatively quiet about their distaste for the democratic principle, then many of their successors are now shouting it from the rooftops.[5]

The third level of the argument lies the practices of the Islamists Iran and Sudan, where they hold power. A brief glance at Iran, where the Khomeinist camp has brutally clamped down on its left-wing opposition with methods used by imperial dictators, and at the regime of Omar al-Bashir, whose practices, even if they are comparable to those of the great 'secular' allies of the West, such as Tunisia, Algeria, Egypt or Iraq, leave a great deal to be desired, are enough to reinforce unproven assertions with empirical evidence.

Therefore, the incompatibility is three-fold: structural, because of the void between the doctrines of nineteenth-century industrial Europe and classic Muslim thought; circumstantial, because of the 'acknowledgment' of some Islamist activists; and empirical, in view of the practices of the Islamists in power. Consequently the 'relationship between Islamism and democracy' is an extremely thorny subject. The reader should be aware of the message that our most famous analysts have for the past 10 years been emphasising, that

> Islamism is the arch-enemy of democracy; as in Iran, its victory in Algeria will herald a bloody dictatorship crushing all those who oppose its message [...] The global cost will be huge: a theocratic-military regime, scientific regression, a cultural inquisition, and people leaving in droves.[6]

All this is nothing new. It is reminiscent of 'No freedom for the enemies of freedom', a justification for all the repressive measures of the past and the future to prevent what the most staunch supporters of democracy have become accustomed to calling 'national-Islamism' or more bluntly the new 'green fascism'. But have we really completed the analysis of this difficult question? Is this all there is to say?

What Islam? What Islamists? What democracy?

In order to debate the matter properly, one must not underestimate the pertinence of these arguments. Of course, the institutional categories and expressions of classic Muslim thought naturally sit uncomfortably with those built up by the European and US constitutionalism of the eighteenth century. There is a fundamental antipathy between all religious dogma and the democratic idea. The initial doctrinal expressions of modern Islamists distanced them from the democratic principle, and some continue to uphold the 'primacy of divine will over that of the people' that appears to be holding back the short-term development of democracy. Finally, there is no doubt that the Iranian experiment and, a few years later, the Sudanese regime of Bashir, were far from being the credible alternatives to the regimes that they succeeded.

The present attitude of Islamists towards democracy ranges from unconditional and unreserved acceptance to total and utter rejection. Some lazy analysts simply throw this first category in with 'doublespeak' and other 'proofs of duplicity', while the second constitutes definitive proof, usually leaving nothing else to discuss. The first expressions of modern Islamists did, in part, denounce the democratic principle. Even if the Muslim Brotherhood was more flexible on this issue before it was repressed with increasing regularity, and if the first writings of Banna did not focus on criticising the institutions derived from Western political thought, rejection of the principle of democracy has at no point been entirely absent from Islamist discourse. From Benhadj to the leaders of the Gama'a Islamiyya in Egypt to the Islamic Liberation Party in Jordan, many of the movements are still explicitly accommodating these ideas. Even if this notion has been discredited by a number of Muslim theorists, the idea that the democracy compromises the primacy of the religious remains a central issue to their argument.

It is in the name of this rejection of majority rule that Benhadj justifies his attacks against what he calls the 'democratic poison'.[7]

> Of all the reasons for objecting to democracy, the most important is the fact that it is based on the will of the majority. What is considered fair and reasonable is decided upon by the majority. As a result of this, we see leaders of the democratic parties trying to attract the maximum number of people, without a thought for faith, dignity, religion and honour, with the sole aim of securing their votes come election day. We Sunnis believe, however, that justice [haqq] can only be drawn from the lessons of the shari'a, not the multitude and their demagogues. The followers of the Prophet are heavily outnumbered by the followers of idols.[8]

'The governing body has no right to change the law [...] Neither do the people. This right only belongs to scholars who understand the rules of itjihad as well as the specific circumstances affecting the societies of which they are members.'[9]

Everything written by the Egyptian Gama'a Islamiyya, the Islamist Liberation Party (Hizb al-Tahrir) and the AIG in Algeria[10] closely follows the same principle of rejection.[11] Despite his differences of opinion with Benhadj,[12] the Moroccan Abdessalam Yassine has also sketched out his position by confirming that there should be no question of abandoning the principle of divine guidance. The idea of bowing to the whims of Western democracy is not entertained:

> Any right that is not based on the law of God has no bearing on our mentality or our hopes. The rights that man has invented over time ignore the funda-mental right of a man to know the truth about the meaning of his presence in the world and the purpose of the necessary and predestined journey towards his death. Materialist ideas of power, economy and of harnessing nature have developed the misguided attitude of relativism, which explains everything by linking it to nothing and which leads to an overwhelming sense of nihilism... We will never exploit modernity to cajole either our people or outsiders. This is not a game for us, it is a matter of life and death for a quarter of the world's population. We support the democratic ideal where the people choose their

government and it is they who dismiss the team, class or ideology that they do not like. Democratic alternation? Why not!...[But] the cries of the propagandists who sing the praises of Western-style democracy as the only system that can satisfy 'rational desire', and the only hope for 'those condemned to work the land' to escape from the rut of under-development, will fall on deaf ears. We will not be led astray and we have seen through their attempts to present themselves as the renewal of tired and crumbling Marxist ideology.[13]

Do these more-or-less radical criticisms of Western democracy confirm that the resurgence of Muslim culture and the respect and development of humanist values are completely incompatible? There is no evidence of this. Why? It is a simple matter of form: when there is no alternative, a hypothesis becomes a postulate. For a postulate to earn its name, it has to have been proved beyond doubt, and this has not been the case with Islamism. If it is not the case, the part played by the postulate in the analysis would be as disastrous as that of having a single party run a supposedly pluralist system.

Beyond its initial logical shortcomings, the impact of which is considerable on Western analysis, the idea of the absolute incompatibility of Islamist forces and the mechanisms of functioning democracy contains a major flaw: not a mistake in logic or methodology, but in the way it deals with empirical reality.

Democracy? 'It belongs to them'

We should remember that the concepts that the north regards as universal are connected in the minds of the people who reject them to both the manner in which they were introduced to the Muslim world and the manner in which they have been exploited by the regimes these people are presently fighting. We know that Islamist rhetoric has prospered because it represents a symbolic rift Western references. It is no surprise, therefore, that it has refused to adopt the terminology of Western thought. When it denounces democracy, Islamism is not necessarily seeking to suppress any independent intervention by human will or proscribe all possibility of regulating the methods of the devolution, transferral and exercise of power using profane laws, or even suppress minorities. In fact, much of this line of thinking is now unlikely to be translated into reality; it has evolved into a marker of identity and, moreover, into a reactionary statement: 'I am against "their" democracy so I am beginning to exist'. 'Foreign' understandings of local culture are largely derived from the meaning they have acquired within the context of their importation to the Arab world. Ghassan Salamé is exactly right when he points out that 'to a great extent, the Arab world is still reacting to a democratic model which is closely linked with the colonising powers that inspired it,' and that 'the use of either of these terms [Islam and democracy] is clearly linked to the cultural and political conflict conducted by the two dedicated and partisan sides'.[14] The rhetoric of the Gama'a Islamiyya militants does not see the prerequisites of democracy (secularism and 'all men are equal in the eyes of the law') in the same light as that of the French revolutionaries or the 'secular' activists who came after them. In their logic, secularism is first and foremost a concept imported from the West which, at the turn of the century, spelt the end for the hegemony of the Islamic norm. Using the very small Christian community for support the prerequisite that 'all men are equal in the eyes of the law' has justified the confining of Muslim practices behind the closed doors of 'personal status'. Therefore, it comes as no surprise to hear that after the electoral victory of his party in June 1991, Benhadj was celebrating a 'victory for Islam, not for democracy'.

Moreover, the Arab regimes and their faithful Western allies have lost all credibility by their highly selective application of the definition of democracy. The treatment of Algerian elections in December 1991 and of the subsequent crushing victory of the FIS succeeded in popularising the idea that these 'foreign' concepts, alien to the indigenous culture, had failed to produce the slightest positive effect. It was an idea that became even clearer when numerous Islamist leaders experienced the repression of the self-proclaimed 'democratic', 'popular' regimes, which are passionate about 'human rights' – or are labelled as such by the West. Has France not tended to label as 'democratic', any regime which seeks in one way or another to stamp out the Islamists?

Is it not true that George Bush went into the Gulf with arms and aid in order to 'restore democracy in the Emirate of Kuwait'? The arguments of some defenders of the eradicatory thesis and those for whom 'the illiterate' should not have the 'same right to vote as the educated, the company worker the same rights as the managing director, or benefit-claimers the same rights as tax-payers'[15] must be discussed. By seeing things from 'their' point of view, there are many more examples of this contentious issue which certain Muslims promote as a dangerously simplified representation of the democratic idea. The influential Tunisian leader of hizb al-Nahda, Rached Ghannouchi, who is well-versed in the demands of democracy, is therefore in a position to highlight the flagrant contradiction of the regimes' discourse:

The annoying thing is that those countries pointing the finger at us over human rights or democracy can hardly boast about their own records. [They] have continued to suppress freedom, to rig elections and to monopolise the information services. We are surrounded by absurdity [...] The truth is simple. Our adversaries have always found it difficult to accept democracy and pluralism. They used to openly reject such principles, yet today they disguise their contempt. They will only embrace democracy if they are to profit from it. Indeed, let us suppose that we are inveterate anti-democrats and our opponents are irreproachable democrats. If they were sincere, they could make us take part in democracy. In France, the extreme Right, or for that matter the extreme Left, are not known for their democratic tendencies, but no-one would dream of excluding them from the democratic process. The situation could be repeated in the democracies of Israel, America, Britain, Germany, etc. Thanks to democracy, authoritarian parties have been allowed to prosper in every country, even if they are marginalised. Therefore, to re-educate ourselves, we should be allowed our place in 'democracy'. [In Tunisia] they have a Communist Party. No one has asked them to renounce Marxism, if this is a democratic ideology, to be recognised. Yet this is precisely what they expect us, and only us, to do because they are trying to stamp out a large and powerful party.[16]

The pitfalls of (a) historical comparativism

The parallelism of Islam and democracy, or *shura* and pluralism referred to by many symposia,[17] including those of the Islamists, has its uses, but a mechanistic comparison of concepts produced by completely different dynamics and historical environments is relative.[18] Thus, the pitfalls of a confrontation between the classical expression of Muslim culture and the contemporary interpretation of democracy by industrial Europe are seriously underestimated. What purpose is served by the unsurprising revelation that the concept of the *shura*, as practised in Medina from the days of the Prophet Muhammed, is clearly at odds with Bill Clinton's vision of democracy fourteen centuries later? How is it possible to underestimate to such an extent the sociological distance separating the actors representing these concepts from their supposed eternal 'essence'? The juridical instruments of classical Muslim public law cannot exist alongside the judicial process developed in Europe 14 centuries later. Yet is this really the heart of the matter?

The strictly comparatist view not only results in manipulating slightly incompatible categories, but also chooses to ignore the myriad of possibilities offered by historical dynamics and the manifestly rapid and clear changes which occur in the modern Islamic movements in particular. If the response is only partially negative – for example, *shura* is incompatible with democracy, as is Islam with secularism – it over-estimates the depth of historical determinations to the extent that it in fact deprives the Muslim community of everything in which its, or any other civilisation's, strength lies: its ability to evolve, even if its system of norms is compromised.

Is Muslim civilisation 'democratic'? The desired reply would be 'no more than the Christian civilisation was before it became democratic', which has only happened recently and only in certain countries. The political practices of Muslims from the classical age or even, as we shall see, the advocates of the new Islamist rhetoric, are far less important than the ability of the Muslim community, including the Islamists, to transform its relationship to the very core of their doctrine. Those who feel the need to disassociate themselves from 'democracy', even if they are leaders, cannot be considered the 'owners' of the future of their community. Some leaders of some groups might publicly defy democracy, but that is not enough to shape the conduct of all those who today and in the generations to come, are influenced by his teachings. Where the controversial view is logically content to enjoy the Islamist disavowal of the democratic idea, the analytical view has to go even further to be able to measure the exact scale of the rejection. Is the intention of the arch-enemy of democracy to establish the law for the majority by abusing the rights of the minority? Is its intention to deny all independent human thought and reject any possibility of 'profane' leadership? Is its intention to deprive the majority of the opportunity for political participation? Whatever its intention, any investigation must look beyond the terminology and the rites of European political practice in an attempt to measure the concrete effects of adopting or rejecting a particular concept. This involves the principle of recognising the political arena and the methods of ensuring its survival, the institutionalisation of contestation, respect for religious or ethnic minorities, a degree of political participation, respect for humanist values not just economic values etc.

Another thesis has emerged in the broad spectrum of the Islamist attitudes to democracy at the opposite end of the 'anti-democratic' scale, which chooses to assert the structural unity of the community expressed in the consensus (*ijma'*) of its *'ulama* and the recognition of one 'divine' sovereignty. Here the principles of pluralism are presented as wholly compatible with respect for divine 'guidance'. For example, there are two doctrinal schools in opposition to each other: on one side, there are those who believe there is an irrefutable link between political philosophy and religion; on the other, those who think that an autonomous political space does exist and therefore can perfectly accommodate the use of profane methods for conflict resolution.[19] The Quranic verse most often used to highlight the differences between members of the Muslim community and the legitimacy of their political expression refers to the 'peoples' and the 'tribes' that make up the fabric of the community, thus underlining its pluralist structure.[20] This pluralist vision demolishes the idea of human infallibility in the interpretation of the (divine) reference and guarantees the process of political debate, the idea that 'if there is only one book and one truth, it does not necessarily follow that man is capable of reading and finding this truth without making mistakes' and that consequently 'no Muslim has the right to monopolise the interpretation of a text or the truth when there have always been so many interpretations'.[21]

The most widespread of the exegeses have also established an analogy between the political parties of the democratic system and the doctrinal schools in Islamic law, 'differences of opinion' that Islam has always tolerated. Obviously, these differences do not affect the eternal and unchanging essence of the doctrine, only the part of the belief which must be interpreted and therefore adapted by man to suit the social and political demands of the time and the place. Yet again, the removal of this essential barrier between the eternal and the changing, between the *thabit* (that which does not change) and the *mutaghayyir* (that which changes), between what some prefer to call 'religion' and 'the knowledge of religion' – which in this case is remarkably similar to the border between religion and politics – is left entirely to a balance of power that is affected by all the dynamics.

The most vocal proponent of this dynamic appears to be Ghannouchi, to the point that it fuels fierce hostility of the most conservative section of the Islamist movement.[22] 'Stop saying that democracy is foreign to our culture. Stop saying that it belongs only to the West. You are mistaken, as democracy is Islam,' Ghannouchi would regularly plead to the eastern audiences, whom he also advised to observe the Islamic communities of the West coast of the US instead of those of the Gulf countries.

What can be said about those Islamists who think that democracy is a *kufr* concept?[23] If it is a simple matter of linguistic disagreement, there is a definite problem…Democracy is simply a way of resolving political and intellectual disputes in a peaceful manner…If there are to be no constraints on the Muslim religion, then it is even more important that there should be none in politics…Liberties should not be seen as a threat to Islam because they are the essence of Islam…People who think democracy to be *kufr* are wrong. This question has been pondered over by the eminent specialists of the *ijtihad*. To call democracy *kufr* is a misguided *ijtihad*.[24]

At present this position is shared by a broad sample of Islamist groups, particularly the arm of the FIS led by Abbassi Madani, whose declarations have been explicit:

> [In the event of electoral defeat], our position will be to accept and respect the will of the people…In this country there are people who follow Islam and there are others who do not. Therefore, to avoid falling into a situation similar to that in Lebanon, we have to agree on a minimum, namely on the will of the people.

Even Benhadj has considerably modified his initial impressions. The backing given in January 1995 to the platform signed by the Algerian opposition in Rome, when it does not clearly oppose the emblematic formulations of 1989, has a considerable effect upon them. For Benhadj, the leaders chosen by Muslims without restriction cannot be foisted upon them by either 'military force or tribal affiliation or by so-called divine law'. He goes on to recognise the principle of popular sovereignty by recalling that 'it is the community of believers that is the source of power', and that the Imam must be 'someone who can unite Muslims behind him'. The right to 'objective' opposition is recognised as it is 'inscribed in the *shari'a*', Benhadj also declares, citing a speech by the Caliph Abu Bakr asking for help when he trod the right path and correction when he erred. Finally, he refers to the distinction made by the political model of Islam between 'the constant and the evolutionary', between 'the Commandments of God which are unchanging and the interests of the Islamic community which can evolve'.[25]

In Egypt, the Labour Party of Ibrahim Shukri and Adel Hussein as well as the Muslim Brotherhood, have always supported the pluralist option, although they use a different terminology.[26] Hussein stresses that the Islamist demands are more a desire to restore the symbolic sphere than a single, intangible political ideology:

> Every country has a general framework, a constitution or general principles which co-ordinate effort and regulate politics. The rules, the general principles that govern the political game are clearly defined and consequently the political game is played peacefully and constructively. That is what we need. We need a general ideology, which means general principles that regulate the game as a whole and which act as a guide for the different participants, which is a condition for the game to run smoothly. I think that in this country Islam represents these general rules or these general principles […] That does not mean, however, that there should be a single party. The Muslim Brothers should be included, as well as the Nasserists, etc. Yet we should all stand under the flag of Islam, because that is our identity. We should not allow the Muslim

Brothers to monopolise Islam. They represent a certain section of Muslim society, but they are not and should not be the only representatives. We should work together from the same base and compete with each other from the same base. Of course, we argue over detail and even more fundamental differences, but it must all remain within the framework of Islam.

The vision of relations with the Christian community held by this sector of the Islamist movement (see Chapter 6) similarly demonstrates the ideology needed to involve the non-Muslim minority in the dynamic of re-Islamisation.

The law of God, pluralism and secularism

However, there are some precepts which explicitly and definitively forbid the expression of democratic values in the supposedly intangible core of the doctrine of the Muslim community. As Leonard Binder asks, 'Is Islam capable of liberal thought without losing its essence?'[27] When the highest priority is given to the unity of the community, how can Islam allow for pluralism of political expression? How can the primacy of divine law and the primacy of popular will live in harmony?

If the essence of democracy is thought to lie in the primary principle of the human will, then there seems to be insurmountable conflict between the secular West and the religious Islamic countries. However, it is not as grave as the two camps often believe it to be. To show this, we should remember that the undisputed principle linking Islam with 'divine sovereignty', which apparently rules out all forms of political autonomy, has led to a huge range of interpretations, including of course the interpretations of Muslim thought itself. It cannot be denied that since the efforts of Ali Abd al-Razzaq at the turn of the century the modern incarnation of this political autonomy within Islam has aroused the suspicion and hostility of oppositional Islam.[28] In the reactionary context of the resistance to the invasion by the West, followed by the conflict caused by the emergence of the Islamist opposition groups, any criticism of using the concept of 'theocracy' to govern the Muslim community has been met with a barrage of protests.

Nevertheless, the whole of Muslim history demonstrates the validity of such an approach. Chérif Ferjani notes that

> The status of politics and the judiciary are no more fundamental in Islam than they are in other religions. If you need proof, look at the evolution, and some-times the involution, of the political and legal systems of Muslim societies and

note the disparity between these systems: it is only the ignorance of the specialists that can confuse them and conclude either that Islam, its law and its divine figure are unique, or that it is incapable of evolving.[29]

Jacques Berque insists,

I defy anybody to find an example in Islamic history of a *faqih* (a specialist in Muslim law) holding power. The Umayyad Caliphs, the Abbasid Caliphs, the Mamlukes, all masters of war, and the Ottoman sultans, the solemn and conquering Asiatics, none of them were *faqihs*! ... But, seriously, *religious* power has only been held, falteringly, by sects: the *Hashashiyyin* ('assassins') or the Qarmatians. Mainstream Islam has never experienced direct political power from religion.

Many recent initiatives, even if they have failed 'politically', have shown that Islam has always sought to recognise an autonomous political space.[30] The difficulty is in forcing a public admission by Muslims that such a space exists, especially since it is identified as a notion produced by Western culture. Mohammed Arkoun expresses a similar idea when he stresses that 'to think of Islam as the separation of the spiritual and the temporal and the separation of the religious and political [is] much more a political obstacle than it is a psychological or even cultural one'.[31] Secularism is not a scientific concept: it has become a mark of identity 'shielded' from all rational management.

Once the extent of the affirmation of the 'supremacy of divine law' of the politics of Islam has been measured, logical thought must also consider the range of the secular principle and the principle of popular sovereignty in the West. Has the democratic West really raised these principles to a supreme value? Does the expression of public sovereignty know no limits? Do constitutionalism and Western political practice allow real free will to the authors of the laws that govern society? Have these laws really succeeded in cleansing politics of all 'religious' influence? Apart from a few rare exceptions, it seems that there are terms and conditions for this to be so.[32] This is primarily because in the West there appears to be huge variations in how the secularist principle is imposed and how widespread it is. This is particularly the case with Israel. Israeli democracy, even if other religious denominations are tolerated, is based on a state whose foundation is rooted in religion. Apart from France, very few Western countries have fulfilled their vision of secularism. The leading lights of Western liberal thought, the US (In God we trust!), the UK and Germany, have always allowed the survival of principles higher than human will, be it based on both the collective and the majority. In these countries, references to the divine corpus are explicit. But nearly everywhere else, including in republican France, it has only disappeared in a formal capacity, even if there is a distinct difference. 'Universal declarations', 'general principles of law' and other 'natural rights' have continued to impose principles that are supposedly higher than the will of any parliamentary majority on the people. Even when the majority is overwhelming, in several 'secular' democracies the public will is submitted to a body of rules over which the 'sovereign people' have no control. To limit the possible excesses of a 'majority', there is recognition of the existence of immanent principles which are not drawn from the human will: an irrefutable way of admitting that there are other sources that define the norm.

The refusal to qualify these references as divine undoubtedly represents a significant difference. Again, remember that such a difference is the result of the shape and the context of its formulation – the emancipation from ecclesiastical supervision – as it expresses the will to confirm an essential principle. Of course the formal precision of the Quran is altogether more restricting than the ever-changing principles of natural law. But one should not underestimate the extent of the autonomy that Muslim jurists have, or the potential of the techniques of *ijtihad* to interpret the sacred text. There are many examples of such an exegesis: a restrictive interpretation of the conditions of imposing the *hudud* (the Quranic penal sentences that the West often associates with all of Islam), the distancing from polygamy and acceptance of the rules of political pluralism. For these interpretations to become 'Islamic norms' they need the support of a socio-political majority.[33] Therefore, the emergence of 'democratic' behaviour is not so much a question of Islamic studies as it is a question of the nature of the countless political, economic, educational etc influences that make themselves felt upon the different Islamic actors.

No freedom for the enemies of freedom?

Does religious law have more of a 'totalising' potential than human law? Does its absolutism tend to victimise minorities more systematically if they happen to reject it? What about the people who oppose not only the expression of Islamic law, but also the whole system? In this regard, the verbal reassurances of some leaders are simply not enough.[34] Evidently, if you read between the lines of the democratic Islamist discourses, you will see the 'reservations', which bear witness to their persistent difficulty in recognising the political legitimacy, of those who have been declared the adversaries of Islam, and therefore find additional proof that the Islamist rhetoric is fundamentally 'different'. These reservations are well-known. For example, the leader of the FIS, Abbassi Madani, has said:

> We believe that elections are crucial for everyone. Whatever the result, we will respect the majority even if it only represents one voice. We think that the people elected by the people reflect the will of the people. On the other hand, what we find unacceptable is that the elected body not serve the interests of the people. They should not contradict the *Shari'a*, its doctrine or its values. They must not wage war on Islam, as the enemy of Islam is the enemy of the people.

Meanwhile the Algerian moderate Mahfoud Nahnah has stated: 'From the moment that democracy does not affect the heart of Islamic faith, it becomes the quest of the believer'.[35] This is why it often seems that the democratic Islamist potential is at its limit when it reaches the boundaries of the system: anything goes, 'as long as it does not go against Islam'. Such an Islamist leader, trying to convince the Western interlocutor that he is open-minded, will make a sincere declaration that 'he hopes that once the FIS has seized power they will be able to respect the point of view of other ... Islamist movements.' However, this is doubted by those militants among the Islamists who are convinced that universal suffrage is an instrument destined to bring down a corrupt system which has so far hidden behind the smoke-screen of democracy, so that they can put in place their own system which has different terms.

However, to measure the degree of incompatibility between democracy and Islam, a close examination of Western democracy, which has served as the yardstick, is advisable. Of course, we should not ignore the parts of the Muslim doctrine that limit the status of non-Muslim minorities or 'anti-Muslims', namely the actors who, by their affiliation, have declared themselves 'outside' of, indeed hostile, to the system. Yet, to measure this supposed Islamic specificity, we should also bear in mind that Western liberal thought has always sought to limit the liberties of those who are 'foreign' to its own system. Some of the ways to protect the dominant symbolic system – which vary according to the seriousness of the threat to the system – are to be found throughout the history of democracy, even if they are serious infringements of the general principles on which democracy is supposedly founded: the Constitution of the Federal Republic of Germany does not recognise the rights of anyone who does not recognise its principles; until recently, communists, or those who were thought to be communists, were denied entry to the US; the Swiss and Norwegian constitutions exclude non-Christians from being appointed to the highest legal positions; the Queen of England must also be the head of the Anglican Church.

What guarantee does Islam agree to give to people who reject it? What guarantee does the dominant normative system give to people who refute it as such? Someone who rejects the system altogether cannot expect to achieve the same central position as someone who accepts it. But, in similar circumstances, would their position be any more marginal in Islam than it is elsewhere? In today's Arab world, what status would be given to an intellectual who has chosen to be an atheist? Or to a woman who, in front of Western television cameras, compares the dress-code of Islamic women to the 'yellow star' that the Jews had to wear as a prelude to their physical elimination? No doubt these people would be in a very precarious position. Yet no more precarious – although this should not serve as an excuse and even less as an encouragement – than it was for communist intellectuals in the US in the 1950s, where McCarthyism was the height of liberal thought.

What 'freedom' does the person who portrays himself as 'an enemy of freedom' have? One side says: 'There are no guarantees of democracy and freedom for the enemies of democracy and freedom'. The other side replies: 'There are no guarantees of Islam for the enemies of Islam' – or words to that effect. Is this a reason to tolerate it? Certainly not. Is this a reason to reintroduce a degree of relativity into the automatism of our comparisons? Of course it is. With all due respect to the die-hards on both sides, if the terms used to compare – or to cause discord – are reassessed (and reconnected with their historical background), then it will be shown that the distance between democracy and Islam is relative. In fact, the intention of the Islamist surge appears mainly to be forcibly to reaffirm a certain number of humanist values for the benefit of a Western secularism which appears to be driven above all by materialism. Is this 'difference' incompatible with the democratic contribution of which Western political thought is justifiably proud? That is still undecided. In Islam, the function of 'divine' law is not dissimilar to that of the 'natural law' or 'general principles' in Western thought, a collection of intangible principles encompassing human normative activity. The increasing significance of the sacred therefore seems to be much more in keeping with what, in secular terms, the West considers to be legitimately universal. The rest is just a matter of 'politics', namely the individual and collective will that in this sense is expressed in a socio-political context and at a given moment in 'Muslim' history. Has this process come to an end? Not at all. When the Islamists seize power, are they, in the space of a few hours, going to break with the methods of the dictatorial regimes whose downfall they are inevitably going to produce? Absolutely not.

Nevertheless, the outsider persists in refusing to acknowledge any progress or change, no matter how small. Instead, sterile denunciations of majority rule which could result from the Islamists' coming to power persist.[36] Many observers, both Arab and Western, have seen the proclaimed rallying of the Islamist leaders to pluralist values as diversionary 'strategy' or other 'tactics' of circumstance. Mohsen Toumi, who summed up the state of mind of a sector of the Arab political class and the argument of the 'eradicators' of all persuasions, wrote:

> At first, there seems to be some democrats among the Islamists. They might be genuine. It could also be that this is a Trojan horse, occupied by people sent by the fundamentalist movement and assigned this mission: to become involved in public life, to run a successful business, to allay suspicion, to calm hostilities and to take advantage of the opportunities offered by the democratic institutions of other groups that have remained underground, until the moment is right to drop everything to take up the fight with the state system. This strategy is based on an assumption, the knowledge that democracies are fragile and that they are open, more so than other regimes, to conquest.[37]

Islamism or democracy?

There are those who condone the shameful acts perpetrated by the regimes that are fighting the Islamists today by warning of the perversions of democracy that certain Islamists, once in power, might one day be responsible for. Their argument shall not be refuted here with a response as equally peremptory. Rather, in the absence of conclusive evidence, it is suggested that evaluating the relation between the values (which, as has been stressed, are quite separate from vocabulary) of democracy and the different pieces of the vast Islamist movement that are involved in the different Arab political scenes at the end of the twentieth century, is an operation which should be questioned on many levels, beyond the web of simplification in which the relationship between Islam and democracy is usually entangled.

Once the problem of the compatibility of the 'essence' of Islam and democracy and the range of discourses of the actors has been addressed, our attention must inevitably turn to the concrete socio-political conditions, that are variable in time and space, in which these actors evolve. Therefore, it is less a case of knowing if Islam is compatible with democracy, a fairly unrealistic proposition, than of trying to understand whether contemporary Arab societies – namely the different Muslim communities – that have evolved from different histories have reached a point in their political development where 'pluralist' behaviour, that respects individual or collective differences, can emerge and develop to a greater extent than has been the case since the colonisers 'flew the nest'.

However, answers to the question of the compatibility of Islam and democracy will not be clear-cut. They can only be partial, mitigated, multiple and hesitant. But once these answers have been reconciled with this plurality, this dynamism and critical doubt without which objective analysis comes to resemble partisan polemic, they can no longer, more importantly, be limited to refining the myth of the 'Islamist threat to democracy'. The Algerian Islamists emerged after France had conducted a policy of deculturation over a period of 132 years, and who felt the blind and savage repression of the FLN. They were drunk on nationalist legitimacy, leading to the inevitable radicalisation of some of their members, and are therefore certainly not the best people to suggest immediate and decisive measures that respect the differences that exist in Algerian society. However, does Islamism really represent 'the arch-enemy of democracy' and, wherever or whenever it holds power, will it ultimately dissolve into a process of 'scientific regression, cultural inquisition, and a mass exodus', as portrayed by the most celebrated analysts of the Algerian scene?

To try and wrap up this impossible debate, the position of the author, and the response to this position that is reflected throughout this book, will be clarified. Today, many people identify the chances of reform and modernisation and therefore, in one way or another, of democracy itself, with the end of the process of re-Islamisation or its banishment to the fringes of political expression. On the contrary, the author believes that two major processes occurring in the Arab world are anything but incompatible: the reconciliation of political discourse with Muslim culture on the one hand, and the slow and laborious emergence of pluralist and tolerant conduct in line with the democratic world on the other. There is of course absolutely no guarantee that a modernist conduct which respects democratic thought will emerge, but nor is their any certainty that the rise of the Islamists will affect or condemn this emergence. In the present environment, in which the political elites of the region are experiencing a transitional period, there has hardly been a challenge to this view that is, conversely, almost certainly threatened by the 'fossilisation' of the dominant elites and the criminalisation of the intellectual activity of the opposition.

Contrary to what the 'secular democrats' in power have been trying to tell us for the past 30 years, 'democratisation' and 're-Islamisation' are today following paths that meet at many points. In the thick of confrontations, it is difficult to separate the 'grains of identity' from the 'extremist chaff', to take the time to note that the indulgences of the Islamist rhetoric are just as reactionist as they are reactionary. It is also possible to miss the fact that, behind its vocabulary of rejection, it awakens values and energies that are not as harmful to the humanism of our 'democratic modernity' as we have sometimes the imperious need to believe.

The existence of political forces which use the rhetoric of Islam can no longer be considered the sole criterion for assessing delays to the process of modernisation while the rest of the political class (miraculously pardoned for decades of authoritarianism) is considered the natural defender of individual and collective liberties simply because it has publicly distanced itself from the Islamist movement. If there is a line of demarcation in the Arab world that separates the 'good' and the 'bad', or rather, the 'democrats' and the 'anti-democrats', the tolerant and the intolerant, the defenders of the rights of men, women and the confessional minorities and those who only have a slight interest in them, then this line follows a far more sinuous path then that of the line distinguishing the Islamists from the rest of the political class.

It is simply not enough, as some Islamist leaders have, publicly to declare that majority rule will be respected, in order to boost one's 'democratic' credentials. Nor is it sufficient to oppose the Islamists (as Saddam Hussein did at the time of the war with Iran), to be 'anti-Saddam' (like the Emir of Kuwait), or a soldier or a Francophile (in Algeria), in order to join the so-called 'democratic camp', which is today monopolised by discredited regimes or by a secular opposition marginalised by the Islamist surge with the blessing of the West.

It is because it represents one of its intrinsic ingredients that the involvement of the Islamists appears conversely to be an indispensable condition of a truly democratic transition, which would lose all significance if it were denied the input of an entire political generation.

CHAPTER ELEVEN

Islamism and Women

The hijab is like a yellow star for women, the first step towards their physical elimination.

Khalida Messaoudi[1]

A woman to an Islamist is like a Jew to a Nazi.

Rachid Mimouni[2]

The position of Islamism on the question of the 'female cause' is subject to particularly passionate debate. If *homo occidentalis* is disturbed by the allegiance of men to the Islamist credo, it is nothing in comparison to the distaste aroused by women joining the Islamist movement. It also inspires people of the West, and not just 'feminists', to make some bizarre assumptions.

The most classic assumption is to reduce the entire dynamic of the ideological repositioning of the south to an 'anti-woman' movement and to condemn it outright in analysis as a form of 'misogyny', even a form of 'apartheid'.[3] When the caricaturists of Western media draw pictures of bearded villains forcing young women to cover their tear-stained faces with a *hijab*, they reflect a common perception. However, this image is as simplifying as it is divorced from reality, for it ignores the fact that there are millions of women who have consciously and deliberately joined the Islamist cause. Throughout the Arab world, women's rights in general, and the wearing of the veil in particular, are subject to wildly differing perceptions, a point that it is important to remember. The media has feasted on the legitimate and wholly understandable disarray of some Arab women, who feel threatened by the Islamist upsurge, with the result that there is now a huge smoke-screen dividing Western public opinion and the complex reality of the area.

'To simply point the finger of blame at the radical Islamist discourse for the way women are treated, without re-examining the male-female relationship,' as Sa'ida Rahal Sidhoum, not noted for her complacency, explains, 'is pure manipulation and poppycock'.[4] Rather than being the 'stumbling block for the Islamist movement' that the most automatic of its detractors believe it to be, is the 'question of women' more a question of the Western view of Islamism?[5]

What do we really know about the political attitude of women to the forces that are identified with re-Islamisation? What has been the true impact of policies that tend to restore the hegemony of Muslim culture on feminist dynamics and in particular on the claim by women to be granted access to public life? In other words, how does Islamism approach the question of women, and how do women approach Islamism?

To respond to this last question, with all the limitations arising from a presentation which will inevitably mean over-simplification, we propose to consider that the attitudes of the female population are split into two large groups that will be called the 'traditional' and the 'modern', the latter being further subdivided into 'Islamists' and 'anti-Islamists'.

Between traditionalism and Islamist modernisation

The traditional women shall be qualified as those who live in harmony with the intuitive 'pre-modern' culture. This is mainly because they have had limited access to the education system, largely – but not exclusively – living in rural areas. The antipathic effect of Islamism on this section of the female population is limited, even non-existent. However, although they are not exactly the same, the demands of re-Islamisation, particularly with regard to the dress-code and relationships between the sexes, do not differ much from traditional norms. With the exception of a few extremist and therefore rare practices (such as the wearing of the niqab, which covers the face), traditional women do not perceive these demands as violent or as an attack on their freedom. On the contrary, they regard Western practices, such as women, and even men, parading their naked arms and legs, as unacceptable innovations.

The political behaviour of these 'traditional' women will vary according to which ethnic grouping or clan they belong, their clientelist or political affiliations or those of their family. In Algeria, for example, the eventual decision by a woman to distance herself from the FIS will not be based on the fact that she is a woman, but rather situations similar to the following: her husband or one of her close family might work for the police and therefore be a possible target for the armed groups, or may be a member of the FLN whose social status is threatened by an eventual change of government, or she or her family may feel concerned about the Berber cultural claim to which some 'anti-Islamist' groups have had recourse. She could also quite easily be 'pro-FIS' for many other reasons, her gender irrelevant to the formation of her political attitude and behaviour.

The second group of women will be defined as those who have adopted the 'modern' references of society, because of their access to the educational system, and have internalised the partially 'Westernised' behaviour that such references bring, most notably their role in professional life. These 'modern' women are to be found throughout the Muslim world divided into two groups. Firstly, those who have chosen to adopt the Islamist symbolic system. These women have made this choice according to the intellectual, social and political determinations that, to a certain extent, are shared by their spouses, sons, brothers and fathers. It is always this first group of 'modern' women, you could even call them 'feminists' – of whom the Western view has a clear and systematic mis-reading. These women, who will quite logically vote Islamist, have not had the *hijab* imposed upon them: it was their free choice to wear it, sometimes against the will of their family or class. They did not have to be convinced to submit to it 'out of fear' or even 'because they have finally given in', so that 'they go unnoticed', or 'because it's cheaper than a perm' etc. Instead they have claimed it and brandished it and advocated it in their professional or family lives. They do not wear it 'because it's not that different from traditional clothing', but they are on the other hand willing to take full responsibility for the relative split that it represents with traditional society.[6] For them, the veil is a symbol of their allegiance to a system of representation and socialisation.

These women, who in general are wrongly identified by the Western view as 'victims of the macho violence of the Islamists', or even as the 'alienated',[7] are denied in the most up-to-date analyses the basic right to exist as women. Yet all the available studies show that the number of women in the Islamist movement is rising sharply. The reports of humanitarian organisations show that they too are subject to contemporary 'male' violence, a symbolic violence which deprives them of the right in Algeria, Tunisia and Egypt to wear the clothes of their choice. This violence is also political, because there is nowhere for them to hide from the repression of the judiciary and the police, which is often accompanied by the physical violence that the regimes in Algiers, Tunis and Cairo claim is protecting 'secularism'.[8]

Of course the multiple symbolism of the veil[9] and the obvious diversity of meanings that the Islamist movement has for its female members should not be underestimated.[10] In a society where the imposed integration of the sexes (particularly on public transport) is culturally ill received, the veil can offer protection that everyday clothing can no longer guarantee. Mohammed Tozy emphasises that

> When a young woman chooses to wear the *hijab*, and therefore to denounce the integration of the sexes, she adopts a cultural identity [...] But this identity is effective to the extent that it is a response to the countless obstacles that block her path. In the never-ending queues for the university refectory, or in crowded buses where physical integrity is often threatened by bodily contact, the *hijab* is a vital statement.[11]

Pressure exerted by a woman's family or fellow students and the response to a vague social expectation also play a role. The proselytising efforts of the activists are seldom in vain. The activists of the mosques in the Muhandesin district of Cairo zealously explain to the new recruits at the weekly 'women-only' sessions that transformation 'must begin from outside (the *hijab*), before it can enter within (the soul)'. It is also said that 'Wearing a *hijab* is a message that you are sending to everyone, which shows that Islam is coming back'. Moreover, although it is 'silent', a *hijab* is a 'vocal', destabilising signal since it is a permanent reminder to a broad range of audiences, both at home and abroad, a dimension that the most zealous of the Islamist activists have understood perfectly.

Pressure can also lead women to try to anticipate the preferences of potential husbands who have been working in the Gulf or to please Arabic teachers, brothers, neighbours or relatives. The impact of the economic situation (rising prices at hairdressing salons or the cost of imported jeans) can perhaps also have an effect. But in general, and in all seriousness, membership in the Islamist cause probably occurs like any other profane method of socialisation for the modern Arab woman. Rather than being a manifestation or an implication of their imprisonment, it is increasingly the case that the veil allows them to go out, and not just to listen to the Imam's *khutba* (sermon) on Fridays – a traditionally male practice that today has been largely adopted by many of the *muhajjabat* (women who wear the *hijab*) living in towns. By exhibiting their rejection of the most disreputable types of socialising (bars, nightclubs, bumping into someone on the street), and despite the reservations of their family circle, the *muhajjabat* are not cutting themselves off from public areas where they would like to go. This is their wish, and the vast majority of them express it just as effectively as the wishes of their 'emancipated' sisters.

One of the two main conclusions drawn by the research of Djiehida Imache and Inès Nour is that the expectations of women who wear the veil are almost identical to those of women who do not.[12] Zakya Daoud, in the preface to her work dedicated to this research, found the similarity between the following statistics to be 'absolutely stunning':

> 91 per cent of veiled women and 96 per cent of non-veiled women envisaged following a career after their studies, 44 per cent of both camps think women should be able to work where they please, including paid work, 96 per cent of veiled women and 75 per cent of non-veiled women reckon that there are jobs for women, 49 per cent of veiled women and 66 per cent of non-veiled women believe that both sexes should receive the same level of education, 71 per cent and 96 per cent respectively for the same level of religious instruction, while 84 per cent and 96 per cent think that women should be able to participate in sport.[13]

'Of course, the *hijab* represents a rejection of imported and imposed modernity, but it has a far greater meaning than that', explains Fariba Adelkhah once she has ridiculed the

> folly of the Western discourse that considers the imposition of the *hijab* to be a sure sign of the repressive nature of Islamic regimes [...]: it is the materialisation of a continuity between human nature and Quranic revelations, which governs the relationship between the private and the public sphere, and between the family and the social domain.[14]

Dominant perceptions in the West rarely understand such subtleties. As the French Minister for National Education recalled in 1994, the veil is not only synonymous with religious affiliation, it is also 'a sign of woman's submission'. As one journalist elaborated the point, 'It symbolises the inequality of the sexes and the imprisonment of women'.[15] The paradox for Western feminists is thus: it denies the right to self-determination to the women that it claims to defend from abuse by masculine domination ...without any reference to femininity, to be a thinking individual who has free choice. Yet we are led to believe that women become 'involved in Islamism' for the same reasons as men. Today there are female activists as well as passive supporters, all of whom have joined the Islamist system of representation for the same everyday reasons as their brothers, fathers, sons or husbands, their gender not relevant to their choice.

The feminist resistance

The second of the two groups of 'modern' women brings together all the women who perceive the beliefs that the Islamist movement is trying to install (and for some of its most radical members, is trying to impose) to be a personal assault. Pressure exerted by the family, social and political environment, the bully-boy tactics of the proselytising and the counts of physical intimidation are examples of the methods of the Islamists who do not always respect the boundaries of individual liberties. Sympathisers of the Jordanian Muslim Brotherhood have adorned billboards with the pertinent question 'The *hijab* or hell?' Even if they are far from representing the essence of the Islamist movement, the Cairo militants of the Gama'a Islamiyya – who have been brutally transferred from the rural areas of upper Egypt, where interaction between the sexes outside of the family is strictly forbidden – extol practices that appear to be openly segregationist in the context of the modern urban environment. Moreover, since the escalation of the clashes in Algeria, there has been a radicalisation of the methods used to defend and promote the symbols of allegiance to the two camps involved in the fighting. In the context of the maelstrom of repression and terrorism, the 'war of the veil' has sometimes echoed the language and actions of a real war – even taking account of the provo-cation and the manipulation by the authorities. Refusing to wear the veil is not only an expression of an ideological disagreement, it could also be a gesture that indicates allegiance to the 'other side', namely the repressive state and therefore the enemy.

Logically, this section of female society sees the ethical and symbolic demands of the Islamist forces as a double blow to their identity and their freedom. Even if their understanding of some of the symbolic demands of re-Islamisation encompasses more than just the refusal to wear the veil, it is no surprise that these women are politically opposed to the Islamist movements.[16]

The 'anti-Islamist' stance of the feminists is even less surprising when you consider that it often confirms a political and social reservation: 'modern' women are better represented in the political and economic elites than in the middle or lower classes. 'Anti-Islamist' women, usually come from socio-politically privileged backgrounds, which means that all are threatened by the Islamist ethic that they reject, and at least some are threatened by the political alternation that it will entail, which would put their status as the social and political elites in doubt. However, the author has yet to see a single study that has identified a strictly women protest vote against the Islamist surge.

Although numerically they are in the minority, Western observers are nevertheless most familiar with the anti-Islamist feminists. They represent their principal and sometimes their only source in the analysis of the relations between the Islamist movement and women's causes, and, on a broader level, of the dynamic of re-Islamisation itself. As Fernand Braudel and others have brilliantly demonstrated, the machismo of Mediterranean culture does not need religious caution for it to be inter-woven in social practices. The group of 'women who are fighting fundamentalism' is nevertheless the only group that appears to have any legitimacy. It has monopolised the entire Western perception of reality for Arab women, the extremely simplified presentation that it brings, and the complex dynamics that affect it.

The group of female anti-Islamist activists provokes such passion in both 'camps' because it employs a terminology similar to that used in the West. The blind and unconditional support of Western observers can be compared with the heightened resentment of the Islamist activists who are well aware of the vital role that this group plays in stirring the hostility of the West, which regards them as a guarantee for the all-repressive option. All the regimes that are threatened by the Islamist upsurge have encouraged the emergence and the development of a rash of feminist movements that rarely have any social foundation. In the case of Algeria, Sa'ida Rahal Sidhoum explains lucidly that:

The women's movement, which is echoed in France, has been unable to attract the audience that some people are convinced it has. Its failure is primarily an image problem that the Islamists are helping to discredit: women who work in executive positions, women who have reached the same level as the esteemed administrators of the state, female blue-collar workers who are adjudged to have taken men's jobs (especially if they have a family), single women who lead a life of depravity, and economically privileged women who inspire covetousness. It has also failed because of the stubborn belief that if it is sufficient to say something for it to be so: they are few of them among the women of lower social classes, who some look upon with condescension and even contempt, as they have little in common with them, they know nothing about rural issues or the vulnerable urban classes, and they have little experience of what ordinary life is like … they prefer the French media, when Arabic has become the language read by the less educated, they hold supposedly popular meetings in French while Algerian Arabic and the Berber languages are preferred by women, they have to contemplate the anathema rather than the instructional explanation … they prefer the state system as interlocutor … they are members of parties without obtaining guarantees about their position on the female cause … the list of mistakes made by women fighting for a real place … in society is long.[17]

In Algeria and Tunisia in particular, some of these women have courageously tried to inform the new political regimes of their fight.[18] There are others, whose struggle is no less worthy, who have not demonstrated the same concern and prudence. The war waged by at least some of them has been inexorably linked with the unconditional defence of the repressive hardline policy of the regimes.

The respective size of the different groups – traditionalists, modernists, Islamists and anti-Islamists – which varies slightly from country to country, has yet to be determined. The number of women for whom wearing the veil is a simple matter of continuing traditional practices is undoubtedly greater in Egypt, even more so in North Yemen, than it is in Aden, Tunisia, South Yemen or Algeria. Yet globally the size of the first two groups is far greater than the other. Today the majority of women in the Arab world seem to have chosen, by their own will more often than by force, to adhere to the demands of Islamism.

What do we know about their future as women? What do we know of their ability to preserve their autonomy at the heart of the family unit, or of their capacity to gain and maintain access to the public arena, professional life and into politics? Have they really opted for, or are they condemned to, 'enslavement', as our more outspoken observers have predicted?

Islamism and tradition

In all societies, with the exception of 'matriarchal' models, and most probably particularly in those surrounding the Mediterranean, women can in many ways be considered as the 'weak link' in the social and family chain, without underestimating the importance of their role: it is not so much that they are affected most directly by social tensions but rather that they, more systematically than men, are often on the receiving end of such tensions. It has long been demonstrated that in Mediterranean culture the honour of social or family group lies in the hands of its women. Women in Arab societies were particularly affected by the breathtaking speed at which the system of references was transformed by the cultural invasion of the West: whenever the Western model of socialisation came into conflict with the traditional model, it was women who were the most natural target of the violence that resulted from the conflict of allegiance, as they have less autonomy vis-à-vis the dominant system. In the current climate of critically re-appraising a form of modernisation that is perceived as being too Western, the 'weak link' of the Arab society, once again, pays the price more than any other. Thus, the literalist and authoritarian reintroduction of the normative system of 'pre-colonial' culture, in this domain more than others, often disavows certain forms of modernisation, whose only crime is to have taken place during the period of Western 'imperialism' and under the cover of its language.[19] It is also undeniable that women have sometimes become the target of certain types of violence. But there is no evidence that re-Islamisation alone is responsible. The machismo of Mediterranean culture has never really felt the need for the ideological blanket that the literalist interpretation of certain Islamic forces would like to apply. The physical elimination of women who are alleged to have violated a norm, with the consent of the family or social group, has long been a part of North African life. For a long time, the press ignored such practices. At the very most this sort of violence rose from obscurity in the current of 1989, every time that media manipulation could pin the blame on the FIS.[20]

It is not the FIS which is responsible for the parliament voting for the Algerian civil code in 1984, but those who today zealously fight the FIS because of its 'anti-feminism'. The great liberator of Tunisian women, that is the heir of Habib Bourguiba, divorced a wife he considered inadequately 'media-friendly' just as quickly as the 'fundamentalist' Omar Abd al-Rahman took a second wife during his exile in the US. Obviously, there would be a very long list if we were to count all the contradictions that separate the rhetoric of the 'pro-feminist' champions of the fight against the Islamists from their individual practices on the matter.

On the other hand, there is absolutely no proof that the women who have internalised the ethical standards promoted by the Islamist upsurge are spared the sexist violent attacks.[21] This shows that the most emblematic discriminatory practices that have been attributed to re-Islamisation are, in all probability, more a product of the particular socio-historical conjuncture of the appropriations of Muslim culture and religion, than of the essence of that culture. Tradition and religion must therefore be kept separate in analysis, as far as possible. If the Islamic doctrine of the social status of women is evaluated with reference to the practices that were in force before the period of Quranic revelation, then there will be subtle variations in how this is interpreted. 'Compared to North African tradition, Islam is progress', one female Algerian psychiatrist conceded.[22]

In this area, as in many others, the impact of the re-Islamisation dynamic has been characterised by its ambivalence. On one side, the Islamist upsurge has exacerbated the discrepancies between two models of socialisation, and has created or aggravated tensions for which a section of the female population will pay the heaviest price. But it has also fuelled the rise in stature of social groups that have closer links with traditional society and its conservative ethical references, particularly on family matters. Yet, on the other side, it has a tendency to alleviate the divisions between the systems of reference and the tensions that they cause: by reconnecting it with the symbolism of the intuitive culture, the process of modernisation, which has long been limited to the educated urban elites, can extend to much wider components of the society. We will return to this point in the next chapter.

Under the veil, the struggle continues

There is nothing within this new (Islamic) symbolism to prevent the reformist dynamic – which would improve or guarantee the access of women to public life – from following or retaking its path. In this domain as in others, the existing apparent legal restrictions do not possess the permanent character which is often attributed to them. There are many indications that the exegetic construction, produced from within Islamic references and permitting the restriction and even the prohibition of polygamy – to refer to one significant example alone – has been formalised long ago.[23]

Fariba Adelkhah writes that

[The] dual role [of the *hijab*] has led Islamist women to claim...some elements of a modernity that has taken place over the last few decades: the unconditional right to a modern education and to work, recognition outside of the family unit, and the implication that women should be involved in all debates held in Iranian society.[24]

Fatiha Hakiki Talahite also notes:

On an individual level...wearing the *hijab* is not necessarily the sign of regression that it might appear to be at first glance [...] You could say that the *hijab* is a woman's affirmation that they submit to God before they submit to man. Here, submission to man means submission to a social order in which man has the dominant role...Of course, she is not going as far as to question her submission to man since religion has preordained it. But to claim her direct submission to God, with reference to man, can be interpreted as an affirmation of the self, the start of the emergence of women as individuals, in a society where even the male individual is still in its infancy.[25]

Fariba Adelkhah concludes:

The greatest contribution of Islamic women in Iran was certainly not their numerical weight. It was the critical dimension that they brought to the support of the revolution and, in the post-revolutionary period, their crucial involvement from inside the Islamist movement in the restoration of reformism and the fact that today every text is discussed, debated and, if necessary, amended under the pressure of their intervention, by a feminist movement whose activism could not be matched by a pre-revolutionary movement.[26]

Indeed, the symbolism of Islamist 'feminism' seems increasingly to alternate between two sets of references. Patrick Haenni says that 'The women's movement alternates between two principal levels: on one side, there is the reversion to Islamic symbolism from a reformist perspective, and on the other, there are international conventions'.[27] It is becoming increasingly clear that the bridges that unite the two movements are congested with renegades: 'It was very difficult to persuade the women I know to take part in the big feminist demonstration in March 1990', explains Salima Ghezali, who was then the chief editor of the bilingual Algerian weekly publication, *Nissa*.

> Women were afraid of what their neighbours or their husbands would say and they did not think it was worth taking the risk...[Oh well], I had the courage of my convictions, but all the women who turned up to my demonstration swapped their feminist banners for *jilbabs* [a long flowing garment] and became the most active supporters of the FIS.[28]

In order for the process of reform to begin again, the unwise and clumsy interventionism of the West must again desist from constantly claiming some sort of cultural monopoly over the emancipation of women, as it has done for a long time. The 'citadel of Islam', as Bishri calls it, should not feel besieged again:

> You cannot advance if you are on the defensive. You cannot go forward when you are defending your positions. Still, the essence of the debate between the advocates of the veil and its detractors is not a question of the length of clothing or of whether or not hair should be covered. It concerns, or should concern, the necessity for women to have access to education and employment. The Western mentality, however, wants to place this argument in terms of progress and retardation. The *hijab* is thus considered as the expression of the ill treatment reserved for women, but also as the result of under-development. It is both the origin and the expression of a woman's inferiority, while the fact that you don't wear it becomes a sign of progress, equality and the recognition of freedom. As we are talking about freedom, the Western reader will want to believe me when I tell him that no one has ever forced the women of this generation [of the 1970s and 1980s] to wear the veil and that all the women who wear it have deliberately chosen to do so.
>
> This insistence on approaching the problem in terms of the veil and not in terms of education and employment coincides with a wish to tackle the

question within the confines of the system of reference, instead of seeing that it is a simple social question that deserves discussion. For some, this insistence is indicative of a desire to depose one set of references to impose another. For others, it is a rallying call to protect this set of references from destruction by the other. It is not a fundamental disagreement that divides Islamic thought from Western thought: both recognise the 'particular' nature of women and the fact that this specificity justifies the prevention of women from doing certain jobs. The disagreement is simply a question of numbers: which jobs are on that list?... But instead of being posed in terms of a debate, that is open to discussion - the reference being that if women are granted access to education and teaching, both women and society will benefit - the Muslims are asked this question in terms which offend their essential beliefs. On the other hand, for the secular West, it is posed in terms of behaviour patterns, life references and value judgements.[29]

When it comes to the question of women, as on so many other matters, the process of reform that was on the agenda before the Western invasion was interrupted by it and has hardly moved on since then. This is why, when a system is under threat of invasion by outside forces, an introspective, critical and reformist approach often turns into a reflex of absolute conservatism.

The problem of women, like any other problem produced either by our own weakness or the will of the other, results from nothing but the acculturation and the waves of trauma that have been inflicted upon us by the one-sided encounter with the dominant civilisation two hundred years ago.[30]

The answer to how to successfully meld Islamism and modernisation is to be found in the internal dynamics of the Islamist movement much more than in the dialogue of the deaf between 'feminists' and 'fundamentalists' on both sides of the Mediterranean. From this point forth, they reveal, as we shall see, a future much more promising than dominant analysis might suggest.

CHAPTER TWELVE

From Imported to Imposed Modernity

The historian Benjamin Stora has written that:

> In a country such as Algeria or Egypt or Tunisia, the battle is being fought between, on one side, the 'modernists' who want to be separate from the state, to install new models of development, to reform agriculture in order to create 'industrialising industries' and to restructure civil society and its links with the state from top to bottom, thereby bringing an end to populism and, on the other side, the Islamists who propose a return to the community-based model of the past.[1]

Is it really all so simple? Is Islamism no more than a manifestation of resistance to the process of modernisation, of 'those left behind by development', or is it a stumbling block to modernisation and 'a return to the past'?

What is the relationship between Islamism and the so-called values of 'modernity', which are perceived (even though they are in fact the culmination of a long process of accumulation in which all civilisations, including Islam, have played their part) as originating in the West, the very alter ego from which it wants to 'distance itself'? Even if it is only at a symbolic level, the restoration of references that have been absent from the societies they intended to regulate clearly provokes a rupture over what technical progress, as well as intellectual and political progress, have brought to these societies. Does this apparent rejection therefore allow us to conclude that the 'essence' of these modern values, or more precisely, the vested interests that they serve, are systematically and continuously threatened? Are concepts such as democracy, secularism, human rights, the access of women to public and economic arenas and the political integration of the individual and the masses characteristics of modernity doomed to disappear from the landscape of societies that are 're-Islamicised'?

The new pastures of modernisation

For the moment, the powerful reactionary wing of the Islamist rhetoric is 'fanning the flames' of passionate misunderstanding. The double resonance of the notion of secularism on Western or Islamist soil constitutes, as we have seen, a primary and eloquent example. When they denounce secularism, are the Islamists really claiming that they will suppress all independent human thought, that they will outlaw any possibility of dealing with the questions of devolution and the handing over of power using a profane legal system, or that they will clamp down on individual liberties? Will they leave the Christian community (which has, it is often forgotten, survived for more than 12 centuries under the sway of Islamic law) to fend for itself? Here, a rather different hypothesis will be introduced into a debate that can be particularly passionate. Even if it is the very condition of its effectiveness, the rejection of some of the values of modernity which characterises Islamist discourse is not necessarily a true reflection of its genuine logic of action on the subject. Of course, the components of modernity that originate from its European stronghold, in particular the historical references which legitimise it in the collective consciousness, have been strongly rejected in societies to the south of the Mediterranean: the south will not use the same historical and symbolic terminology to describe modernity as the north. But, does this mean that this is the last we shall see in the south of the values of 'Western' modernity? That remains to be seen.

In the former territories of Western colonisation, it is more probable that to distance oneself from the West, which is still too close, equates less to rejecting it point-blank than returning to it its attributes of alterity, to differentiate oneself from it, rather than deny it; to allow all or a part of the West's heritage to be reappropriated rather than cutting oneself off from it. The values of 'modernity' are not so much rejected as 'rewritten' using the categories and terminology of Muslim culture. The Islamist surge is involved in more than 'the resistance of the traditional society to modernisation': it is participating in a complex process of reconciliation which actually extends the boundaries of modernisation rather than causing it to stall or preventing its progress.

If the 'passing of the baton' between West and East, the 'transmission' of what, in Western modern values, can claim to be truly universal without being tied solely to the cultural destiny of the West, seems so far to have failed, it is perhaps because modernisation within the context of colonial aggression has been defined from outside the Muslim symbolic system, or in preference without it. Since imposed secularisation has never taken the time to conduct a necessary 're-writing' of modernity according to the local culture, this is probably what, in this hypothesis, the Islamists are today striving to do behind the veil of their discourse of rejection.

For the majority of analysts, the dogmatic withdrawal of Muslim societies from some of the products of modernity arises because of – or has been shown to be caused by – the 'closing of the gates of the *ijtihad*' in the tenth century. Jacques Berque reminds us that

> '*Ijtihad* is the 'supreme accolade' of Muslim societies, giving the possibility for its scholars to break new ground in doctrine. Something that until recently was considered as illegal, and which practically drove these societies to the brink of stagnation. An untenable situation during a period of regeneration of social conditions and a rapidly changing world... While the world has moved on, the law has been left behind. Finally, these societies have often found that they are left with a medieval *fiqh* when dealing with situations that have emerged from the Industrial Revolution. As you know, these situations are changing with increasing rapidity. It is logically untenable in as much as, in line with Muslim thinking, the Quran is considered valid at all times and in all places: is it not contradictory to mention the constancy of the transformation of time and the diversity of places? But our religious authorities have no intention of such a contradiction. What they call the *shari'a* is simply the reification of Muslim law from the tenth century.[2]

The dynamic of modernisation nevertheless re-emerged in the 18th century, says Bishri.[3] If Islam did indeed cease to be modernised, it is perhaps because the societies that had been traumatised by the Western invasion no longer believed that the changes entailed by this modern-isation displayed any endogenous characteristics, but rather that they had been triggered by a foreign influence. 'At the turn of the century, when our experience of the West was already fraught with conflict, the Nahda movement was engaged in a contest with colonialism, and it was colonialism that won', Daoud quite rightly declares. The net result of this interruption was that reform, namely 'political democratisation, scientific and technological advancement and the role of women', was suspended for many years. 'Only scientific and technological advance, because of its importance in education... managed to transcend the complications and to affect the elite during the period of colonisation, while the masses were to benefit later on.' The questions of the status of women and political democratisation were tainted by the

> danger of a foreign model of modernisation, especially since the West used reform to justify their policy of colonisation... each time colonialism claimed that women played a pivotal role in the process of modernisation, and North

African societies must realise this if they are to move forward, North African women took a step backwards.[4]

It is not a case here of any sort of structural incompatibility with the invariable core of the Muslim doctrine; it is the circumstances under which modernisation spread through the Arab world that have prevented it from taking root there. It is the fact that reform has been promoted by a foreign culture, that it is not a product of the local Islamic fabric, but instead has been pre-fabricated outside of its target destination and made out of foreign materials. For Tareq al-Bishri:

A thought can only renew itself effectively from within, with the help of its own material or with intellectual material extracted from its fundamental components...If we look at the history of Muslim thought from the point of view of its capacity for reform, and if we compare the situation between 1750-1850 and 1850-1920, we will notice that during the first period there was a significant decline in the sectarianism and dogmatism that had at one time prevailed and that there was a return - which was highly innovative - to the primary sources of Islamic thought, namely the Quran and the *Sunna*. The first of the two epochs of reform employed materials, principles, references and methods based solely on Islamic thought which had come from within the 'Islamic framework'. There was no other philosophy pertaining to social dynamics that could interfere. On the other hand the second era, since about 1850, was marked by the development of the Western cultural and military threat and it was to degenerate over the coming decades. It was in this context that the conservatism of Islamic thought began to emerge and become more resolute, as a result of the influence of its defensive and defiant attitude and out of fear of being uprooted, as well as out of its determination to protect its beliefs, its framework of references and the sources of its civilisation. Any display of dogmatism was simply a result of the obsessive fear that it would be usurped. It was a self-defence mechanism. So, how can you go forward when all your energy is taken up with defending the *status quo* and holding your position? There have been many Muslim thinkers [who were] reformers up until the point when they felt that the foundations of their thought were under threat. That is when they defected to the conservative camp. Islamic thought has been on the defensive and it has ignored what it could have exploited to its benefit.

The return to prominence of the references of the intuitive culture, even if it also means some rejection of an imported modernity, does not necessarily mean that the individual cannot be involved in the dynamic of modernisation. On the contrary, depending on the nature of the social forces that have adopted it, which vary from country to country, it has enabled individuals to get involved and has speeded up the process. At a time when the division imposed by secularism between the intuitive culture and the 'modern' public arena limited the accessibility of the latter, the resurrection of 'popular' terminology in fact assisted in restoring and expanding the legitimacy of the vectors of modernisation.

Up until then, it was clear that there were many limitations to the acceptance of modernity, in urban as well as rural areas. If the chaos of the huge network of backstreets in Cairo contrasts with the tidiness of the grand avenues of the city, it is because the 'secular' modernist state has only been capable of imposing itself in the 'avenues' of power. Yet, in the huge network of backstreets, which make up the threads of the political fabric, it has never sought to offer anything other than repressive intervention. In its ambition to completely control the public arena, the state has often shown itself to be more adept at forbidding certain types of movements that it thought were opposed to it than at replacing them with an effective alternative, more used to destroying the internal political fabric than truly investing in the void left by its intervention, quicker to ban associative networks from the localities, that are too readily deemed subversive, than to install in them an administrative apparatus of equal stature.[5]

But wherever the Islamist associative network springs up today, socio-educational policies, which are undoubtedly pro-modernity, are winning over areas where modernisation 'from above' has never succeeded in taking hold before. The reintroduction of certain codes of the intuitive culture thus contributes to diffusing the 'modernising' conduct that the state failed to inspire and which it had even discredited. Of course, this approach is fraught with paradoxes.

When in 1979 Islamist militants at the University of Cairo ended the sexual integration of the coach excursions that were put on for the students, their initiative had a double impact. As the outsider saw it, this was an attack on the rights of a female student population which had adopted the practice of socialising with men outside marriage. But although it was disturbing for a few people, the restoration of the codes of the dominant ethic also, paradoxically, allowed women students for whom the integration of the sexes was a far-from-everyday occurrence, the chance to escape the circle of family acquaintances. Conversely, there were occasions when voluntary modernisation brought up new obstacles to women gaining access to the public sphere. Fariba Adelkhah recalls that

The ban on the veil in Iran, in 1936 persuaded many of them not to leave the house and it has often been suggested that the settling of the nomads or urbanisation led to the 'dangerous half' of the population being even more strictly controlled and to the loss of any effective social skills.[6]

By contrast, this reconciliation means that all those women who think that what happens 'behind the veil' happens, in many ways, 'thanks to it', will have access to the benefits of an undeniable 'modernisation'. To avoid confusion, the restoration of an 'ancient' norm is not necessarily synonymous with a return to traditional methods. Thus, if a growing number of young Egyptian couples adopt the particularly austere formula of marriages organised by Islamic groups, it is not simply a 'return to the past'. On the contrary, the formula allows them to separate themselves from tradition and its constraints. For thousands of young people, it relieves the enormous financial burden that today is placed upon their matrimonial ambitions in order to respect the particularly costly forms of a 'traditional' marriage.

The modernising component of the Islamist movement can also be demonstrated in the field of politics: the paradox is that the activists of the FIS, when confronted by their exclusion from the elections by the military, did more in a few months to promote the legitimacy of the institution in the collective imagination than all the Algerian 'democrats' of the past 30 years put together. '[They] explained the superiority of the state of law in the straightforward manner which is their trademark', Pierre Guillard notes. 'At last, the Algerian masses could hear the democratic idea.'[7]

Access to universality

When it comes to economic practices, finally, the simple addition of the word 'Islamic' to the word 'bank' has been enough over the past few years to enable the peasants of upper Egypt or elsewhere to rise out of the subsistence economy and join the financial circuit on a national level. A strictly ideological decision, namely to restore a norm that evolves in symbiosis with the wishes of the social majority, rather than being 'divine' or 'from the past', is able to push in this case an economic actor outside the circle of his primordial associations, and thereby to extend the scope of this modernisation. The Egyptian regime was thus not mistaken when it quickly recognised the danger presented by an economic movement that worked to the detriment of the circuits that it controlled, and opted, whilst benefiting from the crass errors of some of their leaders, to abort the experiment of the 'Islamic investment fund co-operatives'.[8]

In terms of a political movement this time, it is more often than not the case that entry into Islamism can also be clearly seen as a sign of a split from traditional allegiances: for example, by joining the Islamist movement (where they are far more numerous than it is often supposed[9]) the Algerian Berbers are leaving the political ghetto in which they are imprisoned by any display of their ethnic background. In Sudan, where the network of brotherhoods of the first political movements was very similar to the tribal network, conversion to Islamism is widely seen as a radical departure from traditional allegiances, and is therefore equated with modernisation.

The socio-professional profile of the Islamist elites, even if it does become harder to define, such is their presence in all layers of society, also reinforces the hypothesis of 'Islamist modernisation'. As we have seen, the engineering union was one of the first to be conquered by the Muslim Brotherhood in Egypt. The fresh recruits are not, as has long been thought, old religious professionals in turbans, but are much more likely to be university-educated and in particular to have a scientific background: the executives are engineers, doctors, lawyers or teachers, and they are swelling the ranks of an increasingly diversified section of Islamist intellectuals.[10]

At a time when many people were still reinforcing the old maxim of 'Islam against the state', Olivier Carré was among a handful who quickly understood the probable evolution that would result from these dynamics 'Once it is sure of its footing, Islamic radicalism will fully integrate - perhaps without saying so in as many words - the modern approach to politics... The modern secular state is in the process of becoming a naturalised "Islamic state".'[11] The possibility that an endogenous process of modernisation could unfold, which is much more productive than that initiated by the first generation of the nationalist elites, is certainly not inevitable. But it is just as likely to happen as that curbing of civil liberties which we are systematically told is the only possible outcome of the encounter between Islam and modernity. Of course, the debate is far from over. But is the essence not precisely that, contrary to the peremptory assurances of the dominant view, we are again debating this issue? Furthermore, the perspective of the 'impasse of modernisation' and other 'regressions' that so often hamper analysis leads subtly onto another hypothesis: the Islamist protest is less a manifestation of a 'return to the past', that Muslim societies claim, than of the tensions that are a natural by-product of the period of conflict, pain and contradiction that is today affecting these societies as they build their modernity.

The challenge that the north faces at the end of this century is therefore to allow the reappraisal of the virtual ideological monopoly that it has held during the course of the past two centuries, as well as to measure the exact meaning of this reappraisal. The north is not being asked to deny or even to minimise its contribution to history in general, or to political thought in particular, but rather to historicise it and to renounce its arrogant claim to hegemony over what is and what is not legitimate. It is being asked to admit that the history of ideas does not amount to the itinerary of 'sub-cultures' from its colonial periphery that have fed on its science and its rationality[12] and by so doing to shatter the illusion that 'a civilised being is a Western being'.[13] It is being asked to recognise the right of a southern culture to formulate its values based upon its own historical heritage, and to express these values by drawing on a wide range of references that are specific to it. It is being asked to understand that it should never have monopolised access to universality, and should never again do so.

However, this major and necessary cultural evolution does not rule out a precise evaluation of the political perspectives held by the Islamist parties and movements of today. From this point of view, the contentious thesis of Olivier Roy deserves a closer look.

The failure of political Islam?

In 1992, the valuable insights gained in Iran, Afghanistan and Central Asia by Olivier Roy, who has been at the forefront of the thought on Islamist movements, were put into perspective and they were beautifully summed up in the title of his work, The Failure of Political Islam, whose argument is regularly fielded in the current debate over the Islamist future.[14]

It is perhaps surprising that Roy should adopt such a position, as he was undoubtedly one of the first to see that, behind the noise of the Islamist protests and the shortcomings of Western interpretations, there was the more complex, less predetermined, more evolutionary and in any case less fragile architecture of 'cultural re-appropriation'. Roy has certainly never denied the reformist potential of the Islamist thought he so brilliantly highlighted in his first works. Yet, as he tells us, more than 10 years have passed since the foundations of the Iranian revolution were laid, and the sterility of this first decade justifies the present conclusion that Islamist thought has not been able to deliver its promises. In a roundabout way he tells us to drop the subject. 'The Islamic revolution is behind us now'; political Islam has failed.

Of course, he concedes, Islamist thought holds itself to be 'in conflict with the questions of the imported state and segmentation', of course it represents 'the next stage on from the "timeless" thought of the 'ulama', and it has noted 'quite correctly that secularism and nationalism do not guarantee modernisation'. And even its 'rejection of history' (which has yet to be established) and its reference to the archetypal society should ensure that it is seen as archaic, since 'another fundamentalist thought, Protestant reform, has proved to be one of the best ways of attaining economic and political modernity'. But this attractive programme has not been fulfilled. Islamist thought has failed because, 'at the end of an intellectual journey which forces the issue of modernity, it finally reunites the "Islamic political imagination" of tradition and its fundamental blind-spot: politics can only be founded on individual virtue'.[15] The proposed model 'presupposes the virtue of individuals', but 'this virtue can only be acquired if it is a truly Islamic society'. Now the star has fallen. The Islamists had 10 years to become what they said they would become and they have not done so, Roy explains at length. 'The modernity that [the new Muslim intellectuals] brought to the interpretation of Islam was worn down by the repetitive, uncritical and undemonstrative praise of Islam, which would solve all the problems of the modern world'. That would be enough to establish a catalogue of failures.

Should we really speak of this 'intellectual journey which forces the issue of modernity' in the past tense, as though it were a completed process? Should we – and this is the crux of the matter – tar all Islamists with the literalist brush and thereby deny the existence of everything that does not fit in with this pattern? It is impossible not to notice how circulations are developing, more rapidly than it is said. This is apparent from the fact of the formidable diaspora that repression feeds a little everywhere, between the 'Western' side and the 'Arab' side (and not necessarily the two extremes) of Muslim thought. The hardcore of the Islamist rhetoric has largely demonstrated its ability to mobilise a wider range of opinion than can be identified with this hardcore, including during elections. Thus, in the recipe of the so-called 'God-fearing maniacs' there are other ingredients than those that their adversaries are prepared to see. The keys to the future interpretation of Islamism today lie, not just in the incantations of the 'fundamentalist' core, but also in the imperceptible shifts which lead so many (lay) political actors to reconcile themselves with the universe of this 'religious' thought that was once disqualified.

Roy goes on to say that 'With the exception of the Iranian revolution, Islamism has not had a profound impact on the political scene in the Middle East'. The regimes that were in power in 1980 remain there in 1991.

> They have maintained their stability in the face of the Islamist opposition; their leaders have had long political careers: from Morocco to Pakistan (but excluding Lebanon, Sudan and Afghanistan), the only reason why we lost political leaders in the 1980s was through illness or death. All the others retained their positions throughout the decade.

Moreover, the terrorist attacks that have been attributed to the Islamists over the past 10 years 'have not caused as much outcry as those of Western terrorists, such as the IRA, ETA, the Baader Meinhof gang, etc'. Can this really be the definitive evaluation of 'the capacity for unrest' that is cast upon the newcomers to the political scene, that the 'effectiveness' of the outburst of violence of the 1990s in Algeria has already started to wane?

Roy then suggests that Islamism is not condemned to vanish. It will regenerate itself. One day the Islamists – notably in Algeria – will even come to power. But Islamism has lost its 'original impetus', and it has evolved. In fact, it has become mundane and, worse still, it has become 'social-democratic'.[16] It is impossible not to follow Roy's line of reasoning on this point as on many others. But it is more difficult to follow its conclusion: the Islamists have already lost, they have failed even before they reached their goal. They 'will not invent a new society. The world order will remain after the revolution. For the rich countries (Saudi Arabia), the Islamic model means profit plus the shari'a, for the poor (Pakistan, Sudan and later Algeria), it means unemployment and the shari'a.' Is Roy not a little hasty in his conclusion? Or is it a way of stressing that the Islamist discourse should never have been and should never be taken literally, and that its promises of a brighter future and of growth in three figures should never be taken seriously?

On the other hand, it could be a way of recognising the fact that the literalist and 'fundamentalist' core of the Islamist rhetoric, which is the product of an interpretation of religious references that lacks any sense of history and is accepted without question, has evolved and is now involved in, and has itself accepted, the much broader dynamic of the reconstruction of identity? If so, this should come as no surprise. It has been clear for a long time (particularly to the readers of Olivier Roy) that 'fundamentalism' was never the real force behind the Islamist movement and that it was not only bound to evolve, but was also capable of doing so. There were even signs that it had begun to do so. And even if the imperatives of political combat had endowed them with an undetectable hardiness, the most stereotypical intellectual argument and the most literalist dogmatic attitudes that the West had used to paint the picture of the first Islamist bogeymen are shaped more by the history of this phenomenon than its present-day reality or its foreseeable future. Instead of a failure by the Islamists, perhaps we will one day have to accept that it is the outsider's dominant view which has failed, because it has chosen to ignore, if not to fight against, the possibility that Islamism could evolve.

The growth of the 'nationalist left wing'

Since it contradicts the dominant perception of the phenomenon, the 'reformist' or 'modernist' dynamic of Islamism has long been underestimated, indeed it has been overshadowed, in the same way as doctrinal dynamics and internal tactics have generally been ignored; yet these are the crucial elements of analysis. Still Islamist credos do evolve, at rhythms which vary from nation to nation. Their common trait in this respect is the attenuation, of the reactionary dimension of the Islamist rhetoric, and consequently the bridging of the gap between classical Muslim thought and Western-style political modernity, whereas it has long been thought that it was impossible to resolve the differences of the two. In Algeria, the FIS has certainly not put political radicalisation at the top of its list of priorities, but the terms agreed by Benhadj when he signed the Rome Agreement in January 1995 reflected steps taken long ago by the Muslim Brotherhood. If one was to look behind the smoke-screen of the politicking discourses and the demands of the partisan movement, one could have seen the changes taking place.

To a certain extent, the doubt over the Islamist future is also determined by the secular intelligentsia. Its attitude has swung from the aforementioned radicalisation, which has acted as ammunition for the 'eradicatory' faction of the Algeria intelligentsia,[17] and another, less-defined tendency which has emerged in less dramatic circumstances. In Cairo, Rabat and Gaza, 'nationalist left wingers' and Islamists have been looking, to settle their differences in ways other than open war.[18] The number of conferences and meetings organised in an attempt to bring the 'nationalist' and 'Islamist' perspectives together has increased since the end of the 1980s. Both camps have expressed self-criticism.[19] Throughout the Arab world, a small section of the secular intelligentsia has begun to adapt its semantic and tactical position to fall more in line with the Islamist movement.[20] Their reluctance over the direct interference of religion in politics has certainly remained intact. But when faced with the loss of credibility that Marxism has suffered, from the Soviet Union to Beijing to Cuba, the Arab left-wing parties have been forced to find new ideological references. The collapse of the political satellites of the Soviet Union, the ideological suicide of the leading light of communism itself and the increasing demands for religious identity from inside the communist camp have all combined to cause its downfall.[21]

Apart from when they no longer want to be seen as the opposition, it is difficult for the heroes of the first social and political struggles in the Arab world not to distance themselves in their dealings with the Islamists from the narrow-minded discourse and the repressive methods of the regimes in power. It is also hard for them to ignore some of the changes that the doctrine and practices of some of these groups have undergone, especially in relation to their calls for democracy. This is why some Nasserist Egyptians insist on qualifying their group as both Nasserist 'and Islamic'. Their activists have looked on gleefully as their old nationalist rhetoric has been bolstered by certain culturalist dimensions they had long neglected. And some opinion leaders have chosen to build bridges: 'Even if I disagree with the Islamists, it is important to remember... that they are the leading political party in this country and that they have responded to the great historical problems faced by Egypt: national independence, social justice and development', declares the economist Hussam Isa, one of the leaders of the Egyptian Nasserist movement.[22] From 1989, there has been a process of relative 'Islamisation' of the legal opposition parties, not to mention the internal dynamics of the ruling parties. In 1987, the Egyptian Neo-Wafd Party decided to form an alliance with the Muslim Brotherhood, which afforded them their first electoral break-through. In 1989, when Hassan al-Banna's successors bypassed the electoral ban by merging with the Socialist Workers Party, the Wafd tried to entice Sheikh Omar Abd al-Rahman, the ideologue of the Tanzim al-Jihad organisation, into an alliance so that it might preserve its Islamist flavour.

Just as the Islamists have been able to make full use of the previously underestimated discourse of social justice so that the left does not gain the monopoly, the left can no longer allow its principal adversaries to monopolise tradition. Even if they speak a different language, it is on the nationalist dimension of the recourse to local culture (as well as on the 'ashes' of the socialist dream) that Islamist and nationalist discourses are destined to recognise one another. The fact that the Arab nationalist discourse is changing its attitude toward the symbols of Muslim culture brings the Islamists in turn to modify their traditional rejection of the discourse of nationalism. This tends to narrow the distance between the two main political ideologies of the contemporary Arab world, and it marks out the political forces that will build the internal political stability of southern Mediterranean states. It is, of course, very difficult to predict the outcome of this process. But it is in the hugely variable socio-political situation of each country that we will find the results.

For the rest, that is for the most part, it is difficult to disagree with Olivier Roy. The Islamists will never be able to add two and two together and make five. But if their aptitude for social mobilisation can reduce the administrative paralysis and other political obstacles that prevent the regimes in power from doing their sums correctly, if the puritanism of their activists makes them capable, if only for a short while, of preventing the leaks which affect the channels of state action, then at least it is a step in the right direction. And then perhaps we will have to take a new look at this 'failure' of political Islam.

CONCLUSION

Islamism Today

The current translation of *Face to Face with Political Islam* allows the author to re-examine conclusions last published in French in 1996. Three types of development in particular need to be re-evaluated.

First of all, there are the political facts. Regimes have generally enjoyed considerable stability in the Arab world, a stability which is primarily the result of their persistent authoritarianism. If some space for liberalisation has been opened up, it is neither in ballot boxes or political institutions that it should be sought.

Secondly, there are developments within the Islamist movements themselves, whether they be in power, as they are in Iran and Sudan, or, as is more often the case, in opposition. These developments may be tactical or doctrinal. If the old divide is still in place between jihadist groups (which favour direct action and are thus closed to legalism) and the successor of Hassan al-Banna, the Muslim Brotherhood, then the numerical superiority of the legalists has become obvious, at the same time as their increasingly flexible attitude to the demands of parliamentary democracy has been made explicit.

Finally, there have been changes in the perception of Western media and academia. Western research institutes remain entranced by the Islamist currents, and the idea of their being a purely pathological phenomenon has remained pervasive. Nevertheless, a number of dedicated academics have continued to attenuate this 'politically correct' vision, also found in the rhetoric of secular regimes themselves. Whereas those who maintain that Islamism is solely a cancerous body persist in transferring violence or doctrinal literalism from the radical periphery to the epicentre of the movement, those whose theses take into account the identity dimension of Islamism over its narrowly religious component emphasise its changing, dynamic character, the importance of its legalist component and the vital question of the role frequently played by the regimes in the escalation of violence.

From the triumph of the authoritarianism of secular regimes to the example of the 'fundamentalist' regime in Iran

For six years, elections have proven a firmly established tenet: only with rare exceptions does the road to power pass through the ballot box. A large majority of Arab leaders continue to take advantage of the benefits pluralism accords them in the arena of international opinion, without taking on any of its drawbacks. Whatever name might be given to this façade of denying the right to political representation, it is increasingly difficult to smooth over profound political crises.[1]

Some regimes still refuse to allow the existence of groups legally independent of the single or dominant party (for example the Iraqi Ba'th, the National Progressive Front in Syria), from the throne (for example the Saudi monarchy) or from the People's Committees which are the repository of 'direct democracy' in the Libyan Jamhiriyya.[2] Qadhafi has felt no more need than the Gulf monarchs for elections to keep himself at the head of the 'State of the masses' for over 22 years; it seems that he, too, has been toying with the idea of familial succession.

Those regimes which have long vaunted their belief in the pluralist system – Egypt, Algeria, Tunisia, Jordan and Morocco – have managed to preserve the *status quo* by manipulating certain loopholes: taking heed of the electoral success of the Algerian FIS in December 1991, occupiers of the Arab 'thrones', whether royal or republican, have all succeeded in putting their power well beyond the reach of their fellow citizens' electoral whim by the means of timely constitutional reforms (which had to be approved by purportedly popular referendums, of course).

In Algeria, where the legal dissolution of the FIS, winner of local and national elections in June 1990 and December 1991, had already been considered a principle worthy of enshrining in the constitution, the constitutional referendum adopted in January 1996 completed the process of closing off the state system to all but the head of state. The head of state would effectively appoint a third of the second chamber created by this amendment to the constitution, and the fact that legislative procedure required a quorum of 75 percent of votes cast meant that the president would thus be protected from any unpleasant surprise that might pop up in parliament. Similarly, a constitutional revision which took place in

Morocco in 1996 created a high chamber and reintroduced representation based on union and profession. As in Algeria, the aim was to reduce the opposition's capacity to mobilise by dividing it. In order to maximise the effect of this constitutional buffer, the principle that the ruling power selects its own legal opposition candidates has been adopted everywhere, with the exceptions of Lebanon and Kuwait.[3] Morocco, Algeria, Tunisia and Egypt have thus continued to avoid any legal competition with their Islamist challengers. More than ever, the weight of the legal opposition (of whatever political persuasion) depends less on its own political beliefs than it does upon those of the regime, for which the temptation is great to turn the democratic threat represented by the Islamists' demands into a simple security threat. The strategy of those holding the reins of power, especially in Algeria, has increasingly been to do everything to ensure the Islamists with bombs are more visible than Islamists with ballot papers. The existence of an extremist fringe in each opposition movement then 'justifies' certain methods (states of emergency, torture or summary executions by 'state-sponsored death squads'[4]), the temptation of which some regimes find impossible to resist in order to guarantee their survival. Apart from a few ideological counter-offensives by 'state Islam',[5] effective or not, regimes have continued to respond with a common array of repressive measures, most often pre-emptive and largely disproportionate to real security requirements. Across the Arab world (with the possible exception of Lebanon), elections have served less to select the rulers than to denote the quality and number of opponents that those rulers agree to tolerate in line with a democratisation which is only cosmetic ('for the Yankees to see'[6]).

Where some Islamist groups have been legalised, for example in Morocco, following the lead of Egypt or Algeria, it has only been to hide the exclusion of the more cumbersome amongst them.[7] While Abdessalam Yassine's organisation al-'Adl wa'l-Ihsan remains forbidden from activity and its leader under house arrest for over seven years, the Moroccan regime has chosen to legalise a rival group less firmly entrenched.[8] Significantly, it is not the ideological profile of candidates which is the deciding factor; it is the Islamic opposition's estimated political power which determines their fortune for good or for ill. Members of the Muslim Brotherhood working for the Algerian Nahnah (whose own political career began in the protests against the secularism of the Algerian National Charter of 1976, with the dynamiting of electricity pylons) were declared 'moderates' and 'legalists' by the regime of General Zéroual after their fragile support base had been (repeatedly) ascertained. Members of the Muslim Brother-hood working for Ghannouchi, himself unanimously considered one of the most progressive thinkers of the Islamist movement, are for their part definitively labelled 'extremists' by the neighbouring regime of General Ben Ali, in just the same way as the Egyptian Mustafa Mashhur.

As far as longevity is concerned, rulers of the republics are not far behind their royal counterparts. The Syrian Hafiz al-Asad holds the record so far: borrowing from his Moroccan and Jordanian homologues the dynastic formula which ensures the survival of his political and familial legacy, he succeeded in having his son Bashar appointed – 'with popular acclaim' – head of the Ba'th Party and the Syrian state, thereby founding the first hereditary republic of modern times.

Five years of change within continuity

Re-elected in 1999 with 99.4 percent of the vote after a constitutional reform adopted precisely to allow for a variety of candidates,[9] the example of the success of the Tunisian president Zine Al Abidine Ben Ali gives a better idea of the quality of Tunisian political life than any commentary. On 21 September 1995, Mu'adda sent an open letter to the President of the Republic in the name of the Mouvement des Démocrates Socialistes, to draw his attention to the serious setbacks to electoral procedure, public freedom and right to information that the country was facing. Imprisoned, then freed under international pressure, he again denounced such practices in April 1996. Civil society appeared to him at that time as if 'each part of it were in the grip of the single party, in every field; this party identifying itself unreservedly - administratively, materially, personally - with the state apparatus'.

> One of the consequences is the impossibility of creating a group in whatever area- cultural, humanitarian, sport - without the approval of the party in power and the direct supervision of local official institutions over each one of its public meetings. The evident result has been the disappearance of all civil society, even if the government boasts of the existence of several thousand such associations [...] The area in which the contradiction between the official rhetoric and the daily practice of the state is most blatant is the defence of civil liberties and human rights.

Five years later, this picture has not been proved wrong. On Thursday 15 June 2000, the European Parliament passed, for the second time, an emergency resolution regarding the human and civil rights situation, proposed by five parliamentary groups.[10] Testimonies from a small number of exiled opposition activists allowed Members of the European

Parliament fully to weigh up the implications of the 'struggle against fundamentalism' which has served as policy for the regime of Ben Ali for over 10 years, with the active support of the West.[11] The situation in Egypt has remained very close to the regional standard: emergency powers introduced after the assassination of Sadat are still in force, the main Islamist opposition movement remains as forbidden as ever and the parliament has never dreamed of challenging the president in his successive re-elections.

The rotation of power which has allowed the socialist opposition to lead the Moroccan government should be viewed with a great deal of circumspection, as not only the base of royal power, but also governmental power, have been kept out of reach of the opposition 'in power': the key Ministries of Foreign Affairs, the Interior and Religion have been held by intimates of the royal court. The royal succession following the death of Hassan II is still too recent to allow anything but peremptory conclusion. It is, however, difficult to see, even after the initial honeymoon period, how the new king could avoid the obvious contradictions so strongly and unreservedly made clear to him by Abdessalam Yassine[12] without a fundamental overhaul of the system.

The situation in Algeria, at the heart of the West's perception of the Islamist phenomenon, calls for particular attention. In the home of the FIS, both the more frequent re-election of the president (four times in 10 years) and the apparently modest gains obtained in 1999 (60 percent) are deceptive: they are more a testimony to Bouteflika's profound understanding of political necessity, an understanding which escapes his Tunisian neighbour. Let us not be mistaken: Bouteflika's 60 percent is indeed the direct equivalent of the Tunisian president's 99 percent. Behind the smoke-screen of talk of amnesty and national reconciliation, the regime has continued to attribute the violence to one party alone. Its refusal to allow institutions to play a role other than purely formal – particularly in passing off a mouthpiece of the military as a national representative in rigged elections – thus remains the underlying cause of the current crisis and the main explanation for its duration. There is nothing really new in the Algerian political climate. Like each one of his predecessors in his time, Bouteflika has been tempted to reform the system which elected him into power. Just like Chadli Ben Jedid, Mohammed Boudiaf or Liamine Zeroual, he has dreamt of cleansing himself of the sin of being co-opted by the military apparatus (in elections which are only nominally popular), of abstracting himself from the system of which he is the product in order to survive it, if needs be. Unsurprisingly, Bouteflika, too, became rapidly aware of the dangers of such an ambition. He understands only too well that it has cost others their position, or even – in the case of Boudiaf – their life. His room to manoeuvre resides solely in the indubitable awareness of the military clan (or alliance of clans) in power of the growing difficulty it will face in maintaining a political system which requires a degree of manipulation impossible to conceal forever and, confronted by an international body of public opinion a little less blind than in the past,[13] in again having recourse to the extreme solutions of deposing or assassinating the mandated president.

This equation has only slight variations. The relative liberalism of Lebanon must have attention drawn to it, as it has allowed all political forces, including Hizbullah, to participate in the parliamentary process and allowed presidential power to be passed on peacefully. At the opposite end of the spectrum, the president of unified Yemen called the 'first presidential elections in the Arabian Peninsula'[14] but chose a member of his own party to represent the opposition in a purely symbolic nod to the value of competition and political pluralism.

If international public opinion has been hesitant in bestowing political legitimacy upon the Islamist opposition it has also begun to investigate, with the same suspicion, the legitimacy of authoritarian regimes which have hardly been touched: in Tunisia, the mounting number of testimonies[15] has undeniably begun to tarnish Ben Ali's reputation; and in Algeria, the veil over all manner of manipulations is being lifted, revealing, to those who care to face it, the extent of the violence orchestrated by the military authorities and their various bureaux.[16]

Conquered liberalisation and imported liberalisation

It would be reductive not to see spaces of liberalisation appearing or emerging in arenas other than the ballot box and political institutions. As well as the rise of civil associations, women's groups (when they manage to escape the mortal constraints of the regime and the invasive sympathy of Western ideologue-supporters) and professional struggles (crushed in Tunisia, reinvigorated in Algeria), it is perhaps the unstoppable rise of a transnational radio and television news network, immeasurably more credible than the monotonous voice of the state, which constitutes the most noticeable expression of this liberalisation. In the closed spaces controlled by the state, under the false colours of 'pluralism' (Algeria, Tunisia) or even without that fiction (Libya), the state has kept an amazingly tight rein on the press. Against this, the birth and considerable impact of the Qatari Al-Jezira channel marked a seminal moment in the liberalisation of political discussion and the end of the state's monopoly. The Internet, even if too often limited to the elite and susceptible to new, particularly insidious forms of control by regimes,[17] also contributes to this dynamic. The opposition, including Islamists, have quickly come to understand this, and the clumsy counter-offensives made by regimes have failed to silence these new voices.

The comparative performance of fundamentalist Iran and secular Tunisia

If it were necessary, by way of conclusion, to bring out the paradoxes of the Western reading of the vices of 'fundamentalism' and the virtues of 'those who stand against it', it would be tempting to contrast the performance of Tunisia's 'secular, modernising' system with that of the 'fundamentalist' Islamic Republic of Iran founded by Imam Khomeini. It is not enough to consider the 1999 elections, which brought about a rebalancing of power relations at the apex of the Iranian system, as tantamount to the 'rejection of the Islamists' that some Western observers saw it as being when they cited it as one more proof of the supposed failure of political Islam. For that, it would be necessary to demonstrate that the election of President Khatami represented a counter-revolution of the Shah-supporting 'secularists' against the 'Islamists' of Khomeini, which was far from the case. The fundamental import of the Iranian elections was in the fact they allowed the first real instance of political change via the ballot box in Middle Eastern history, attesting that the regime born from the Islamist rupture of 1980 was hiding something more complex and more sophisticated than the 'theocratic dictatorship' which has monopolised attention, and that the religious vocabulary of political actors in Iran has never obstructed the complex dynamic of political liberalisation from making progress in society. On the one hand, there is Tunisia, with a system seen until recently by the head of the French state and an overwhelming majority of the Western intelligentsia as an 'exemplary experiment at modernisation',[18] which re-elects its president with over 99 percent of the vote. On the other hand, an 'Islamic Republic', with the reputation of being the embodiment of 'fundamentalist totalitarianism', has allowed its citizens profoundly to alter the balance of power at the highest levels of state by presidential and legislative elections. The Iranian experience seems in many respects to be an awkward interruption to the seamless notion of 'secular' political modernity.

Paths of Islamism: Between attentism, reformism and diaspora

It is impossible to sum up six years of changes in the currents of Islamism under one headline, one tendency or one single evaluation without questioning the importance given in this book to the diversity of recent expressions of the meeting between Islam and politics.

As far as tactics and strategy are concerned, from the Muslim Brotherhood of Egypt to the Hizbullah of Lebanon, the trajectories of the Islamist opposition is very logically affected by the topography of the political situation, which varies from one country to the next. In the course of the last six years, the Islamist tide has found itself in the position of occupying sites very different in nature. Consider the following: whereas hizb al-Nahda had only its leadership exiled in London to rely upon for activity (from which stems the reformist openings of its often-remarkable ideological stance[19]), the Turkish Refah Party has seen its leader, albeit briefly, at the head of a coalition government. Whereas the Algerian FIS, under the impact of repression and disinformation, has seen its agenda divided between the concessions made by those who have to pay the price of their continued presence on their national soil and a critical conscience (itself divided[20]) only allowed to find voice in exile (in Germany, Belgium, Britain or the US), the Hizbullah found itself in the position of being able to relaunch, reinvigorate and ultimately win an armed nationalist struggle against the Israeli occupation of the south of the country, whilst making headway in a confessional political system unparalleled in the Middle East.[21] It is worth remembering that the Hizbullah had the benefit of a degree of tolerance from the Lebanese state which its Hamas counterpart and the majority of Islamist groups in the region (with the exception of the Yemeni 'Islah' and the Muslim Brotherhood in Jordan and Kuwait) have always been refused. Since the second Palestinian Intifada of autumn 2000, Hamas has nevertheless had the satisfaction of seeing the logic of its refusal, motivated by the limits and contradictions of the Oslo Peace Agreements (which ended the creation of Palestinian *Bantoustans*), adopted as a national position by forces across the entire political spectrum, including the PA. Elsewhere, in Yemen, Kuwait and Jordan, others have had the comfort of becoming legal opposition and even, occasionally, receiving some real power.

In spite of this, if it were necessary to delineate a general tendency, it could be said that, faced with exclusion from the legal political scene, there is a realistic and prudent wait-and-see policy (attentism) common to all the major 'centrist' currents. If the route of extremism, encouraged by the state or not, remains adhered to, it is only done so by an extreme minority.

This situation is especially relevant in the case of Algeria, but also in Palestine and in various civil wars or other international conflicts, such as those in Bosnia, Chechnya, Kashmir and Iraq. The tendency is also present amongst the Afghani Taliban,[22] whose exaggeratedly pedantic moralising and flagrant attacks on the most elementary of women's rights embodies the extremist component of the Islamist current. Its opposite reflection within this framework can be found in the movement of the former Turkish Prime Minister Erbakan, head of the 'fundamentalist' Refah Party. Whether or not they have looked at it as an alternative to legalist politics, certain segments of the Islamist current have relied, from Egypt to the Arabian Peninsula, on a rigorous body of neo-Salafi morality. In Yemen, for a centrist movement long associated with power which seems reluctant to re-enter into active opposition, the impossibility (or perhaps just the fear) of attacking the president is sometimes manifested as inglorious offensives against isolated intellectuals[23] in the name of their supposed apostasy, and as such much easier targets than corruption or social inequality. In Egypt, the sad case of the philosopher Nasr Abu Zayd has revealed the darker side of purportedly legalist movements, unless it is a question of one of the sinister manoeuvres of 'state Islamism'.[24] The rhetoric of Islamist opposition to the richest of Gulf petromonarchies has persisted. It shows particularly well the malleability of Islamist discourse and its capacity to adapt its opposition function to highly differentiated ideological environments, including those heavily determined by religious references.[25] In Saudi Arabia, the sense of identity shaped by use of religious vocabulary does not stand in the way of the elites in power frequenting the company of Western political actors, whose presence, a fortiori a military one, is perceived as an attack upon that very identity. The fact that the ideological response (or the attempt at ideological outbidding) of 'state fundamentalism' fails to satisfy Islamist demands confirms that these demands have not only ideological, moral, religious or even identity implications, but that they have succeeded in becoming the frame of reference for even purely social or political demands, including the demands for democracy.

In the small number of cases where they are in power, contrary to the masses of hostile propaganda, Islamists in Iran and Sudan have not led populations to economic ruin, as predicted by their adversaries. They have, however, had to face a serious weakening of their ideological resources, inasmuch as the distance which separates the utopian force of oppositional discourse from the compromises of a governmental programme of action is considerable, especially when that programme must be implemented in a peculiarly hostile international (and regional, in the case of Sudan) environment.

More clearly in Iran than in Sudan, this deterioration has manifested itself as an acceleration of certain dynamics more generally observed in the mainstream of the movement.

The Islamisation of modernity

Within legalist movements, doctrinal attitudes are far from monolithic. The convolutions of the 'old guard' of the Muslim Brotherhood (Egyptian, for the most part) contrast with openly reformist trends (in another element of the same Egyptian Muslim Brotherhood, and in the writings of Rached Ghannouchi and Abdessalam Yassine,[26] but also of Adel Hussein, Fathi Yakan and the Shiite Hussein Fadlallah). It is impossible to provide a fully documented list here, but examples of this are Rached Ghannouchi, taking the symbolic step of denouncing the death penalty traditionally reserved for apostates from his London exile, and the Egyptian Wasat Party in seeking a more explicit integration of Christians into the politico-cultural dimensions of the Islamist movement. For this reason, reformist trends within the Islamist movement face the resistance of both the doctrinal old guard of the Muslim Brotherhood and of the regime in power. There are numerous examples of the way in which oppositional Islam is being slowly reconciled with liberal values formerly rejected because of their identification with colonial deculturation.[27] This should not be over-emphasised: if some of its premises have been re-appropriated, Western modernity has not been accepted unconditionally. It is above all a question, as Abdessalam Yassine was one of the first to put it, of the 'Islamization' of modernity by re-empowering it with the force of God's name and, faced with its unbridled nature, by then reaffirming the need to take more account of the safeguarding of moral values. Apart from 'smoothing the hackles of modern sceptics', Yassine intends to continue 'speaking about God and the afterlife...to a modernity deafened by its modern din, blinded by reflections of the coloured image, dazzled by instant flashes, seduced by the magic of electronic highways, exhausted by the explosion of the virtual world'.

On the edge of an inaccessible political arena, social action continues to be an important field of activity for the Islamists. Islamisation 'from below' of the associative and educational world and the institutions of civil society still goes on: in fact, it touches all the spaces of collective or social action capable of at least partially eluding the administrative grip of the state: unions, professional and student associations, educational struc-tures, research centres, sports clubs, welfare or co-operative organisations, and human rights groups, but also lawyers' groups, unions of the liberal professions and the banking sector. The vectors of mobilisation are traditional (mosques, pilgrimages, door-to-door calls, meetings etc) but are becoming increasingly modern (in the form of audio and video cassettes, television programmes, newsletters, fax, websites, etc) and innovative (mass marriages designed to alleviate financial constraints of those entering married life). Such forms of extra-political action have seen significant growth into new areas over the last few years. The proliferating research and study centres, the burgeoning Islamic humanitarian associations, both regional and international, and systematic investing in the Internet constitute one of the first trajectories which could be illustrated at more length.

The paths of exile

In the context of Algerian, Egyptian, Tunisian and even Moroccan political turmoil, exile has become an Islamist reality so routine as to be banal. The Islamist diaspora has moved not so much to Afghanistan as to Europe – especially Britain, Sweden, Germany, Belgium and Switzerland – the Islamic republics of the former Soviet Union and the US, Canada, Malaysia[28] and Indonesia, in addition to some parts of the Arab world.

The dynamic of exile is primarily determined by security considerations: even if banal family or economic reasons play a role, the departure of activists is first and foremost a means to escape repression, or even, occasionally, the threat of liquidation. If it does not necessarily entail the export of political activism, and much less the 'export of armed struggle', which constitutes the deforming optic of the media approach to the subject today, this does not mean the groups do not experience change on political, strategic, intellectual or ideological levels – whether consciously or not. The Islamists of the 1990s are paying the same high price, in terms of being separated and dispersed, paid by the Palestinian refugees at the end of the 1940s. Yet they will also begin to gain a no less impressive recompense for their ordeal: an intellectual opening and a relational force which will eventually procure them many more national links, allowing them to profit from the relations, contacts and human, linguistic and ideological experiences to which their exile has exposed them, as was the case for the Palestinian diaspora.

The increased proximity of the Western environment is the catalyst for developments within the exiled Islamist elite which appear contradictory. Whereas acculturation reduces communication difficulties and brings closer two frames of reference, 'anti-Western' rhetoric seems simultaneously to be reinforced inasmuch as it gains more 'precision' and 'rigor'. When the powerful dynamic of modernity affirms itself, it is no surprise that it does not necessarily reduce the extent of the divisions, more political than ideological, with the West. If the vocabulary becomes (once again) shared, the political content of demands housed by Islamist rhetoric hardens in this new proximity: feelings of the inherent justice of the international order as dominated by the apparent US–Israeli alliance,[29] or the denunciation of the lack of representation allowed some Muslim communities in Europe not only fail to be calmed, but actually mount as the language in which they are expressed 'modernises' itself on a daily basis, gaining in precision what it loses in exoticism. Today, the most astute Islamist writings do not come from the depths of the Egyptian Sa'id, but from the suburbs and inner cities of Europe and the US.[30]

Another important political dynamic today is the way in which the Islamist movement is having increased communication with at least some of its secular opposition counterparts. International meetings between 'nationalists' and 'Islamists' have multiplied, effecting a thaw in relations between two previously hostile camps. The National Pact signed in Rome by the main Algerian opposition groups in February 1995 sketched out the ideological architecture of this rapprochement, which sanctified a new polarisation of the Arab political scene. On one side, there is the camp which 'refuses elections', grouping together the military authorities in power, their secular, 'eradicatory' allies and the most radical fringe of the Islamist opposition. On the other, far from the attention of the media, there is the vast majority of political forces, ready to submit themselves to the verdict of the electorate, whatever their ideological hue.

This fundamental evolution can now be detected in places other than Algeria alone. By co-ordinating their actions, the Libyan exile in opposition have regularly proved themselves capable of overcoming their ideological differences. Tunisia offers another example of this dynamic, with the slow defection of members of the secular opposition, after their dangerous position of blind support for the 'fight against fundamentalism', first to disillusionment, then to the re-establishment of relations with their Islamist counterparts.

This evolution – partly tactical and strategic, but also doctrinal – generally supports the idea of some type of gradual 'normalisation' of the Islamist movements as the process of 'reappropriation' or 'cultural re-articulation' of the universal components of modernity serves to marginalise the literalist (harfi) groups, confirming the expression and affirmation – albeit a slow, even contradictory process – of the 'Islamic' nature of political liberalisation (social justice, the protection of individual and collective freedoms, defence of minorities, the institutionalisation of mechanisms guaranteeing the transmission of power) and social modern- isation (principally women's right of access to the public sphere, in a political or professional capacity) which will not necessarily be contested by 'secularist' politicians. This evidence is beginning to be taken into account by external observers.

Slow changes in the approach of Western academia and media

The question of Islam as a political force is a vital question of our times, and will be for several years to come. The precondition for its treatment with a minimum of intelligence is probably not to start from a platform of hatred.

Michel Foucault[31]

Communication with Western modernity, very much of the 'North' and tried and tested against Islam, smacks of impossibility when you speak of God, wear a beard, and come from the 'South'.

Abdessalam Yassine[32]

I find insupportable the persistent line of questioning that implies the Algerian state could be responsible for the massacres.

Max Gallo[33]

In the Western reading of the political dynamics of the Muslim world, an excess of ideology has made the language of Islamist political actors more prominent than their behaviour and practice. In its uncoding of Egyptian, Algerian and Tunisian political life, the media and sometimes elements of academia still persist in applauding 'victories' which the so-called secular regimes, however discredited and authoritarian they might be, continue to achieve over the relentless 'fundamentalist threat'. These victories are achieved by a subtle combination of ideological counter-measures here, legal and constitutional tweakings there, police terror and media dis- information pretty much everywhere.

In the Mediterranean region, the fundamentalist card has continued to be played by almost all of the state-actors in concert. The ideological criminalisation of those who frequently find themselves on the front line in each of the Arab political systems, as well as in the regional and global political orders, is a tactic which works like a machine expressly designed to drown those who resist leaders of national, regional and international political orders in waves of emotion and irrationality, however legitimate such opposition might be. Leaders of a previous military junta in Algeria, masters of manipulating violence, managed to acquire the unlimited confidence of international financial institutions and stuff full their prisons and ballot boxes with impunity, so carefully had they established their credentials as a 'buffer to fundamentalism'. Each time the Israelis managed to pass off their opponents as 'fundamentalists', they succeeded in de-legitimating the considerable number of Palestinians disillusioned by the walkover of Oslo, and the Russians have used similar tactics to rain bombs upon the slightest suggestion of autonomous tendencies within their crumbling empire. Western leaders themselves know that the recipe of the 'fundamentalist threat' contains active ingredients capable of converting all manner of concerns held by their citizens into electoral dividends.

However, the dominance of the first generation of interpretations of the Islamist phenomenon and the damage they inflicted upon the under-standing of regional and global political dynamics has begun to lose ground.

The first signs of convergence

To simplify the matter somewhat, it may be said that academic writing on Islamism, in French as well as in English, has produced two types of reading. The first – with most media exposure – has relied upon the radical wing (of which one of the most final expressions was the assassination of Sadat) to construct an explanation for the entire phenomenon. The other, which this book follows, has emphasised its cultural, national and identity-based aspects, putting the purely religious dimensions of the phenomenon into perspective and considering its extremist component as marginal and consequently denouncing its supposed antipathy to the dynamics of social modernisation and political liberalisation.[34]

At the dawn of the third millennium, academic expertise has begun to adopt several basic explicative principles. This is not to say that there has been any reconciliation between the camps symbolised in the US by the virulent, dismissive arguments used by Daniel Pipes,[35] Martin Kramer[36] and Samuel Huntington, and the infinitely more nuanced and historicised approaches employed by John Esposito,[37] John Entelis[38] and a growing number of other authors. However, there is some agreement emerging on several fundamental points: the quantitative importance of the Islamist movements and their relative centrality to the ideological spectrum of Arab oppositions are hardly contested any more. As Darwich and Chartouni-Dubarry have pointed out: 'In the space of two decades, religiously-based political opposition, in other words Islamism, has enforced itself as the unique language of social protest and opposition to the powers that be in most of the Arab Muslim world'.[39]

There was a time when the social base of the Islamists was held to be no wider than a few small groups of its radical fringe, themselves supposed to be primarily the product of economic difficulties (or those 'excluded from development') and deliberately excluding themselves from political institutions (as they 'feared facing the verdict of the electorate'); this time is long gone. Purely 'monist' interpretations of the phenomenon are increasingly difficult to argue. Darwich and Chartouni-Dubarry say that 'The term 'Islamist' today covers highly diverse projects, from manifest legalism to overthrowing the powers that be, some using the mosques and others assassinations, some preaching moral regeneration of the Muslim man and others the establishment of the Islamic polity'.[40] It has been conceded that Islamist rhetoric, under the aegis of religious discourse, can convey a limitless amount of purely profane demands – both economic and social, but also, increasingly, democratic. Along with its relative and pluralist dimensions, the new generation of observers of Islamism has begun to recognise the malleability of the phenomenon, 'from the Taliban to Erbakan'.[41] its extreme diversity, as well as the importance of its internal dynamics. Talk of a global religious revival is today forgotten, even by its former proponents. Dangerously simplistic antipathies ('Islamism vs. modernity' or 'Islamism vs. democracy'), too long used as a way to open any attempt at interpretation, are being slowly but surely abandoned. This trend is quickened by the fact that Western writing is losing the monopoly of academic representation of the phenomenon. This is also true of the first generation of secular Arab authors, whose work is similar to their Western counterparts. Muslim Arab intellectuals, even 'Islamists', have taken the baton from their Western counterparts and 'secular' compatriots in order to defend their own vision of the reality, in which they are the actors, writing works too numerous to list here. In Europe, Tareq Ramadan adds a voice as powerful as it is dissonant (and nevertheless acknowledged by the university[42]) to ongoing debates about the place of Islam in European society. Efficiently diffused on the Internet, allowing it to circumnavigate the circuits of publishing and broadcasting, this new pluralism is undermining an old monopoly. Obviously, the effects of such a meeting are not one-way. Islamic thought cannot face the world without being obliged to meet its questions and its gaze.

The hidden assumptions of 'Post-Islamism'

The coming together of various Western academic approaches is also the result of a paradoxical development: that section of French academic writing which gets most media coverage regards the Islamist phenomenon as being now 'in decline', even 'overtaken' – the era of 'post-Islamism' has now arrived. The question of the 'failure of political Islam'[43] was in many respects the forerunner of the 'decline' announced today[44] as well as one of the founding stones of 'post-Islamism'.[45] Gilles Kepel has made the problematic begun by Olivier Roy his own.[46] For adherents of the post-Islamism thesis, in whichever of its guises, the failure or 'irrelevance' of Islamism is primarily a result of the inability of various movements to defeat dictatorial regimes. This failure is moreover explained by the social isolation into which the recourse to violence has supposedly put them. Gilles Kepel, moving away from the approach developed in *La Revanche de Dieu*,[47] thinks that it was an alliance between the religious bourgeoisie and disaffected youth which sparked off the political rise of the Islamists from one end of the Muslim world to the other in the 1980s and 1990s.[48] From Algeria to Afghanistan, it is the shattering of this very alliance – the bourgeoisie fearing the violence of the armed groups – which explains the current 'decline' of the Islamist phenomenon as a whole. Last but not least, for each one of the adherents of 'post-Islamism', the decline also develops, or reveals itself, both in the inability shown by the Islamists to follow the route laid down for them by their political discourse and in the obligation which they now have to side with the forces of democracy.

Now that they keep their activity within the framework of the nation-state, and reconcile the vocabulary of Islam with the values of modernity, Islamists no longer merit consideration as a religious group. This is what the promoters of the theory of post-Islamism are telling us, each in their own way. This book, researched for the most part in the late 1980s and early 1990s, has conversely sought to show that the processes of 're-Islamisation' and modernisation are far from being mutually exclusive. The problem comes less from post-Islamism's recognition of modernity than from the belated nature of this recognition: this modernity has long been evident, even if deliberately and explicitly denied in the discourse of the political actors concerned. This fact has been noted by a significant minority of academic observers.[49] The men and women that are today described as 'no longer meriting the name of Islamists' actually bear a strange resemblance to those whom many scholars have long described as perfect examples of the phenomenon since its very beginning. In some cases, the 'new' findings that are supposed to illustrate the transition to 'post-Islamism' have even been previously designated as part of the very essence of the old Islamism. For Roy,[50] the end of Algerian Islamism depends, amongst other things, on the fact that the FIS, following the lead of some other Islamist parties (including Hizbullah), has transformed itself into an 'Islamic-nationalist' party. Have the disciples of Abbasi Madani really become nationalists, or has the 'cultural' comeback of 'the South' always been at the heart of their mobilising power,[51] much more that any hypothetical 'revival of God'? The same can be said of the representation of 'feminist' currents: have Iranian women really had to wait until the year 2000 to be able to handle social symbolism 'explicitly combining Islam and the values of modernity'?[52] It hardly seems to matter that the dynamics of the 'revolution beneath the veil' have long been described to us with brilliance;[53] it is obviously preferable to see in it something new, attesting to the arrival of the new era of 'post-Islamism'. Otherwise, how on earth could the 'dictatorship of the Mullahs' founded by Khomeini manage to acquire an institutional system which allowed Iranian voters to send their rulers home, a feat that no 'secular' system has been able to accomplish in the entire region (with the possible exception of Lebanon, which remains confessional, however). Has the reconciliation of Islamic terminology with social modernisation and political liberalisation only come to pass in the twenty-first century, or was it already perceptible in the very essence of the Islamist reaction?

This ambiguity is more than one of mere terminology; if it is not raised, serious misperceptions in the analysis of a still-significant factor on the Arab political landscape may persist. If the modernity of the Islamist movement was really inherent at its very inception, as numerous authors have long shown, the sudden retreat of the 'Islamist' label as applied to its representatives in the current generation would seem to be no more than the simple reconciliation of an academic construction with a social reality that, for many years, refused to conform to the vision that social scientists had of it.

Let us now further determine the notions of 'defeat' and 'failure' of the Islamist movement. Besides the truth that the Islamists are not in power, such notions have two obvious limitations, particular to a Western, external viewpoint: firstly, that simple security successes of the regimes have been imbued with the air of the ideological defeat of their opponents; secondly, that of according some sort of civilisational 'pat on the back', echoing the supposed 'end of history', to those who today proclaim the failure of the Islamist trend – a failure which they themselves have largely fabricated by way of their summary arguments. To look more closely, it can be seen that the literature on the 'weakening of the Islamists', which sometimes has a hint of payback about it, is not new. Since 1992 and the military coup in Algeria, there have been uncountable multitudes on the verge of removing the Islamists from the Algerian, and the Arab, political map – women, Sufis, Kabyles, the army, students, democrats etc. But let us rely upon the facts. If the Turkish Refah Party is almost reduced to silence, it should not be forgotten that this stems from its legal dissolution, implemented at a time when its increasing support (not its decline, as local elections demonstrated) and its persistent legalism were causing concern to the Turkish military tribe and its US supporters. The same can be said of Hamas in Palestine, which is caught in the crossfire of Palestinian and Israeli security services. The Lebanese Hizbullah enjoys a high level of legitimacy both within its home country and abroad, across the confessional divide, as the French prime minister found out in Palestine.[54] In Morocco, Islamists processions continue to attract the support of a strong majority of the female population. The principle holds true for most of the Arab countries. The notion of an Islamist monopoly on illegitimate violence, which is supposed to have alienated the descendants of Hassan al-Banna from their political base, is rendered invalid both by the revelations of dissident Algerian army officers and by innumerable testimonies from other quarters that it would be unwise to ignore for much longer. Those who do not feel it 'obscene'[55] to search for truths about this phenomenon now have at their disposal a significant amount of material (relating to Algeria, Egypt and elsewhere) that illustrates exactly how such a notion was originally given weight and subsequently manipulated. Supposed bourgeois terror of a disenfranchised (and Islamist) youth in their countries has served those forces that purport to oppose it very well indeed.

In order to be able to speak of an Islamist defeat as opposition, it would be necessary to prove that other political forces had replaced them – 'secularist' forces which would thereby show themselves to have a superior capacity to mobilise support. We are far from such a situation, especially if we seek to generalise about the whole of the Muslim world. In contesting national political orders (just like the Palestinian resistance in the face of Israeli intransigence), the Islamists implacably continue to be both advance guard and main body of mobilised activity. In the Arab world, the conjectural success of state violence only now serves, in all probability, to reveal the society's general difficulty in making progress along the arduous road to democracy – a difficulty for Islamists, certainly, but also for the regimes and forces which claim to oppose them in the name of secularism.

All this should not be taken as a denial of the fact that times change, for Islamists as much as for the regimes which they oppose. The contradictions which the militant wings of these movements (who lock themselves into the familiar territory of the strictly reactionary, highly ahistorical position of the facile 'rejection of Western modernity') will be facing in the future must not be underestimated. The force of the Islamist dynamic in its involvement with identity, proceeds from the reforging of symbolic continuity between the process of modernisation expressed in Western terminology and an 'authentic' indigenous culture which has been marginalised for several decades.[56] This dynamic, reactionary in nature, will therefore not last indefinitely; simply reintroducing an old indigenous language to current 'modern' political discourse will no longer have the same politically motivating power, especially when, as in Iran and Sudan, it will be taken on by elites who exercise power in coalitions. It is therefore evident that, one day, there will be room for an expression of 'post-Islamism'. That day has not yet arrived.

Beyond Islamism

'Islamism' as a political discourse is active in two areas: in the internal contestation of Arab political orders and, internationally, in the context of East–West relations. In both cases, the language privileged by the current political generation will be eventually made redundant. The generation which today employs the rhetoric of Islam to work towards the ideological destabilisation of elites emerging from the secularist post-independence generation of Nasserists and Ba'thists, still has a good few years ahead of it. When these activists will be integrated into the legal political arena will depend less on how people change than on how much the regimes change: like any opposition in any part of the world, Islamist oppositions are both the product of and instrumental in shaping with the political environment in which they grow. In this respect, the regimes themselves only have the (Islamist) opposition that they deserve. Only meaningful democratic openings will allow them to take root inside the legalist institutional framework that a large majority of them are ready to or already do accept. It is this inevitable participation in power which, in bringing activists and ideologues to face the challenges of implementing their political agenda, will very probably see the successors of Banna lose their unique character – a uniqueness (due, in large part, to the utopianism it allows) that in the current climate, gives them significant ideological and political strength.

Internationally, it is necessary that the symbolic arsenal of Muslim culture has its role reinstated in the production of universal modernity for the appeal of reaction to Western cultural hegemony to begin to wane. This would imply a considerable shift in behaviour, on the Muslim side as well as on the side of that Western alter-ego and defining Other which lies at the heart of Muslim political identity. A consensus on modernity would need to have emerged, which Muslim and non-Muslim need to be able to perceive as founded on common values and as issued from a plurality of cultural co-operation, instead of being seen as the unilateral imposition of one sole civilisational model, as it is at least partially at the moment. This modernity would allow each of its participants to feel that their cultural and religious heritage was still a relevant factor in a universal history, but would simultaneously disallow that heritage from setting unilateral limits upon their ability to innovate. It would respect their cultural and religious identities in some ways, even whilst permitting them to overcome and transcend them, from which it would be seen as 'shared' by all and therefore effectively universal.

For everyone, Western or not, Muslim or non-Muslim, such an achievement implies that parallel convulsions over identity, whether active (in the case of the West) or reactive (in the case of the Muslim world) be overcome. For the West, it is a question of unreservedly admitting the possibility that values as universally valid as its own can be equally well expressed with the symbolic resources and historical references of non-Western cultures. Without renouncing these values, it must abandon the pernicious idea that it has once and for all acquired a monopoly over the production of modernity because its terminology, language and codes are alone able to innovate, modernise and provide access to universality. On the Muslim side, the danger of falling into the trap of a purely reactionary response to Western ethnocentrism must be avoided, as must the danger of adopting the same irrationalities as the West. This reactive version of the ethnocentric withdrawal, frequent in at least part of the Islamist movement, even today shelters a certain reticence as regards those humanist principles and values which, at one particular historical point, seem linked to Western civilisation. It leads in some way to 'throwing out the baby' (modernisation) 'with the bathwater' (colonial acculturation). It also confuses the substance of these values, much more commonly accepted than might be thought (social justice, the woman's right to act in the professional or political public sphere etc), with their symbolic baggage, taken from respective histories with all their specifities, which serve to give these values their social legitimacy at a certain point in time by grounding them in the individual or collective conscience. This injurious confusion is hardly a recent development. Kamel Ataturk did it in reverse when he thought to impose headwear popular in Europe to the detriment of the *fez* traditionally worn in his country, in order to ensure Turkey's modernisation. He obviously confused the substance of the values of modernity with their symbolic trappings.

The challenge of developing a consensual modernity demands national political actors capable of abstracting themselves from the instinctive membership of their own symbolic universe and accepting the legitimacy of a formula which uses symbolic resonances other than those with which they are familiar; in this way they recognise the commonality of modernity, beyond the specific countries which have expressed its content.

For believers of all faiths, the ecumenism of such a step is often considered as an intolerable concession, or even an unforgivable sacrifice. It would demand that they renounce the supremacy of what they consider as the (sole) legitimate system of reference. These people should perhaps be reminded of a principle honoured by each one of the major religions, even if the history of the mortals who claim to abide by it shows they have but too rarely respected it: 'There is no compulsion in religion'. Even the most fervent belief of the most sincere of devotees should, in theory, be able to make room for the respect of others' convictions and the search for a humanist *modus vivendi* founded on those values which unite religious and cultural groups, rather than on that which divides them. It would then remain to identify and, if possible, regulate those very material conflicts of interest between nations and other groups which shape the population of the planet. Let there be no mistake: this task is more than sufficient to occupy ideologues, politicians, strategists and diplomats for a long time to come.

NOTES ON THE TEXT

Notes on Introduction

1   Karthala, Paris, 1988: revised and updated version by Payot, Paris, 1995. Some of the developments in this essay were published in certain reviews, collections and journals, notably in *L'Encyclopédia Universalis, L'Encyclopédia Quillet, L'Encyclopédia Rousset, L'Etat du monde, Le Monde diplomatique, Liberation, Maghreb-Machreq, Passerelles, Relazioni Internazionali, Le Genre humain, Esprit, Géopolitique* and in an extended English version of Burgat, *The Islamic Movement in North Africa*, translated by William Dowell, University of Texas Press, Austin, TX, 1993.

2   This book has benefited greatly from the viewpoint of the 'Islamist subject', notably because in 1992 an extended version was published in Arabic in Cairo, which gave greater access to the authors' theses and the opportunity to gauge the reactions of the Arabic-speaking world: Al-Islam al-Siyasi and Sawt al-Janub, François Burgat, *L'Islamisme au Maghreb: la voix du Sud,* translated by Laurine Zikri and Nasr Hamid Abu Zayd, Dar al-'Alam al-Thalith, Cairo, 1992, with the collaboration of the translation centre, led by Richard Jacquemond.

3   The Egyptian Secret Services seemed to make up a few *fatwas* of their own: cf. their list in Kamel Issam, *Omar Abderrahmane: le seisme qui a secoue le monde,* Cairo, October 1993 (not for resale).

4   Cf. for example Phillipe Aziz, *Le Point,* 18 February 1991, p. 53. In Tunis he is called Mr Valium, the reassuring Islamist who bores us rigid with his moderate approach and his fondness for legality. What he says is surprising, and completely unorthodox for an Islamist leader. In Robert Laffont's *Les sectes secretès de l'Islam de l'ordre des assassins aux Frères musulmans,* Paris, 1983, the same specialist proposed a grid of analysis for a long time which does not allow for this type of nuance; the dissension that is presently dividing the Arab world is largely explained by the action of these active minorities. The Muslim Brotherhood, which constantly causes trouble in present-day Egypt, Syria and other Arab countries, is a political and religious secret society whose action is directly inspired by the ancient order of the Assassins (p. 8).

5   He does this in those pieces selected by Mohammed Al-Ahnaf, Bernard Botiveau and Frank Fregosi in *L'Algérie par ses islamistes,* Karthala, Paris, 1991. As Michel Camau is at pains to point out in the preface, this collection was not intended as a summing-up before sentence was passed. One might easily be excused for this misapprehension.

6   Georges Corm, *L'Europe et l'Orient,* La Découverte, Paris, 1989, p. 378. Corm also writes – just as correctly – that 'ever since the emergence of the Eastern

Question at the end of the 18th century that saw the decline of the Ottoman Empire, the stubborn refusal of Europe to discuss these people who surround them in the south Mediterranean without any reference to geographic, historical or social territoriality is remarkable: "the world of Islam", "Islam", "the call to Islam", "the Muslim people", in a way that entirely disregards any notion of history and geography, as well as that of ethnic roots. There is no distinguishing between Arabs from the Maghreb and the Mashreq, Turks, Iranians and Afghans' (p. 371).

7   Cf. notably Henry Laoust, *Essai sur les doctrines sociales et politiques de Taqi Eddin Ahmad b. Taymiyya*, *'Recherches d'archéologie, de philologie et d'histoire, IX'*, French Institute of Oriental Archaeology, Cairo, 1939; Michot, 'Textes spirituels d'Ibn Taymiya' I–IX in *Le Musulman* 11–25, June 1990–February 1995, AEIF, Paris; Emmanuel Sivan, 'Ibn Taymiya: Father of the Islamic Revolution. Medieval Theology and Modern Politics', in *Encounter*, t. LX/v, 1983, pp. 41–50; Bruno Etienne, in F. Chatelet *et al.*, *Dictionnaire des oeuvres politiques*, PUF, Paris, 1986.

8   Cf. notably Olivier Carré, *Mystique et politique, lecture révolutionnaire du Coran par Sayyed Qutb, frère musulman radical*, Presses de la FNSP/Editions du Cerf, Paris, 1984.

9   *Maghreb-Machreq-Monde Arabe*, September 1990.

10 Fouad Zakariya, *Laïcité et islamisme: les Arabes à l'heure du choix*, presented and translated from Arabic by Richard Jacquemond, La Découverte-Dar al-Fikr, Paris–Cairo, 1990.

11 But the best example of the limits of such a classification is undoubtedly to be found in the exceptional self-righteousness of the French political scene – faced, for example, with the Gulf crisis – offered to us by the outsider Ghassan Salamé.

Notes on Chapter One

1   *Le Monde*, 22 October 1990, column written by Gisèle Halimi, Alain Carignon and Dominique Jamet, who add: 'Algeria has stalled at a crossroads where it must make a painful choice. Its people, men and women who are already living and trembling in the shadow of fundamentalist Islam, and its young devotees are far from being completely receptive or resigned to discontent, repression and imprisonment.'

2   Cf. notably Alain de Libera, 'Comment l'Europe a découvert l'Islam', in *Connaisance de l'Islam*, Syros, Paris, 1992.

3   Western colonies in the Arab world:

Colony	Dates	Years	Colonised by
Algeria	1830–1962	132	France
United Arab Emirates	1892/1916–71	55/79	Great Britain
Egypt*	1798–1801	3	France
	1882–1936	54	Great Britain
Iraq	1920–32	12	Great Britain
Jordan	1922–46	24	Great Britain
Kuwait	1899–1961	62	Great Britain
Lebanon	1920–46	26	France
Libya	1912–51	40	Italy, UN mandate from 1943 until the end of December 1951
Morocco	1911–56	45	France
Mauritius	1907–60	53	France
Sudan	1898–1956	58	Great Britain
Syria	1920–46	26	France
Tunisia	1881–1956	75	France
Yemen (south)	1839–1967	128	Great Britain

*54 years (under the supervision of the Ottoman Empire from 1882–1914; protectorate from 1914, followed by a formal independence in 1922; more than 20 years of British military control over the Suez Canal from 1936 to 1956).

4   'The largest of the groups, the FIS, has recruited from the hordes of people on the margins of society, who have nothing to lose by giving it a chance and who are ready to risk all' (Jacques de Barrin, 'D'un totalitarisme a l'autre', Le Monde, 31 December 1991).

5   Gilles Kepel, Le Prophète et Pharaoh, La Découverte, Paris, 1984; new edition, Le Seuil, Paris, 1994.

6   This theory was notably in preference to two 'local' works whose approach is markedly different: firstly Olivier Roy's account, which delivered a real theoretical insight by outlining the problem of cultural reappropriation in Afghanistan: L'Afghanistan, Islam et modernité politique, Le Seuil, Paris, 1985; secondly Olivier Carré's Radicalismes islamiques, L'Harmattan, Paris, 1985, co-edited by Paul Dumont. At the time of publication of this work, Carré was one of the first people to look at modern Islamism without adopting the usual 'pathological' approach. Thus, Carré clearly assumed the idea that the dynamic of re-Islamisation consisted of more than its 'reactionary' facade and was not intrinsically negative. At the other end of the scale, Gilles Kepel has for a long time regarded the entire process of Arab re-Islamisation as an 'impasse' in which the Arab 'victims' of 'modernisation' have got lost (cf. notably 'Impasses arabes', Le Monde, March 1991), a thesis which today is still favoured by the general public. The other notable figure of the Orientalist

scene is Bruno Etienne, whose approach is again completely different; the analyses of his *L'Islamisme radical*, Hachette, Paris, 1986, are more difficult to encapsulate in a single thesis.

7 Kepel, *Le Prophète et Pharaoh*, new edition.

8 This view was expressed by a high-ranking Algerian civil servant several months after the event: interview with the author, December 1992.

9 Cf. Baudouin Dupret, 'Qualifier, disqualifier; de la fonction des mots dans le discours sur l'Autre arabo-musulman', in Espace Arabesque (ed.), *La Peur et la séduction: l'autre dans l'imaginaire occidental et arabo-musulman*, Sabir, Brussels, 1992, pp. 64–73.

10 A major French television channel broadcast archive pictures of Lebanon to document a peaceful march by the FIS in the centre of Algiers.

11 The Egyptian authorities were not fooled. In July 1994 they deported Ali Ben Si Ali, a young journalist who had specialised in putting the special envoys of the foreign press in contact with a sample of mainly Islamist interlocutors that the regime thought were dangerously diversified.

12 Press conference at the FIS headquarters, Algiers, 14 June 1990.

13 The presence of the Christian community, which represents between 8 and 10 percent of the population, tends to adversely affect the reading of the civil war in action by giving it a virtually exclusively confessional dimension, which is actually far from being the case. The conflict escalated again not so much from the resistance of the 'Christian South' to the Islamisation of laws as from the disagreement over the control of oil reserves. However, the Western public was only shown the representation of the conflict in the south once it had been 'confessionalised' and inscribed in the dichotomy of a discord between Islam and Christianity. At the same time the confessional factor is becoming increasingly important, thanks to certain types of missionary interventionism and the propensity of the south to take advantage of this simplistic dichotomy to attract foreign aid – this importance was initially lacking.

14 Cf. Ahmed Manaï, *Supplice tunisien: Le jardin secret du général Ben Ali*, La Découverte, Paris, 1995.

15 Egypt has been governed by the 'emergency law' since 1977, which did not stop the President of the French Senate in 1990 from solemnly awarding the Egyptian President Mubarak a Louise-Michel prize in recognition 'of his service to democracy and human rights', between two rounds of legislative elections boycotted by the majority of the opposition. When in 1993 he was elected – as the only candidate – for his third presidential term, none of the major French news services dared put a figure on the election turnout, officially quoted at 84 percent, but probably closer to the 5 or 7 percent quoted by Reuters.

16 This thesis is insufficient on two accounts: globally it overlooks the internal reasons for the Islamist surge, and circumstantially it gives the impression that the phenomenon emanated from the Arab-speaking university

departments, which is wholly inaccurate. The dreadful conditions under which the 'Arabisation' policy of universities was implemented are, on the other hand, responsible for the lack of education of a whole generation of students. It could be just as easily proposed that abandoning any policy of Arabisation would have magnified the demands for 'identity', which the Islamists have successfully exploited politically.

17   Cf., for example, Nadia Ramsis Farah, *Religious Strike in Egypt: Crisis and Ideological Conflict in the Seventies*, Gordon and Breach, Montreux, 1986; she believes that if Islamists exist then it is in some way owing to the existence of Copts.

18   The Pakistani thinker regarded as one of the founding fathers of contemporary political Islam.

19   Literally translated as 'those who transmit'. The members of Jama'at al-Tabligh, established in Pakistan in the 1920s, have since been travelling the length and breadth of the Muslim world to convert believers to a strictly pietistic faith: cf. notably Gilles Kepel, *Les Banlieues de l'Islam*, Le Seuil, Paris, 1987, pp. 179 ff.

Notes on Chapter Two

1   Tareq al-Bishri, *The Political Movement In Egypt*, Dar al-Shuruq, Cairo, 1992, in Arabic.

2   As noted by François Massoulié in one of the rare studies in the French language of the works of the Egyptian writer Tareq al-Bishri: *Un intellectual égyptien et sa problématique*, Mémoire de Maîtrise d'Histoire sous la Direction de D. Chevallier, Paris, 1987; see also Léonard Binder, *Islamic Liberalism, a Critique of Development Ideologies*, Chicago University Press, Chicago, IL, 1988.

3   At the Labour Party Congress in May 1993, Adel Hussein was elected general secretary of the party and gave up his position as chief editor of the twice-weekly journal *Al-Sha'ab* to his nephew Magdi, the son of the founder member of Young Egypt, Ahmed Hussein.

4   Interviews with the author, Cairo, 1990.

5   Interview with the author, London, February 1992. Rached Ghannouchi's political vision has long been recorded in a collection of interviews with Qusaï Salah Darwish: Khalil Media Service, London, 1992, in Arabic.

6   Interview with the author, Cairo, 1990.

7   The Wafd, the 'party of 'delegation', was established in 1918 when a group of nationalists led by Saad Zaghoul went to London to plead the Egyptian cause.

8   At the beginning of the war, during which Ahmed Hussein was imprisoned, the name of the party was changed to the National Islamic Party.

Notes on Chapter Three

1   For the relation and the limits of the 'modernist' and 'reformist' reaction to the Western surge, see the book written by one of the fathers of Algerian Islamism: Malek Bennabi, *Vocation de l'Islam*, Le Seuil, Paris, 1954.

2   Abdelkader led the resistance to French invasion until 1847: cf. notably Bruno Etienne, *Abdelkader*, Hachette, Paris, 1994.

3   Interview with the author, Khartoum, December 1993.

4   Cf. Richard Jacquemond, 'L'édition d'ouvrages traduits du français en Égypte; pour un point de vue biculturel', *Égypte-Monde arabe*, 5 March 1991, Cairo, p. 163.

5   In Michel Camau, *La Tunisie, une modernité au-dessus de tout soupçon*, Presses du CNRS, Paris, 1989, p. 301.

6   Mzali was first Minister of Education, then Prime Minister of Bourguiba: interview with the author, Paris, March 1988.

7   A civil servant for UNESCO in the 1980s, Rachid Ben Aïssa was one of the first supporters of the Islamist movement at the Algerian University: interview with the author, Paris, 1988.

8   In Camau, *La Tunisie, une modernité*; see also François Burgat, *The Islamic Movement in North Africa*, translated by William Dowell, University of Texas Press, Austin, TX, 1997, pp. 63 ff.

9   François Burgat (with the collaboration of Baudouin Dupret), 'Cacher le politique: les représentations de la violence en Égypte', *Maghreb-Machreq*, Paris, December 1993.

10   Colonel Qadhafi thus evokes the system of direct democracy extolled in his little Green Book as the 'third universal theory', in reference to the capitalist and socialist experiences which he transcended.

11   For all that, it will be objected, he is part of the Muslim majority (90 percent), since Christian references of identity, even if they are far from being totally different to the Muslim equivalents, are not exactly identical.

12   On the Islamic current in Jordan see notably Moussa Zied Al-Keilani, *The Islamist Movement in Jordan*, Dar al-Bashir, Amman, 1990, in Arabic; Mahmoud Salem 'Oubaidat, *The Impact Of the Gama'a Islamiyya in the Twentieth Century*, Dar al-Madrasa al-Haditha, Amman, 1990, in Arabic.

13   Cf. notably Rémi Leveau, *Le Fellah marocain et le trône*, Presses de la FNSP, Paris, 1985.

14   The brutal domestication perpetrated in 1961 by Gamal Abdel Nasser to prevent the old al-Azhar University – the nomination of its sheikh by the state – completing the restrictive texts of 1911 and 1930 (which had respectively confined the activity of the Azharists solely to religion, and predicted a regime that sanctioned them) was not enough to wipe out its ability to mobilise, especially in the most traditional sectors of society. Cf.

notably Ola Abdelaziz Zeid, 'Al-Azhar and the appeal for democracy', in *Democratic Challenges in the Arab World*, Cairo, Centre for Political and International Development Studies, September 1992; Pierre-Jean Luizard, 'Al-Azhar, institution sunnite réformée', *Communication au colloque La Réforme Sociale en Égypte*, CEDEJ-IFAO, Cairo, 10–13 December 1993.

15 Cf. François Burgat, 'Algérie, la longue marche de la société civile', *Encyclopœdia Universalis*, Paris, 1990.

16 Cf. notably Mohammed Mzali, *Tunisie, quel avenir?*, Publisud, Aix-en Provence, 1991.

17 Jean-François Bayart, 'L'Énonciation du politique', *Revue Française de Science Politique* 35, June 1985. Cf. also Jean-François Bayart, *Le Politique par le bas en Afrique noire: contributions à une problématique de la démocratie*, Karthala, Paris, 1990, and *L'État en Afrique: la politique du ventre*, Fayard, Paris, 1989.

18 Before straying towards more ambivalent formulations, as Gilles Kepel did in the collective work *Exils et royaumes, les appartenances au monde arabo-musulman aujourd'hui*, Presses de la FNSP, Paris, 1994, p. 30: 'The development of Islamist protest is not taking a linear path. Earlier, until the mid-1980s, the movements that preoccupied the attention of the authorities and the media [...] favoured a process of re-Islamisation from above.'

19 Olivier Roy, 'De l'islam révolutionnaire au néo-fondamentalisme', *Esprit*, September 1990: 'The failure of the revolutionary model is above all the failure of the Iranian revolution symbolised by two dates: September 1980 and June 1989 [...] The death of Khomeini denied a charismatic leader to the remnants of the revolutionary movement'; 'The Islamic movements have undergone a profound transformation during the 1980s: the political revolutionary model, whose objective is to seize power through violent action as was the case in Iran, has been replaced by a strategy of re-Islamisation from below of the entire society, in morals, culture and behaviour.' Cf. also Gilles Kepel, *La Revanche de Dieu: chrétiens, juifs et musulmans à la reconquête du monde*, Le Seuil, Paris, 1991.

20 Cf. Chapter 2.

21 Cf. notably Salah al-Wardani, *The Islamist Movement in Egypt: the Facts of the 1970s*, Markaz al-Hadara al-'Arabiyyaa li'l-'I'lam wa'l-Nashr, Cairo, 1989.

22 Sayyed Qutb, executed in Cairo in 1966, is often considered as the father of radical Islamism, if only because he adopted the idea of an 'excommunication' of the political system which persecuted him and of the society which tolerated this system. Cf. notably Olivier Carré, *Mystique et politique, lecture révolutionnaire du Coran par Sayyed Qutb, frère musulman radical*, Presses de la FNSP/Editions du Cerf, Paris, 1984.

23 In Egypt, the weekly *Rose al-Yusef* is behind most of the fabrications attributed to the practices of Islamist groups, the least of which being the 'droit de seigneur' supposedly enjoyed by the emirs. This is enough to make anyone with direct experience of these groups smile.

24 The 'platform affair', as the assassination of Sadat was called from then on in Egypt; Abboud Zummer, who was partisan of doing nothing before 1984, only went ahead with the operation because the wave of arrests launched by Sadat in 1981 was in danger of uncovering the network.

25 Kamel Said al-Habib, interview with the author, Cairo, 1993.

26 Hosni Mubarak was the victim of a double assassination attempt, generally accredited to members of Gama'a Islamiyya. In 1994 a bomb was discovered in the hall of an airport in the east of the country through which he often passed. Two officers were condemned to death and executed for their part in the conspiracy. According to Talaat Fouad al-Qassimi, the exiled representative of the Gama'a Islamiyya, a second attempt, the details of which he refused to divulge, was aborted.

27 Interviews with members of the Gama'a Islamiyya and Tanzim al-Jihad. The numerous publications devoted to the Tanzim al-Jihad organisation demonstrate this reality. Cf. notably Mostapha Hala, *Political Islam, from reformism to the violent groups*, Markaz al-dirasat al-siyasiya wa'l-istratejiyya, Cairo, 1992, which highlights the doctrinal differences between the Gama'a Islamiyya and Tanzim al-Jihad. See also the documents collected by Rifaat Sayyed in *Al-Nabi al-musulah: Al Rafidun* and *Al-Nabi al-musulah: al-Tha'irun*, Riad-al-Rayyes Books, London, 1991. See also Sayyed's *Al Islambouli, Ru'ya jadida li-tanzim al-jihad*, Madbouli, Cairo, 1987. Some of the interviews with Abboud Zummer, who was jailed in Torah (south of Cairo) were published by Ahmed Ragab, *Abboud Abbdellatif Hassan al-Zummer; hiwarat wa watha'iq*, interview and documents, Markaz al-Hadara al-'Arabiyyaa li'l-'i'lam wa'l-nashr, Cairo, 1991, and Mahmoud Fawzi, *Abboud al-Zummer: how did he kill Sadat?*, Dar al-Nachr-Hatier, Paris–Cairo, 1993. On the doctrinal tensions between Tanzim al-Jihad and Gama'a Islamiyya, see a series of pamphlets: 'Al-Hasad al-Murr' ('The Bitter Harvest'), by Aïman Al-Dhouari, one of the Gama'a leaders exiled in Pakistan, 'Batlane wilaya al dharir' ('The blind do not lead', a reference to the blindness of Sheikh Omar Abd al-Rahman) the *fatwa* of the Tanzim al-Jihad organisation, to which the Gama'a Islamiyya replied on the same level with 'La imara li'l-asirin' ('A prisoner does not lead'), a reference to Colonel Abboud Zummer.

Notes on Chapter Four

1 The fact – already mentioned – that competition from the customary norms has restricted it, in the reality of the history of Muslim societies, to only fleeting moments of monopoly, changes nothing. This is firstly because competition from the local custom is not as significant in terms of identity as from a set of norms that are considered foreign. This is particularly because, as has been stressed already, behind the call for the *shari'a* lies the mythical

dimension of the restoration of a symbolic order which is truly at stake. Because they are divine, the 'Islamic' norms are seen as endogenous in relation to their Western equivalents, and it is in this sense that they satisfy the demands of 'authenticity' that is beyond the norms imported by colonisers.

2 Roger Garaudy, Les Intégrismes, Belfond, Paris, 1991.

3 Often considered as the most radical thinker of the Islamist movement, Rahman gave his backing as an expert in Islamic jurisprudence to the assassination of Sadat. Exiled in New York since 1990, he is still considered as the leader of the Gama'a Islamiyya, one of the principle activist movements of oppositional Islam in Egypt.

4 Rifaat Sayyed Ahmed, chief editor of the review Minbar al-Sharq.

5 Tareq al-Bishri, 'La question juridique entre chari'a islamique et droit positif', translated by Bernard Botiveau, Dossier du CEDEJ 3, 1985, Cairo, pp. 179–207.

6 Roger Garaudy, Les Intégrismes, Belfond, Paris, 1991: 'The Quran is a guide for those who believe in what has been revealed to you and what has been revealed before you'. (S II-2, 3, 4).

7 Jacques Berque, 'Lectures contradictoires du Coran: le figé et l'ouvert', La Pensée 299, July 1994, p. 69.

8 On the critique of the literalist interpretation of the shari'a and the demand for modern rights, cf. Abdullahi Ahmed An Na'im, Toward an Islamic Reformation, Civil Liberties, Human Rights and International Law, Syracuse University Press, Syracuse, NY, 1990; also the commentaries of Ann Elisabeth Mayer, 'A Critique of An-Na'im's Assessment of Islamic Criminal Justice', in Tore Lindhom and Kari Vogt, Islamic Law Reform and Human Rights: Challenges and Rejoinders, Nordic Human Rights Publications, Oslo, 1993, p. 37.

9 Fouad Zakariya, Laïcité et islamisme: les Arabes à l'heure du choix, presented and translated from Arabic by Richard Jacquemond, La Découverte-Dar al-Fikr, Paris–Cairo, 1990.

10 Rémy Leveau, Les trajectoires du politque, colloquium of the National Foundation for Political Sciences, Bordeaux, September 1988, and Le Sabre et le Turban. L'avenir du Maghreb, François Bourin, Paris, 1993.

11 Fouad Zakariya, op. cit., also insists that the Islamists have displayed the 'formalist drift' in their call for religious rites to be respected literally; by doing so, he tends to systematically deny the political and identity dimension of their discourse. He also did so just after the outbreak of the Gulf War, when he stated in an argument – that was dangerously similar to Western wishful thinking – that there were 'two reasons to believe in the decline of Islamism': 'the end of the communist threat for a movement that had close links with anti-communist countries such as Saudi Arabia and the United States' and the fact that 'the failure of Iraqi opportunism will prove to be a giant step backwards for the Islamist current that approved and supported it': Belvédère, April–May 1991. Cf. also Farag Fodha, Qabl al-suqut, Dar al-fikr, Cairo, 1985, and al-Haqiqa al-gha'iba, Dar al-fikr, Cairo, 1986.

12 No 'cultural relativism' should, in the name of 'cultural diversity', bring an end to universal values: cf. *La Défaite de la pensée*, Gallimard, Paris, 1992, as Alain Finkielkraut fears: 'In our desert world, by transcendence, cultural identity has prolonged the barbaric traditions that God can no longer justify [...] However, at the expense of their culture, the European individual has acquired all the liberties one by one. It is finally, and more generally, criticism of tradition that is the spiritual foundation of Europe, but the philosophy of decolonisation has made us forget it by persuading us that the individual is nothing more than a cultural phenomenon' (p. 143).

13 Cf. notably Pierre-Jean Luizard, 'Le soufisme égyptien contemporain', *Égypte-Monde arabe* 2, 1990, p. 36: 'The Sufi brotherhoods are continuing to attract many more recruits than the combined efforts of the currents of political Islam and the modern political currents'.

14 *Ibid.*

15 Smaï Haj Ali, 'Algerie: le premier séminaire des zaouais', *Maghreb-Machreq-Monde Arabe* 132, March 1992, p. 53.

16 Interview with Christianne Souriau, *Le Maghreb musulman*, CNRS, Paris, 1981.

17 Notably, of course, since the arrival of the Islamist scene: Malek Bennabi, *Vocation de l'Islam*, Le Seuil, Paris, 1954, p. 27.

18 Interviews with the author, September–October 1993, Cairo. Abdelharith Madani was a member of the second generation of the Gama'a Islamiyya. He joined the movement after the assassination of Sadat. He became a lawyer in Cairo, after which he was tortured to death at the General Security head-quarters at Lazoghli, Cairo in October 1994.

19 Cf. the description of a *mawlid* (a saint's birthday) in Cairo by Pierre Jean Luizard: 'The atmosphere at the mawlid in the ghost town of the district was in contrast to the indifference, even the hostility of the people [...] where the Gam'iyya Shar'iyya, the Muslim Brotherhood and Islamist associations seem to dominate. It was as if you had to enter this ghost town, where the fewest and the poorest people live, in order to enter the Sufi domain': 'Un mawlid particulier', *Égypte-Monde arabe* 14, 2nd quarter 1993, p. 79.

20 This point was expressed notably at a conference in 1992 at the French Institute of Oriental Archaeology in Cairo.

21 Abd al-Gamal Gawad, 'Deux formes de médiation partisane: Islam traditionnel et Islam moderniste au Soudan', *Égypte-Monde arabe* 2, 1990, pp. 27–34.

22 The spirit of an interview with the sheikh of a small brotherhood to the south of Luxor; a fierce partisan – as are all his peers – of the imposition of the *shari'a*, he shows the significance of traditional comportments and the possible impact of new alliances. 'Is it possible that the members of your brotherhood are voting for the Islamist Party candidate? 'Certainly not!' 'And why is that?' 'Because it is me, the teacher, who decides who they should vote for, and I told them to vote for X.' 'And what happens if one day

you decide to vote for the Islamists?' 'Well, in that case, I swear that there are three thousand of us and every one of us shall vote!': Interview with the author, 1990.

23 Title of a work by Gilles Kepel, *La Revanche de Dieu: chrétiens, juifs et musulmans à la reconquête du monde*, Le Seuil, Paris, 1991.

24 Bruce B. Lawrence, *Defenders of God: the Fundamentalist Revolt against the Modern Age*, I. B. Tauris, London, 1990.

25 Patrick Michel, *Politique et religion, la grande mutation*, Albin Michel, Paris, 1994.

26 The revival of secular fervour, a long-term factor in the rejection of 'ostentatious religious symbols' (such as the veil) in French state schools, should not be misleading on this point. This secularism is more a sign of defiance to the religion and culture of the other than to religion as such.

27 This is the approach taken by Olivier Carré in *L'Islam laïque ou le retour de la Grande Tradition*, Armand Colin, Paris, 1993. For Carré, the Muslim theologians forged a 'great tradition' at a very early stage, which separates political power from religious authority. 'Contemporary Islamic orthodoxy', he writes, 'the heir 'by default' of hesitant reformism from the fourteenth century, breaks with this old, and more open tradition to a certain extent. The Islamic extremists, Sunnis as well as Shiis, are pushing a short-term tradition to its limits, which, in truth, is only a distraction.' Cf. also Mohammed Cherif Ferjani, *Islam, laïcité et droits de l'homme*, L'Harmattan, Paris, 1991.

Notes on Chapter Five

1 Cf. notably Rifaat Sayyed Ahmed, *Les Représentations du pouvoir dans la pensée des groupes égyptiens radicaux*, unpublished.

2 This aroused the suspicion of the most radical factions, which notably highlighted the irony of the fact that the Muslim Brotherhood symbol represents 'a closed Quran and two sabres laid flat' (abandoned) while the symbol of the Gama'a Islamiyya is 'an open Quran and a raised sabre.'

3 A more-or-less formal group, made up of those close to Sayyed Qutb during his imprisonment, did exist; certain members of the organisation have joined this group today. On Tanzim al-Jihad, cf. Rifaat Sayyed Ahmed, *Le Prophète en armes: les révoltés*; t. 2, *Les Révolutionnaires*, Riad al Rayyes Books, London, 1991 (in Arabic); *Pourquoi ont-ils tué Sadate; histoire de l'organisation Jihad*, Dar al-Sharqiyya, Cairo, 1989, in Arabic. Cf. also Mostepha Hala, *L'Islam politique du réformisme à la violence*, Markaz al-dirasat al-siyasiyya wa'l-istratijiyya, Cairo, 1992, in Arabic; Genina No'mat Allah, 'The Jihad, an Islamic Alternative in Egypt', in *Cairo Papers in Social Science*, vol. 9, mono 2, AUC, summer 1986; Salah Ouardini, *Le Mouvement islamiste en Égypte, regard réaliste sur la période des années soixante-dix*, Markaz al-Hadara al-'Arabiyya li'l-'Ilam wa'l-Nashr, Cairo, 1986, in Arabic, and *Le Mouvement*

islamiste en Égypte; les données des années quatre-vingt, Markaz al-Hadara al-'Arabiyya li'l-'Ilam wa'l-Nashr, Cairo, 1989, in Arabic; Salah Ouardini, *Souvenirs d'un prisonnier politique: trois années sous la torture*, Markaz al-Hadhara al-arabia 'ilâme wal-nachr, Cairo, in Arabic.

4   At the beginning of the 1990s, it reminded everyone that it still existed by making an attempt on the life of the director of Torah Prison to pressurise the prison authorities. The attempted assassination of the Minister for the Interior, Hassan al Alfi, by a group that the police labelled Tal'iat al-Fath al-Islami (The Avant-garde of the Islamic Victory) from the name of a text found in the possession of some of the groups members, can however be attributed to it.

5   This group was created in circumstances under which, once again, the repressive option chosen by the regime played a decisive role. Cf. Burgat, *L'Islamisme au Maghreb*, pp. 111, 165.

6   *Ibid.*, pp. 256 ff.

7   On 18 February 1994, three officers with links to the Gama'a Islamiyya were condemned to death for planting a bomb in one of the alleys of the airbase at Sidi Barrani, close to the Libyan border, which President Mubarak often utilises.

8   Quran III-104: 'The formation of a community, whose members inspire good in men, that decrees what is proper and forbids what is blameful, is where you will find the content' (translated by D. Masson). This verse is interpreted very differently by the various Islamist groups. It is a polemic that, for example, in January 1989 pitted Adel Hussein, then chief editor of the weekly *Al-Sha'ab*, against 'Ala Muhieddin, the Gama'a Islamiyya spokesperson in Cairo (who was assassinated in September 1989). Muhieddin accused the joint leader of the PST for ignoring this essential principle – an accusation echoed by the Muslim Brotherhood. Hussein supported the widespread theory that for some it was wrongful to resort to violence in order to enforce it (*Al-Sha'ab*, January 5 1989). The rhetoric most often used to refute the recourse to force considers the deployment of violence as a more serious infringement than the one it is trying to stop. Cf. notably Baudouin Dupret, 'Autorité et consultation en Islam, présentation et traduction annotée des commentaires coraniques de Fakhr Eddine al-Razi, Rachid Redha et Sayyed Qutb concernant les versets III-104 et 159', *Arabica*, unpublished.

9   Garag is the author of the manifesto *L'Obligation absente*, in Arabic, that legitimised the assassination of those who do not govern according to the precepts revealed by God.

10 A native of the Sa'id in Egypt, the Nile valley to the south of the delta. The interview took place in room 25j of the halls of residence at Cairo University: Talaat Fouad al-Qassimi, interview with the author, Copenhagen, July 1994. The third part of the organisation responsible for the assassination of Sadat

was a small group led by a political science student by the name of Kamel Said al-Habib: interview with the author, Cairo, October 1993.

11   Talaat Fouad al-Qassimi: interview with the author, July 1994.

12   This incident is more a case of traditional social violence than of a specific style of the FIS (on the contrary, the mosques had tried to calm the population down that night). Other types of violence, which are just as real, focused notably on the wives of police officers, emerging as a vendetta in response to the systematic attacks by the army against the wives of *maquisards* and the acts of pure provocation by the Secret Services.

13   'This American writer gave a lavish description of the policies of the Moroccan government to neutralise the nationalists by segmenting their groups', wrote J. F. Clément about John Waterbury's *Commander of the Believers*. 'But he completely forgets to mention that there are secret police who practise torture, make men disappear and who put on show trials': 'Les Stratégies des régimes vis-à-vis des mouvements islamistes', IFRI seminar, January 13 1995, unpublished.

14   Cf. Ahmed Manaï, *Supplice tunisien: Le jardin secret du général Ben Ali*, La Découverte, Paris, 1995.

Notes on Chapter Six

1   Cf. notably Christian Decobert, *Le Mendiant et le Commandant*, Le Seuil, Paris, 1992.

2   Islamic law, we should remember, recognises the legitimacy of Christians, who are not prepared to accept Muhammed as a prophet; this is the opposite of canon law, which does not display the same 'courtesy'. To this day, the basis for Christian scholastic teaching in Egypt poses a problem, a fact recognised by some Catholic teachers. 'Even if the situation develops, we have effectively instilled a very unfavourable view of Islam in our young. Muhammed is considered as a sort of Antichrist and therefore all Muslims are condemned to hell': Assyut, interview with the author, Paris, December 1993.

3   Youssef Courbage and Philippe Fargues, *Chrétiens et juifs en Islam arabe et turc*, Fayard, Paris, 1992.

4   Cf. for example Bat Yeor, *Juifs et chrétiens sous l'Islam, Les dhimmis face au défi intégriste*, Berg International, Paris, 1994.

5   For Xavier de Planhol, there was no evidence of the practice of vendettas in pharaonic Egypt. It was imposed by the conquering Bedouin tribes: Xavier de Planhol, *Les Nations de l'Islam*, Fayard, Paris, 1993; Bernard Botiveau, 'Faits de vengeance et concurrence de systémes de droit', *Peuples méditerranéens* 41–2, 1988, pp. 153–66. There are signs of this logic of vendetta in the assassinations of police officers involved in the repression. Thus, one of the

members of the team responsible for the attack in July 1993 on the convoy that was (wrongly) supposed to be transporting the president of a military court that had sentenced seven people to death, came from the same small village (Hujairat, 20 kilometres from Qina) as the seven who had been executed the day before. On August 6, another military commander was attacked in the Qina region, for which the Gama'a claimed responsibility, as they did for the assassination attempt on the Minister of the Interior on 21 August in response to the death sentences passed on their members.

6   On 7 May 1992, for example, the report by the Egyptian Organisation for the Protection of Human Rights indicated that members of the Gama'a Islamiyya in the Dayrout region were 'preventing Christians from practising their faith', imposing by force a tax on Coptic commercial transactions and 'administering corporal punishment on those who broke the law'.

7   'We think that what is happening today between Christians and Muslims is mainly down to provocation', retorts a Gama'a Islamiyya leader. 'The regime provokes them so they have an excuse, in front of world opinion, to strike a blow to the Muslims. They need to be able to say that they are attacking the Christian minority': interview with the author.

8   Interview with the author, Cairo, November 1993.

9   Cf. the responses of Pope Shenouda to accusations regularly levelled at the political role of Copt emigration, in Mahmoud Fawzi, *Le Pape Chenouda et la communauté copte émigrée*, Dar al-Nachr-Hatier, Cairo, 1992.

10   Cf, for example the daily newspaper *Al-Wafd*, 21 April 1993.

11   Since the first reference for their denomination is their Egyptian quality. 'Coptic is only a late and abusive variant of "Egyptian", a word that the Greeks in Egypt in the eighth century based on the temple of Memphis, dedicated to the god Ptah. The Copts are nothing more than Egyptians': Pierre Bourguet, *Les Coptes*, coll. '*Que sais-je?*', PUF, Paris, 1988.

12   Laurent and Annie Chabry, *Politiques et minorités au Proche-Orient; les raisons d'une explosion*, Maisonneuve et Larose, Paris, 1987, p. 52.

13   *Ibid.*, p. 54, 'This was seen more in truly Arab countries than in the future Turkey, where the Ottoman elites (particularly the military elites) had fairly close contact with Western culture.'

14   Guyomarch also underlines in particular that 'communal solidarity does not mean, on either side, that people of the same confessional group no longer exploit each other': Claude Guyomarch, 'Assiut epicentre de la sedition confessionnelle en Egypte', in Gilles Kepel (ed.), *Exils et royaumes, les appartenances au monde arabo-musulman aujourd'hui*, Presses de la FNSP, Paris, 1994, pp. 30, 173.

15   *Ibid.*

16   Although it was extremely rare, this became part of their strategy. In 1992, one exile in the US went as far as to claim the creation of 'a Coptic govern-ment in exile', indeed of an independent Coptic State in upper Egypt, of

which Assyut was the capital. It was a provocation that Pope Shenouda was obviously quick to condemn.

17 On the Copts and politics, cf. notably Carter, *The Copts in Egyptian Politics 1918–1952*, American University in Cairo Press, Cairo, 1986. For a study of the internal dynamics of the community, cf. Dina Khawaga, *Le Renouveau copte: la communauté comme acteur politique*, doctoral thesis, IEP, Paris, 1993 (unpublished).

18 Alternatively, the Christians rather carelessly allowed themselves to become embroiled in the repression against the Islamist current. Therefore, in 1992, the only Copt woman in the Egyptian Parliament (nominated by the President of the Republic to facilitate the representation of minorities) accepted a report of European legislation to reinforce the repressive measures of President Mubarak's regime against 'Islamic terrorism'.

19 Alain Roussillon, 'Entre al-Jihad et al-Rayyan: phénoménologie de l'islamisme égyptien', *Maghreb-Machreq Monde arabe* 127, March 1990, p. 23. 'Violence', Roussillon also notes, 'appears to be that much more prevalent and central to the practises of Islamist groups, on the whole, than the "territories" and "populations" that are more accessible to enquiry – due to the Islamist mistrust of investigations by journalists and social scientists – provided by imprisoned militants or minutes of the trials where they face charges of "subversion" or attempting to unseat the regime'.

20 See, for example, this declaration: 'It is also possible that there was a pact between the Christian extremists and the police, a pact that would breed this type of incident': Talaat Fouad al-Qassimi, interview with the author, July 1994.

21 This appears in his introduction to the report *L'Annuaire de la nation*, presented and translated by François Burgat and Baudouin Dupret in *Égypte-Monde arabe* 11. See also 'Les conditions du dialogue Islam-Occident', interview recorded and translated by F. Burgat, *Égypte-Monde arabe* 7, 1991.

22 Cf. notably the interviews with Pope Shenouda granted to the journalist Mahmoud Fawzi: *Le Pape Chenouda et la bataille au sein de l'Église*, Dar al Nachr-Hatier, Cairo, 1992; *Le Pape Chenouda et la communauté copte immigré*. 'People are demanding the imposition of the sharia without knowing its opinion on many matters. For the moment, the word sharia is open to many interpretations and the religious leaders are still debating many issues, such as the banking interest, etc. Before we talk of imposing the sharia, we should be absolutely certain of its views on women and many other questions. Do working women insult religion, as some people say? Should she simply sit at home, her sole function being to raise the children? This is the point of view, defended for example by Sheikh Shaarawi, that other Muslims fear. If Muslim law is to be imposed, must the Imam and the Head of State be the same person? Must the Imam also be the prince, as was the case for the four Caliphs? What will be the government's attitude to treaties and agreements?

Could we reach an agreement with the Jews? The Muslims are not unanimous on these subjects. As another example, what does the sharia say about art, dance and music?'

23 For a critical review of the position of the Church and the Coptic community, cf. Rafiq Habib, *Le Christianisme politique; introduction aux courants politiques chez les coptes*, Iafa li'l-dirasat wa'l-nashr, Cairo, 1990.

24 Conference held by Mgr Georges Khodr at the headquarters of the review Minbar al-Sharq, in Heliopolis, February 1993. Mgr Khodr is the Greek Orthodox bishop of the Byblos and Batrun region in Lebanon. He encourages dialogue with the Muslim community, as he has been one of the principal intermediaries since the beginning of the 1960s, developing contact with the Shiite Imam Musa al-Sadr (and later Fadlallah) as well as with Sobhi Saleh and Joachim Mubarak. A member of the permanent Commission for dialogue between the Churches based at the former abbey at Balamand (Belmont), he has written many non-conformist works that he expresses notably on the first page of the daily paper *An Nahar*.

25 These meetings were suspended after an article appeared in the London daily newspaper *Al-Hayat*, which publicised the meetings when the participants wanted to maintain their anonymity.

26 Cf. Mona Makram Ubeid, *Allocutions et prises de position*, Hay'at al-Masriyya li'l-Kitab, Cairo, 1992, in Arabic. Other formulae emerged, such as the one used by Father Khodr, who likes to say 'perhaps I am not a Muslim but nevertheless, I am Islamic.'

27 'Communisme, nationalisme, islamisme: itinéraire d'un intellectual Egyptien', interview with Adel Hussein presented by François Burgat in *Égypte-Monde arabe* 5, March 1991.

28 Interview with the author, Amman, October 1991.

Notes on Chapter Seven

1 Tareq al-Bishri, *L'Annuaire de la nation*.

2 Olivier Carré, *Mystique et politique: Lecture révolutionnaire du Coran par Sayyed Qutb, frère musulman radical*, Presses de la FNSP/Editions du Cerf, Paris, 1984.

3 'Remous sur le Nil', *Le Monde*, 28 November 1992.

4 To put the matter in perspective, the explanation for the attacks on tourists in Egypt that was offered to French readers were as close to reality as blaming Georges Marchais for the attacks of Action Directe or Jean Lecanuet for a strike by the CGT trade union.

5 At this time there were 9 political parties in Egypt (10 as of April 1992: cf. note 7), which were, excluding the new arrivals, the National Democratic Party in power, the Socialist Worker's Party (Islamist), the Neo-Wafd (liberal),

the Progressive Unionist Alliance (Marxist-Nasserist), the Socialist Liberal Party (several antagonistic tendencies) and the Umma Party (support restricted to kinship network).

6   Young Egypt, an illegitimate resurgence of the party formed by the brother of Adel Hussein in 1933 (see Chapter 2).

7   Since then, at the beginning of April 1992, one of the Nasserist tendencies has obtained its legal status, yet an 'Arab Socialist Party' had its application refused on the grounds that its programme did not differ sufficiently from those of the existing parties.

8   This happened mainly because the government would have been unable to take the decision to enforce the ban announced in 1949.

9   Cf. notably Imane Farag, 'Le politique à l'égyptienne: lecture des élections législatives', Maghreb-Machreq 133, September 1991.

10   The Islamists won the election to the executive body of the lawyers' trade union on 13 September 1992. They achieved a similar majority in the trade unions for doctors and engineers.

11   In fact, it did not succeed: from then on, the associations' finances, primarily distributed through unofficial channels, were even less likely to be seized. On the social movement, see Sarah Ben Nefissa-Paris, 'Le mouvement associatif égyptien et l'Islam: éléments d'une problématique', Maghreb-Machreq 135, January 1992, p. 19.

12   Sheikh Ali Gad al-Haqq objected to this; consequently this question clearly became an increasingly contentious issue between the leader of the main institution of 'domesticated' Islam under Atif Sidqi's government, under-lining the mounting problems for the regime in maintaining its control over the power of the universities, which ultimately exposed its political shortcomings.

The conditions under which he preferred to call off the conciliatory meetings between a commission of moderate religious personalities and the leaders of the Gama'a Islamiyya – a process that he was more afraid of not being able to control than the supposed convergence between 'moderates' and 'extremists' – is a good illustration of the growing fragility of the distinction between the reputedly 'non-oppositional' Islam of state institutions and the Islamists who were decidedly oppositional. In the same way, several tens of thousands of people representing state Islam as well as the Islamists in opposition, notably the Labour Party and the Muslim Brotherhood, all took part in a meeting at the Azhar in support of Bosnian Muslims where, despite the absence of Sheikh Gad al-Haq, who cancelled at the last minute, the demarcation line between institutional Islam and the currents of the opposition once more seemed particularly vague.

13   Previously, the first recorded victim of the repression against the Gama'a Islamiyya was a student killed on a protest march against the Shah of Iran's arrival in Cairo.

14 Mahjoub was shot instead of the Minister of the Interior, Abdelhalim Musa, who was in a nearby procession. The attack had been preceded in December 1989 by the aborted attempt on Zaki Badr's life. A small group of dissidents from the Gama'a (Al-Naji'un min al-Nar, 'the refugees from hell') whose leaders were arrested in July 1993 after five years on the run, first in Libya, then in Egypt, had themselves tried to assassinate a former minister of the interior as well as the Director of the weekly government publication, Al-Musawwar.

15 Markaz Ibn Khaldun, 'Civil Society and the Democratic Transition in the Arab World', Annual Report 1992, Dar Sa'ad al Sabah, Cairo, 1993, p. 72, in Arabic. Sixty percent of the detainees were considered by the investigating judge to have no connection with the act. See also 'The Security Policy: Political Criminality and Social Criminality', in L'Annuaire de la nation 2, quoted in Égypte-Monde arabe, 1994, in Arabic, translated by Baudouin Dupret. The number of arrests made between 1 March 1986 and 9 February 1989 was officially estimated at 12,472. The prosecution files reveal that the courts returned 12,447 verdicts of mistrial, about 70 percent of which were contested by the Ministry of the Interior.

16 Even the strategic official report by the research centre at al-Ahram had long suggested that the violence between the state and the Islamists was not always as reciprocal as the communiqués of the Ministry of the Interior led us to believe when they talked about the 'difficult' arrests that ended in the death of the accused: 'La violence politique en Egypte, rapport stratégique d'Al-Ahram 1989', Égypte-Monde arabe 4, 1991.

17 This in fact made him rejoice: Le Nouvel Observateur, 7–13 February 1991. The assassination of 'Ala Muhieddin is one of the better known examples of these outbursts, as is the cold-blooded murder of the young Imam Arafa Derwish, who was killed in August 1992 on the minbar of the Sanabu mosque during the Friday call to prayer. The various accounts given to the author mention that procedures were manipulated, and skirmishes allowed marksmen to hit predetermined targets.

18 Embaba, une image intense de la détérioration de l'état des droits de l'homme et du respect de la loi en Égypte, Cairo, 20 March 1993; this report also deals with the abuse attributed to the members of the Gama'a Islamiyya living in the area. See also the Amnesty International report of 23 June 1993, Les Sévères Atteintes aux droits de l'homme en Egypte, in which the organisation writes: 'There has been a sharp rise in the number of murders committed by the security forces over the past twelve months. Amnesty International recorded twenty-nine murders in March 1993 alone [...] Amnesty fears that some, if not the majority of the deaths at the hands of the police, were in reality illegal murders, resulting from the abusive and unjustified use of weapons designed to kill. Some of the killings bear all the hallmarks of extra-judiciary executions, or the deliberate murder of people who presented no danger at the time of their murder.'

19 *Al-Musawwar*, 28 May 1993.

20 It is in this type of demonstration that the strength of the oppositional Islam movement should be measured, rather than in the methods of action that are both more 'modern' – placards, slogans, strikes and votes – and more openly oppositional.

21 On 11 March 1993 a violent clampdown by police led to the deaths of 10 Islamists in Imbaba. In Aswan, police laying siege to a mosque fired on the gathering, killing 16 and wounding several others.

22 In autumn 1992 a number of matters concerning state security were referred to military courts by a presidential decree. On 8 December the administrative court of the State Council adjourned the application of this decree, declaring it illegal on the grounds that such affairs had absolutely nothing to do with the Egyptian armed forces. On 30 January the constitutional court ruled on the contrary, saying that by virtue of the urgency of the situation the president was within his rights to seize the military courts for certain crimes, and ordered the execution of the death penalties pronounced in the meantime by the court in Alexandria.

23 Cf. notably *The Missing Truth*, an allusion to *The Missing Obligation*, the pamphlet by Abdessalam Farag, Dar al-Fikr, Cairo, 1986, in Arabic. Fodha was shot down by a team of two young motorcyclists, one of whom, Abdesshafi' Ahmed Ramadan, was arrested on the spot.

24 Hujairat wa Humairat, 25 kilometres to the south of Qina. A part of the village was bulldozed by the police to force the inhabitants to reveal where the suspects were hiding.

25 A review, *Al-Murabitun*, once published in Pakistan, is still available in Europe.

Notes on Chapter Eight

1 Mohammed Harbi, 'L'ambivalence des relations franco-algériennes', *Le Monde*, 20 August 1994.

2 Cf. Ahmed Rouadjia, *Grandeur et décadence de l'Etat algérien*, Karthala, Paris, 1994; Lahouari Addi, *L'Impasse du populisme: L'Algérie: collectivité politique et État en construction*, ENAL, Algiers, 1990, and *L'Algérie et la démocratie: Pouvoir et crise du politique dans l'Algérie contemporaine*, La Découverte, Paris, 1994; Ignace Leverrier, 'Le Front Islamique du salut entre la hâte et la patience', in Gilles Kepel (ed.), *Les Politiques de Dieu*, Le Seuil, Paris, 1993; Séverine Labat, 'Islamismes et islamistes en Algérie, un nouveau militantisme', in Gilles Kepel (ed.), *Exils et royaumes, les appartenances au monde arabo-musulman*, Presses de la FNSP, Paris, 1994.

3 Jacques Verges, *Lettre à des amis algériens devenus tortionnaires*, Albin Michel, Paris, 1993; cf. also the collective accounts of Reporters sans Frontières, *Le Drame algérien*, La Découverte, Paris, 1994.

4   The results of the first round: 7,822,625 voted out of the 13,258,554 registered. The FIS gained 47.27 percent of the votes cast (24.54 percent of the electoral roll), far ahead of the FLN (23.58 and 12.17 percent respectively) and the FFS (7.40 and 3.85 percent respectively). The RCD received only 200,267 votes (2.90 and 1.51 percent respectively).

5   Pierre Guillard, *Ce fleuve qui nous sépare: lettre ouverte à l'imam Ali Ben-hadj*, Loysel, Paris, 1994.

6   Seventeen by the FIS, 30 by the FFS and 34 by the MDA of Ben Bella.

7   The Council comprised Prime Minister Sid Ahmed Ghozali, Minister for Foreign Affairs Lakhdar Brahimi, Minister for Justice Hamdani Benkhelli, Minister for Defence General Khaled Nezzar, Minister for the Interior General Larbi Belkheir, and Chief of Staff Abdelmalek Guenaizia.

8   This acronym was also used by the Algerian Islamist Movement led in the 1980s by Mustapha Bouyali, who was killed in 1987. Its activists, whose resurgence was witnessed in 1991, were pardoned by President Ben Jedid on 1 November 1989. Apparently they then disbanded and joined other armed groups, the MIA as well as the AIG (cf. *infra*).

9   In the almost total silence of the French-speaking press that supported the eradication option, as highlighted by Abed Charef in *Algérie, le grand dérapage*, L'Aube, La Tour-d'Aigues, 1994. On the ambivalence of the status of 'French-speaking' intellectuals and the origins of their relative marginalisation, cf. the articles of Gilbert Grandguillaume and Lahouari Addi in *Esprit*, January 1995.

10 One of these first armed groups made its existence known in autumn 1991 by an attack on a border station in the El-Oued region.

11 Sa'id Mekhloufi, who became the leader of one of the largest armed groups, took this option.

12 The first assassination claimed by the AIG was that of former Prime Minister Kasdi Merbah (cf. *infra*).

13 There is no proof that these groups were truly united or that they shared a common doctrine. In May 1994, several pro-FIS groups, for example those of Abderazaq Rajjam and Mohammed Sa'id, elected to form an alliance with the AIG, underlining that the ideological and political differences between the different armed branches were not insurmountable. Some members of the ISA returned to the AIG after the signing of the platform of Rome in January 1995. The Secret Services had been attempting for a long time to stir up discord in the Islamist camp by inventing a war that had a minimal effect, inciting 'scores to be settled' within the movement, in order to try and pit the different factions against each other.

14 The AIG was careful to distance itself from the murder of two Spanish nuns in August 1994.

15 Rachid Mimouni, *Le Monde*, 18 May 1994, p. 2: 'The terrorists have sworn to kill the Algerian intellectuals one by one. This is not an idle threat as twelve

of them have already been assassinated … This is the first time in history that we have seen a terrorist movement call for the eradication of a country's entire intelligentsia, as if it were a weed or an illness. Their intention is to brainwash the country.'

16 Cf. Verges, *Lettre à des amis algériens devenus tortionnaires*; the collection edited by a 'Comité algérien des militants libres de la dignité humaine et des droits de l'homme' (affiliated to the Islamists), *Livre blanc sur la répression en Algérie (1991-1994)*, Éditions Hoggar, Plan-les-Ouates, 1995, t. 1.

17 Rachid Mimouni, *De la Barbarie en général et de l'intégrisme en particulier*, Le Pré-aux-clercs, Paris, 1992 (Prix Albert-Camus).

18 Rachid Boudjedra, *Fils de la haine*, Denoël, Paris, 1992.

19 Cf. notably Malek Bennabi, *Vocation de l'Islam*, Le Seuil, Paris, 1954, and *Mémoires d'un témoin du siècle*, 2 vols, ENA, Algiers, 1965.

20 Authors of Reporters sans Frontières, *Le Drame algérien*, who pay particular attention to the historical roots of the present situation by analysing the 'five pillars' – manipulation of history, military security, oil wealth, corruption and regionalism – of the 'paradoxical dictatorship' that has governed Algeria with an iron hand for more than 30 years. Its publication, however, seemed to have little effect on the tone of the audio-visual press. On the mechanisms of misinformation by the French media, cf. also Rabha Attaf and Fausto Giudice, 'La grande peur bleue', *Les Cahiers de l'Orient*, March 1995.

21 The report was extremely cautious, if not to say timid. It is interesting to note that there was serious tension between the members of the humanitarian organisation regarding the violent repression in Algeria and Egypt. In Belgium, some of its members refused to be associated with the condemnation of the repression against the Islamists.

22 Admittedly, this logic reached its limits when – after the hijacking of the Air France Airbus in December 1994 – the increased activity of the armed groups cast doubt in the minds of international opinion that the military regime was able to control its own security forces, and thus conversely attested to the popular support that the Islamists had acquired.

23 Cf. notably Hamid Barrada, '1993: l'assassinat de Kasdi Merbah', in *Le Drame algérien*, p. 98.

24 Some blind reprisals were probably inflicted on the families of activists who had 'repented', or were declared to have done by the police. Vendettas became more commonplace in the structure of the disturbances.

25 *Politis*, 2 July 1992.

26 *Ibid.*

27 Anyone who dared to interpret the dominant perceptions was at risk of being labelled as a 'friend of the cut-throats', as quoted by Rachid Boudjedra on 17 December 1994 on the airwaves of France Culture radio station.

28 The confessions extracted under torture of the prime suspects of this attack have never convinced observers. Cf. notably Verges, *Lettre à des amis algériens*

devenus tortionnaires; José Garçon, 'L'attentat de l'aéroport', in *Le Drame algérien*, p. 186

29 The two women whose 'throats were cut because they refused a temporary marriage' (September 1994) were in fact part of a *mujahidin* family. Most of the arson attacks on businesses are also suspect, as many of them burnt down while subject to a financial evaluation before privatisation. Some districts – even some entire regions – have been punished for voting for the FIS by the suspension of civil servants' salaries, the destruction of the public infrastructure, the confiscation of vehicles, and the embargo on essential medicines etc.

30 The last, but by no means the least, of these are the confessions of a group of Algerian policemen who were in hiding in France. They made sensational claims that the state had a planned programme of terrorism. Dozens of policemen chosen from the particularly popular civil servants in the respective districts were killed by the military security 'to shock and revolt people'. The police militia were involved in all manner of extortion, notably the robbery of jewellers: *Le Monde*, 7 March 1995, report by Dominique Le Guilledoux.

31 It was by chance that this information came out at a public debate in France about Algeria. At the back of the room, having heard one of the eradicators from Algiers use a name that was all too familiar to her, a young Algerian women in tears shouted out: 'First of all, S. was my friend. It was her boyfriend who killed her because she wanted to leave him.' The death of S., 'assassinated for refusing to wear the veil', had 'justified' the shooting a few days later of two female students who had chosen to wear it.

32 *La Nation*, 5 November 1994.

Notes on Chapter Nine

1 On the Islamists in Palestine, see 'Iyad Barghouti, *Islamisation and Politics in the Palestinian Territories*, Markaz az-zahra li'l-abhath wa'l-dirasat, Al-Quds, 1990; Khaled al-Hroub, *Les islamistes en Palestine*, Dar al-Bachîr, Amman, 1994; Aouni Jadou' al-'Ubeidi, *Les frères musulmans en Jordanie et en Palestine, 1945–1970*, Sahafat tarikhiyya, Amman, 1991; Mohsen Mohammed Salah, *Le courant islamique en Palestine et son influence sur la lutte, 1917–1948*, Maktabat al-Falah li'l-nashr wa'l-tauzi', Kuwait, 1998; Abdelkader Yassine, *Hamas, le mouvement de la résistance islamique en Palestine*, Dar Sîna li'l-nashr, Cairo, 1990; Jean-François Legrain, *Les Voix du soulèvement*, CEDEJ, Cairo, 1991; *Maghreb-Machreq* 121, 1991.

2 On the question of Jerusalem, read Agnès Levallois and Sophie Pommier, *Jérusalem; le poids du passé. Histoire et spiritualité*, Michalon, Paris, 1995.

3 Sheikh Nasrallah (General Secretary of Hizbullah): interview with the author, Beirut, 27 July 1992. Ibrahim Rocha (Hamas): interview with the

author, Amman, July 1994. Mahmoud Zahar (Hamas): interview with the author, Gaza, July 1994. On the position of Hamas, see notably the monthly *Falastin Muslima*, London.

4   Cf. Jean-François Legrain, 'Gaza-Jéricho, un accord contre la paix', *Libération*, 7 March 1994; Jean-François Lapaille, 'Bantoustans palestiniens et terrorisme', *Libération*, 28 October 1994. Compartmentalisation has led to an increasing number of terms of status: 'autonomous' Palestinians (Gaza, Jericho), Palestinians 'still under occupation' (West Bank), 'annexed' Palestinians (Jerusalem), Palestinians 'of Israeli nationality' (Israel), Palestinians who have lost their right to residence, Palestinians 'removed' in 1967 and Palestinians 'of the Diaspora of 1948'; to each category its rights or the absence of any rights, its hopes or the hopelessness of any hope.' On the history of the conflict, cf. François Massoulié, *Les Conflits du Proche-Orient*, Casterman, Paris, 1993.

5   Six of the 38 prerogatives of Israel were handed over to the provisional Authority: taxation, tourism, health, education, culture and social affairs.

6   Lapaille, 'Bantoustans palestiniens et terrorisme'.

7   The Democratic Front for the Liberation of Palestine (led by Nayef Hawatmeh) and the Popular Front for the Liberation of Palestine (led by Georges Habash).

Notes on Chapter Ten

1   The ban extends to the creation of parties based on language or a particular region, the theory behind this legislation being to protect the states from any ethno-religious separatism.

2   Cf. *supra*.

3   Cf. for example Francis Ghiles in the *Financial Times*, 6 June 1991, whose analysis follows the somewhat surprising credo of the principal Western analysts: 'Within twenty-four hours, the Fundamentalist Front (FIS) have managed to derail President Ben Jedid's plan to hold the first free elections in three weeks' time'.

4   Plantu depicted the FIS militants as sinister bearded men who were annoyed by the words 'tolerance', 'freedom' and 'democracy' written on the placards of democrats demonstrating in Algiers. After examining a copy of the Quran, they finished by saying 'these words are not in the dictionary'. The French gendarmes killed in August 1994 had come, said Plantu, to uphold 'liberté, égalité, fraternité', which their assassins could not tolerate, and were quoted as saying 'They're after us!'. In the same way, the parents of those children wearing the Islamic veil at a French school were reputedly shocked to hear their children extolling virtues such as 'democracy', 'tolerance' and 'dialogue'.

5   Hassan al-Banna denounced the disunity of political forces inherent to the monarchical system; he believed Machiavellian politicking was a reason

for the division and weakness of the nationalist movement. For the well-documented historical list of positions of the classical Islamic doctrine and the view of modern Islamists on the notion of pluralism and democracy, see notably Gudrun Kramer, 'Démocratie et démocratisation au Proche-Orient', *Islam et pluralisme*, Cahiers du CEDEJ, Cairo, 1992, which pays particular attention to the divisions caused by Rached Ghannouchi.

6 Sami Naï'r, *Libération*, 1 August 1994, p. 7.

7 He said this in a piece published by his newspaper at the time, *Al Munqidh* 23 and 24: extracts appear in Mohammed Al-Ahnaf, op. cit., pp. 95ff.

8 *Ibid.*, p. 94.

9 Mohammed Al-Ahnaf, Bernard Botiveau and Franck Frégosi, *L'Algérie par ses islamistes*, Karthala, Paris, 1991.

10 *Al-Ta'ifa al-Mansura*, the AIG newsletter, 1, 1994.

11 Cf. notably Abdessalam Yassime, *The Islamist Movement and Partisan Activity*, Cairo, 1988, in Arabic.

12 'It is an off-hand decision, an unconsidered proposal, to equate democracy and infidelity': correspondence with the author, 21 March 1992.

13 *Ibid.*

14 Ghassan Salamé, 'Sur la causalité d'un manque: pourquoi le monde arabe n'est-il pas démocratique?', *Revue Française des Sciences Politiques*, 1991, p. 301. 'The terms seemed more palatable to us when the Islamists began to tackle the democratic question having rid it of the controversial culturalist burden (Tareq al-Bishri and Adel Hussein amongst others) by avoiding its imitation and its condemnation [...] It is also interesting to see that the Islamic Republic of Iran was founded, among other precepts, on electoral legitimacy, even if it often appears that the duality between religious legitimacy and electoral legitimacy is not harmonious.'

15 *L'Hebdo libéré*, 23 June 1993, cited by Jacques Verges, *Lettre à des amis algériens devenus tortionnaires*, Albin Michel, Paris, 1993.

16 Original transcription of an interview by Hamid Barrada, Jeune Afrique Plus, July 1990.

17 Cf. notably Gudrun Krämer, 'La démocratie et l'Islam', *Al-Wafd*, 16 January 1992: debate between Ma'moun 'Odheibi, Ahmad Omar Hashem, Hassan Douh and Mohammed 'Amara.

18 Cf. the enlightening remarks of Jean Leca on the 'familiar problem throughout history of how an institution or an idea, developed in a historical context, can be put in another context and from its interpretation in another system of ideas': François Burgat and Jean Leca, 'Les élections algériennes et la mobilisation islamiste', *Maghreb-Machreq-Monde Arabe*, September 1990. Cf. also Jean Leca, 'Democratisation and Social Tensions in the Third World', in *Democratisation in the Arab World: Uncertainty, Vulnerability and Legitimacy. A Tentative Conceptualisation and Some Hypotheses*, University of Madras and Indian Political Science Association, 1992; Jean-Claude Vatin,

'Démocratie et démocratisation dans le monde arabe', in *Les Partis pris démocratiques*. *Perceptions occidentales de la démocratisation dans le monde arabe*, CEDEJ, Cairo, 1992.

19 Cf. the introduction to the two schools of thought in Azadeh Kian, *L'Islam est-il véritablement incompatible avec la démocratie?* (unpublished). The first school of thought identifies with Sheikh Fazlollah Nouri (1843–1919), who believed the constitutionalism imported from the West to be incompatible with Islam; the other school identifies with the constitutionalist Mirza Mohammed Hossein Na'ini, for whom at least a part of the power, the political arena, that he clearly distinguishes from the religious arena, can be attributed unreservedly to the sovereign but must be shared out equally between the sovereign and the people, while the *'ulama* ensure that any legislation conforms to Islamic laws.

20 'O you men! I created you from a man and a woman. I placed you in peoples and tribes so that you would get to know one another.'

21 Krämer, 'La démocratie et l'Islam', p. 341. Cf. an example of a liberal inter- pretation of the political articulation of religion by the Iranian, Abdolkarim Soroush, who believed that ('mysterious' and 'surprising') religion should never be confused with the 'dress tailor-made for a particular society' that is an ideology, and that on the contrary, as a condition for its 'freshness' and survival, it should be the source of many and contradictory inter- pretations in a climate of freedom and exchange between the various schools of thought, cited by Azadeh Kian, *L'Islam est-il véritablement incompatible avec la démocratie?*

22 In *Les Libertés publiques dans l'État islamique*, Markaz al-Wahda al-Arabiyya, Beirut, 1993, he sets out with particular clarity the connections that assure communication between the symbolic and the judicial.

23 This is a term applying to everyone who does not believe in the revelations transmitted to Muhammed.

24 Interview in the Algerian weekly *Horizons*, 22 August 1991, pp. 1, 12. See also his work *Les Libertés publiques dans l'État islamique*, in which he declares: 'We are prepared to respect any legally elected body, even if it is Communist.' Rached Ghannouchi was one of the first Islamists to adopt such a position.

25 Letter dated 20 January 1995.

26 Note in this speech, the position taken by Adel Hussein, the former editor of the weekly *Al-Sha'ab*, in the article 'Nationalisme, communisme, islamisme: itinéraire d'un intellectuel égyptien', *Égypte-Monde arabe* 5, March 1991. The Egyptian Muslim Brotherhood made its position clear on the question of pluralism and the role of women in *La Femme musulmane dans la société musulmane*. *La chûra et le pluripartisme*, Éditions Tawhid, Lyons, 1995, translated by Tareq Ramadan. Cf. also the relatively broad range of positions taken by Egyptian Islamist members of the Muslim Brotherhood (Mohammed 'Amara, Tareq al-Bishri, Mohammed al-Ghazali, Ibrahim Shukri, Fahmi

Huweidy, Kamel Abu al-Majd, Khaled Mohammed Khaled, Mustapha Mashhur, Ahmed Bahgat) on the question of democracy in *Amru Abd Al-Sami*, *The Islamists: Dialogues On The Future*, Maktabat al-Turath al-Islami, Cairo, 1992, in Arabic.

27 And 'if it exists, what does it comprise?': Leonard Binder, *Islamic Liberalism, a Critique of Development Ideologies*, Chicago–London, 1988, cited by Krämer, 'La démocratie et l'Islam'.

28 Ali Abd al-Razzaq, *L'Islam et les fondements du pouvoir*, La Découverte-CEDEJ, Paris–Cairo, 1994, translated and introduced by Abdou Filali-Ansari.

29 Chérif Ferjani, 'La Laïcité et les pièges du culturalisme', *Passerelles* 3, p. 107.

30 This is the theme of the works by the Egyptian magistrate Muhammed Saïd al-Ashmawy, notably in *L'Islamisme contre l'Islam*, preface and translation from Arabic by Richard Jacquemond, La Découverte-Al Fikr, Paris–Cairo, 1990; Fouad Zakariya, *Laïcité et islamisme: les Arabes à l'heure du choix*, presented and translated from Arabic by Richard Jacquemond, La Découverte-Dar al-Fikr, Paris–Cairo, 1990. Cf. also Olivier Carré, *L'islam laïque ou le retour de la Grande Tradition*, Armand Colin, Paris, 1993; Chérif Ferjani, *Islam, laïcité et les droits de l'homme*, L'Harmattan, Paris, 1991.

31 'If one type of culture or intellectual activity is favoured', he continues, 'the question of religion and politics in Islam will encounter serious problems': Mohammed Arkoun, interview conducted by Thierry Fabre, *Al Qantara 2*, January 1992.

32 Jean Bauberot, *Religions et laïcité dans l'Europe des Douze*, Syros, Paris, 1994.

33 For recent examples of reasoning designed to reconcile Islam with pluralism, cf. in particular Rached Ghannouchi, collection of interviews with Qusaï Salah Darwish: Khalil Media Service, London, 1992, in Arabic; cf. also Mohammed 'Amara, 'Concepts islamiques: l'islam et le pluralisme', *Al-'Arabi*, Kuwait, June 1992, p. 97; Rifaat Sid Ahmed, 'Islam and Pluralism', *Minbar al-Sharq* 1, Cairo, March 1992, in Arabic.

34 This does not mean that we should not be aware of them, however. On the two most sensitive questions – the role of women and political pluralism – the Egyptian Muslim Brotherhood attempted to clarify their position by publishing a policy statement which had the advantage of being based on more than mere conjecture and fantasy to justify their standpoint: The Muslim Brotherhood, *La Question de la femme et pluralisme politique*, translated by Tareq Ramadan, FCM, Geneva, 1994.

35 Interview in *Horizons*, 18 November 1990. 'As a Muslim', Nahnah concluded, 'we are expected to find wisdom wherever we can as long as it does not go against our faith. If this point of view tallies with the democrats in this country or elsewhere, then we are the first to call for democracy, but not the Greek version, which has divided society, nor the Roman version which imposed a military regime, we would rather follow the Islamic vision which the weakest people the right to express themselves.'

36 That is to say, the temptation faced by political groups in power with the backing of a solid majority to rule whilst neglecting minority interests.

37 Mohsen Toumi, *La Tunisie de Bourguiba à Ben Ali*, PUF, Paris, 1988, p. 38.

Notes on Chapter Eleven

1 A declaration made on the radio station RTL in 1994.

2 Open conference at the University of Geneva, 1994.

3 'We should not hide the fact that a compromise between the regimes and the Islamists could have a very heavy price for women. Is it right to talk of democratisation about a system of apartheid that is based on sexual discrimination?': Michel Camau, 'Démocratisation et changement des régimes au Maghreb', in *Elecciones, particpacion y transiciones politicas en el Norte de Africa*, Instituto de cooperacion con el mundo arabe, Madrid, 1991, p. 67.

4 Sa'ida Rahal Sidhoum, 'Le Deuil et le fardeau ... la férocité en sus', *Confluences Méditerranées* 11, summer 1994: Are we seriously trying to suggest that the exclusion of women from public life or their subordination to men have been caused by the emergence and then the development of Islamist movements? ... To simply point the finger of blame at the radical Islamist discourse for the way women are treated, an indigestible mixture of unimaginative anathema and spiritless religiosity, without re-examining the male-female relationship in Algeria, is pure manipulation and poppycock.'

5 Cf. Mohammed Al-Ahnaf, Bernard Botiveau and Franck Fregosi, *L'Algérie par ses islamistes*, Karthala, Paris, 1991, p. 239. 'The question of women is undoubtedly the stumbling block that the Islamist movement in Algeria and elsewhere will encounter.' However, this peremptory announcement did not stop the authors from acknowledging a more complex reality a few lines further down, noting that 'Hassan al-Banna, the founder of the association of Muslim Brothers and a contemporary of the first Egyptian feminist association, has had nothing to say, as far as we know, about this movement'; and that 'if it was the old guard in their turbans at the Azhar and Zeitouna who ensured woman's removal from public life and who controlled their behaviour, everyone who thought that social change was an absolute necessity for the Arab world and that it would be better to be part rather than a victim of it, has seen the evolution of the status of women as something that is both desirable and inevitable'.

6 Even if there is no precise norm on this issue, the veil worn by female Islamist militants is generally a sign of the distance taken from one's traditional background.

7 An expression used by former French Prime Minister Michel Rocard when the 'headscarf affair' first surfaced in 1989.

8   As a method of intimidation, the families of militants of the Egyptian Gama'a Islamiyya – including their mothers and sisters – are regularly arrested. In the particularly conservative rural areas, during the waves of arrests and interrogations, the 'honour' of many women is doubted. Cf. for example the 'letter from a soldier' in the article 'Cacher une politique; les représentations de la violence en Egypte', *Maghreb-Machreq-Monde Arabe* 142, 1993.

9   This is particularly the case in Iran, even if the situation there is only slightly comparable to the situation in the rest of the Arab world where the Islamists are not in the majority: cf. Fariba Adelkhah, 'Logique étatique et pratiques populaires: la polysémie du hijab chez les femmes islamiques en Iran', *Les Cahiers du CEMOTI* 10, 1990, and *Une approche anthropologique de l'Iran postrévolutionnaire: le cas des femmes islamiques*, EHESS, Paris, 1990, published in 1992 by Karthala under the title *Revolution Behind The Veil*. For a completely contrasting view, cf. Chala Chafiq, *La Femme et le retour de l'islam, l'expérience iranienne*, Editions du Félin, Paris, July 1991; Andrea B. Rugh, 'Reshaping Personal Relations in Egypt', in Martin E. Marty and Scott Appleby, *The Fundamentalism Project, Fundamentalisms and Society*, University of Chicago Press, Chicago, IL and London, 1992. For a more systematic bibliography, cf. Mireille Paris, 'Femmes et sociétés dans le monde arabo-musulman, état bibliographique', *Travaux et documents de l'IREMAM* 9, Aix-en-Provence, 1989.

10 Cf. the problematic developed by Nilüfer Göle, *Musulmanes et modernes: Voile et civilisation en Turquie*, La Découverte, Paris, 1993.

11 Tozy is renowned for 'Islam et Etat au Maghreb', *Maghreb-Machreq-Monde Arabe* 126, December 1989, pp. 25ff. Interview with Mohammed Tozy, Lamalif, October 1988.

12 Djieghida Imache and Inès Nour, *Algériennes entre islam et islamisme*, Edisud, Aix-en-Provence, 1994.

13 Also by Zakya Daoud, cf. *Féminisme et politique au Maghreb, soixante ans de luttes*, Maisonneuve et Larose, Paris, 1994.

14 Adelkhah, 'Logique étatique et pratiques populaires: la polysémie du hijab chez les femmes islamiques en Iran'.

15 Robert Solé, *Le Monde*, 13 September 1994: 'It is not by chance that great feminist battles in Muslim countries have started over the question of the veil'. This is absolutely true, but what has been omitted is that these 'great battles' often explicitly confuse modernisation and de-Islamisation, which is a probable explanation for their fleeting and limited results.

16 Women who do not wear the *hijab*, and those who oppose it, do not necessarily have a negative view of the principles that it expresses. The second finding, or rather confirmation, of the cited research by Imache and Nour is that representation of these women is experiencing a period of rapid change, as their appreciation of the function of the *hijab* is strangely similar to that of their sisters who do wear it.

17 Sidhoum, 'Le Deuil et le fardeau...la férocité en sus'.

18 In spring 1994, a group of Tunisian women that did not support the Islamist movement spoke out against the methods of the regime and denounced the reintroduction of the repression against female causes. In Algeria, in the review *Nissa* ('Women'), then in the weekly *La Nation*, Salima Ghezali has maintained a militant line that is in stark contrast to that taken by Khalida Messaoudi, the president of an underground Association for the Triumph of Women's Rights, whose struggle was soon to be closely linked with the extremist wing of the Algerian military.

19 This does not imply that the Western approach to the status of women or its morality should necessarily be put forward as the standard of 'normality' or universality. Yet, this is exactly what was being suggested in a report in *Paris Match* in 1993, which applauded the successes of General Ben Ali in the struggle against the 'God-fearing maniacs': the proof that everything had returned to 'normal' in Tunis was the re-appearance of a billboard publicising a pornographic film on one of the main streets in the capital (according to the heading of a photograph taken by Patrick Forestier).

20 'During the month of Ramadan [in 1991], there was an extraordinary outbreak of violence against women. But what was unprecedented was the fact that the written press, and to a lesser extent the other media, made its first declaration on what it considered ordinary to be a private or a public matter (of which the press of the single party were highly suspicious)...Women owe this compassion to a particular situation: the pre-electoral period. Again under the guidance of the FLN, most of the media tried to turn public opinion against FIS. The attacks on "weak women" was an ideal theme, especially in the eyes of international opinion': Fatiha Hakiki Talahite, 'Sous le voile, les femmes', *Les Cahiers de l'Orient* 23, September 1991, p. 123.

21 Even if this information – which was denounced by the FIS with a certain credibility as the work of Algerian security forces – must be handled with the utmost caution, the practice of forced marriage with underground members of the Algerian Islamists has been regularly denounced: cf. notably Sidhoum, 'Le Deuil et le fardeau...la férocité en sus'. Yet we have seen how the FIS has clearly distanced itself from the widely reported episode when two young girls who, in November 1994, allegedly 'had their throats cut because they refused to agree to a mut'a marriage'. According to a credible press release produced by the executive abroad, it was carried out by the authorities as a reprisal against a family whose crime was to have some of its members belonging to the armed groups. The temporary mut'a marriage is recognised by Shiite doctrine, but is strongly condemned by the Sunnis.

22 *L'Express*, April 1993.

23 Notably by Ahmida Enneifer: cf. Burgat, *L'Islamisme au Maghreb*, whose position is similar to that taken by the Libyan Mu'ammar al-Gadhafi – that it is impossible to be fair to several spouses, and that the main meaning of the

Quranic verse that deals with this question is not to be found in the principal proposition, 'Marry... two, three, or four women', but rather in the restriction which follows it: 'and if you fear that you are unable to be fair and equitable, just one'.

24 Adelkhah, 'Logique étatique et pratiques populaires: la polysémie du hijab chez les femmes islamiques en Iran'. Cf. also Nadine Weibel, 'Pour une féminisme islamiste', *Passerelles* 3, 1991, p. 115.

25 Talahite, 'Sous la voile, les femmes', p. 123.

26 Fariba Adelkhah, interview with the author, Cairo, April 1992. 'The theory that Islamist women play a passive role in the Islamist movement under the domination of men and that they are manipulated in the name of the most simple-minded fundamentalism is not convincing when faced with the practice': Göle, *Musulmanes et modernes: Voile et civilisation en Turquie*, La Découverte, Paris, 1993. To illustrate this point, remember that the first woman to be elected to the Sudanese Parliament was an Islamist, as was, more recently (April 1992), the first women to reach the board of the powerful Egyptian trade union of doctors. Cf. also the literary and political experience of the Iraqi Bint al-Huda, Chibli Mallat, 'Le féminisme islamique de Bint al-Houdâ', *Maghreb-Machreq-Monde Arabe* 116, June 1987, p. 45.

27 Patrick Haenni, *Le Théâtre d'ombres de l'action féminine: femmes, Etat et société civile au Maroc*, dissertation for the DEA in political science, Paris, 1993.

28 Limited but active, a surprising number of these women (FIS female activists) were linked to the feminist movement before they opted for a militancy inscribed in the Islamic framework.

29 Interview with the author, Cairo, April 1991: *Égypte-Monde arabe* 7, December 1991, p. 102.

30 Tareq al-Bishri, interview with the author.

Notes on Chapter Twelve

1 Benjamin Stora, *Histoire de l'Algérie depuis l'indépendance*, La Découverte, Paris, 1994.

2 Jacques Berque, 'Lectures contradictoires du Coran: le figé et l'ouvert', *La Pensée* 299, July 1994, p. 69.

3 Interview with the author, cited.

4 Zakya Daoud, *Féminisme et politique au Maghreb (1930–1992)*, in reply to the symposium of the Association of European Journalists, Grenada, 1993.

5 On the problematic of associations, cf. notably Sarah Ben Nefissa, 'Le Mouvement associatif égyptien et l'Islam: éléments d'une problématique', *Maghreb-Machreq-Monde Arabe* 135, January 1992, p. 19.

6 Fariba Adelkhah, 'La démocratie sous le voile?', in Alain Gresh (ed.), *Un péril islamiste?*, Complexe, Brussels, 1994.

7   Pierre Guillard, 'L'équilibre algérien de demain', *Libération*, 15 January 1995. Cf. in particular Guillard, *Ce fleuve qui nous sépare: lettre à l'imam Ali Benhadj*.

8   Cf. Alain Rousillon, 'Sociétés islamiques de placement de fonds et "ouverture économique"': les voies islamiques du néo-libéralisme en Égypte", *Dossiers du CEDEJ* 3, 1988. For a more political interpretation of the failure of the Islamic investment fund co-operatives, cf. Michel Galloux, *Économie et religion, le projet financier islamiste*, thesis for a state doctorate, also in *Maghreb-Machreq-Monde Arabe*, September 1993.

9   Mohammed Sa'id, a founder member of the FIS and then a leader of the AIG, was one of the many people who quashed the claim that there was a dichotomy between being Berber and Islamism that the French media suggested and the Algerian government exploited.

10   Cf. notably Malika Zghal, 'La jeunesse cairote: effets de génération et recomposition du champ intellectuel égyptien' in Gilles Kepel (ed.), *Exils et royaumes, les appartenances au monde arabo-musulman aujourd'hui*, Presses de la FNSP, Paris, 1994, pp. 213–33.

11   Olivier Carré, *Radicalismes islamiques*, t. 1, L'Harmattan, Paris, 1985, co-edited by Paul Dumont, p. 17.

12   Cf. Mohammed Arkoun, in *Connaissance de l'islam*, Syros, Paris, 1992.

13   According to the optimistic formula of Nilüfer Göle: 'Behind what appears to be a movement of political protest, there are signs that the Islamic elites are beginning to find a way to shatter the illusion that a civilised being is a Western being': *Musulmanes et modernes: Voile et civilisation en Turquie*, La Découverte, Paris, 1993, p. 11.

14   Olivier Roy, *L'Échec de l'islam politique*, Le Seuil, Paris, 1992.

15   *Ibid.*, p. 42.

16   'What fascinates us about this movement? Its novelty, the impact it has had in the West, which for the past ten years has been paralysed by the "Islamic threat", and finally its failure. Not that Islamism has disappeared from the political scene. On the contrary, from Pakistan to Algeria, it has spread, taken root, blended in with its political background and defined its morals and its conflicts. It will definitely come to power in Algeria. But it has lost its original impetus. It has become "social-democratic". It no longer offers a different kind of society or a brighter future': *Ibid.*

17   Pamphlets produced by Rachid Mimouni and Rachid Boudjedra illustrate both the content and its limits.

18   The terms of this highly controversial debate were presented by Mohammed al-Ahnaf, 'Religion et État en Tunisie', *Maghreb-Machreq-Monde Arabe* 126, December 1989.

19   One of the many examples is the work entitled *Point de vue prospectif sur le mouvement islamiste: lecture autocritique*, Madbouli, Cairo, 1989. Its authors deal with what the Kuwaiti political scientist Abdallah Nafissi identified as the 'holes' in Islamist thought: the absence of long-term methodological thought,

ignorance of the methods of mass communication, the underestimation of current ideologies (resulting from the misguided belief that the Islamic current is evolving in an 'ideological void' that it is trying to fill), the relative resistance of the Islamist discourse to changes in its environment, the clannishness, the inability to move on from confrontation with to opposition to the government, and the lack of internal democracy (confusion over religious and organisational questions), a lack of respect for the rights of its members). Cf. also Le Dialogue nationaliste-religieux, Centre d'études sur l'unité du monde arabe, Beirut, 1989; Amru Abd Al-Sami', Les Islamistes: dialogue sur l'avenir, Maktabat al-Turath al-Islami, Cairo, 1992; or the countless debates organised by the revue Al-Wasat (London).

20 For example, in Tunisia, after the death of Bourguiba. On this matter cf. Al-Ahnaf, 'Religion et État en Tunisie'.

21 One of the first to be affected, the Tunisian Communist Party announced in 1989 its decision to 'change its identity', namely to cease to exist as a communist party.

22 Al-Ahram Weekly, 1–7 April 1993, p. 5.

Notes on Conclusion

1 For a recent survey of the extent and limitations of elections in the Arab world, cf. François Burgat, 'Représentation et construction nationale: de nouveaux processus électoraux', Maghreb-Machreq-Monde Arabe 168, April–June 2000.

2 In the political theory of the Jamahiriyya, a principle of constitutional value (man tahazzaba khana!) equates the formation of a party with treason against the direct rule of the people through the Popular Committees.

3 Fatiha Dazi-Heni, 'Des processus électoraux engagés dans les monarchies du Golfe: les cas du Koweit et du Qatar', Maghreb-Machreq-Monde Arabe 168, April–June 2000, pp. 76–88.

4 John Entelis, op. cit.

5 This was done by means of symbolic concessions to demands for the 'Islamization' of the public sphere, but also by a certain tolerance with respect to campaigns targeted at secularist intellectuals.

6 Nazih Ayubi, Overstating the Arab State, I. B. Tauris, Oxford, 1995.

7 Some opposition Islamists have however been able to participate under the label of 'independent', a label under which 14.5 percent of the 100,000 candidates chose to run.

8 Harakat al-Islah wa'l-Tajdid of the Movement for Reform and Renewal, founded by Abdellilah Benkirane, was granted the right to revive, to its benefit, the legal body of the tiny Mouvement Populaire Démocratique et Constitutionel (MPDC) which had fallen into disuse. Led by Dr Abdelkrim

Khatib, the MPDC participated in the municipal elections of 1997 and the governmental coalition.

9 Ben Ali, Bourguiba's successor, was elected in 1989 with 99.27 percent of the vote and in 1994 with 99.91 percent.

10 The preceding resolution dated back to 23 May 1996. Several subsequent attempts – in July 1997, April 1999, May 1999 – failed due to the intense and damaging lobbying of Tunisian diplomats (on the 'Islamist danger', the 'promotion of women's rights', the 'economic performance' and 'repeated promises of political liberalisation') made to parliamentary groups. Cf. the reports of the CRLDH Committee (Comité pour le Respect des Libertés et des Droits de l'Homme en Tunisie): http://www.magreb-ddh.sgdg.org

11 Tunisia currently holds approximately 1000 political prisoners. Use of torture and sexual assault on detainees is a daily occurrence. Sanctions also extend to the families of opposition members, who may be denied employment or access to social services.

12 'The backdrop inherited by the sympathetic sovereign (that should not be obscured by popular adoration) is general chaos, mass poverty, offensive luxury for the few, corruption as a method of administration and government, and fiddling around with elections as an institution and a democratic practice. In short, the whole shebang of the makhzan [...] The makhzan of Hassan has not yet breathed its last. When the virus of corruption and deceitfulness characteristic of the makhzan administration has set in, throughout the system, it is no easy matter to renounce intrigue, plots and bribes. Cleansing a corrupt administration will only be possible once the 'great act' has been accomplished, the regeneration of the system able to be envisaged, the organisation of social solidarity founded on development and employment, not on public and private charity': Memorandum 'A qui le Droit', Rabat Salé, 14 November 1999. On the situation of the Islamist movement in Morocco, cf. Mohammed Tozy, Monarchie et islam politique au Maroc, Presses de Sciences-Po, 320pp, Paris, 1999; Myriam Catusse, 'Economie des élections au Maroc', Maghreb-Machreq-Monde Arabe 168, April–June 2000, p. 51.

13 Media attention is slowly but inevitably focusing on the role of the security forces in civilian massacres. Cf. Yocef Bedjaoui, Abbas Araoua and Méziane Ait-Larbi (eds), An Inquiry into the Algerian Massacres, Hoggar, Geneva, 1999; Nasrulah Yous, Qui a tué à Bentalha, La Découverte, Paris, 2000, and Habib Souaidia, La sale guerre, with Mohammed Sifaoui, La Découverte, Paris, 2001. These testimonies confirm revelations made on the Internet by the Mouvement Algérien des Officiers Libres (www.anp.org).

14 Yemen is an exception to the rule of excluding the major Islamist groups from power as is seen in Morocco, Tunisia, Libya, Egypt etc. All the real political forces have had the opportunity of participating in elections, whatever reservations may still be held concerning the regularity of those elections. Cf. François Burgat 'Les élections présidentielles au Yémen',

Maghreb-Machreq-Monde Arabe 168, April–June 2000. On the Islamist movement in Yemen, see Franck Mermier, Udo Steinbach and Rémy Leveau (eds), *Le Yémen contemporain*, Karthala, Paris, 1999.

15 That which Ahmed Manai's scrupulously documented work, *La Tunisie des supplices: le jardin secret du president Ben Ali*, La Découverte, 1995, was unable to do was achieved by Jean-Pierre Tuquoi and Nicolas Beau in *Notre ami Ben Ali*, La Découverte, 1999 and Tawfiq Ben Brick in *Une si douce dictature*, La Découverte, 2000, publicised by that journalist's long strike: the wall of silence surrounding the deeds General Ben Ali's regime is in the process of cracking.

16 The final mysteries of the press falsely named 'independent' have been convincingly exposed by al-Hadi Chalabi's short work, *La Presse algérienne au-dessus de tout soupcon*, Alger, 1999.

17 Most countries' security services today enjoy an unprecedented degree of control over all private correspondence. The majority have free access to not only the correspondence of potential opponents, but also all information contained on the hard drive of any user of the Internet: J. Guisnel, *Cyberwars: Espionage on the Internet*, Plenum PR, New York, 1997.

18 Jacques Chirac, speech in Tunis, 1996.

19 See Al-Hurriya al-'Amma fi'l-Dawla al-Islamiyya, Markaz al-Wahda al-'Arabiyya, Beirut, 1993; 'The Participation of Islamists in a non-Islamic Government', in Azzam Temimi (ed.), *Power-sharing in Islam?*, Liberty for the Muslim World Publications, London, 1993. Other branches of hizb al-Nahda have also moved in favour of a reformist path: see, for example, Salah Karkar, *Al-Haraka al-Islamiyya wa ishkaliyyat al-Nahda*, France, 1998.

20 The division is between an 'executive authority in exile', led by Rebah Kebir from Aix-la-Chapelle, which enjoys a certain freedom of movement (and is represented in most European countries, especially in Belgium) and the parliamentary delegation to the US headed by Anwar Haddam. On 14 July 1997 he was once more refused asylum in the US; Haddam was detained in the US between 6 December 1996 and early 2001, as a result of significant Algerian and international pressure. On the morale of the exiled FIS leaders, cf. Patrick Denaud, *Algérie: le FIS, ses dirigeants parlent*, L'Harmattan, Paris, 1997, and the newsletter *Ar-Ribat* on www.ribat.fsnet.co.uk

21 In forbidding any retaliation against the pro-Israeli militia of the South Lebanese Army then accepting, from the legislative elections of 2000, an alliance with its weakened rival Amal, the Hizbullah has shown a political maturity which has, unsurprisingly, translated into electoral gains.

22 Gilles Dorronsoro, *La Révolution afghane: des communistes aux tâlebân*, Karthala, Recherches Internationales, CERI, 2000.

23 For example, the novelist Muhammad Abd al-Wali. The novelist has in fact been dead for several years; editors of a review which published extracts from one of his novels, in which the hero utters a phrase of exasperation implying he had abandoned God, were prosecuted.

24　Those who sought to disallow Nasr Abu Zayd from remaining married to a Muslim on account of his supposed apostasy were not members of an opposition group. Cf. Baudouin Dupret, op. cit.

25　H. Dekmejian, 'La Montée de l'Islamisme politique en Arabie Saoudite', *Middle East Journal* 48, 4, autumn 1994: 'Although the employment of revivalist Islam as a protest movement against secular state authority has become a pervasive pattern in contemporary Arab politics, in the Suadi case the Islamist protest is directed against an avowedly Islamic state. Thus, Islam has become, once again, a two-edged political instrument - as the Kingdom's primary medium of self-legitimation and as the main venue of protest for opposition elements.'

26　Abdessalam Yassine, *Islamiser la modernité*, Al-Ofok impressions, Rabat, March 1998.

27　Cf. for example Magd Himad *et al.*, *Al-Haraka al-Islamiyya wa'l-Dimuqratiyya fi'l-Fikr wa'l-Mumarisa*, Markaz Dirasat al-Wahda al-'Arabiyya, Beyrouth, 1999.

28　Outside the turmoil of the Mediterranean, Muslim Malaysia frequently plays an important role in ideological exchanges in the Muslim world more generally and between the Islamist movements in particular. The Islamic University of Kuala Lumpur appeals to Arab scholars largely, but not exclusively, drawn from the diaspora of opposition. A good number of students – Algerians, Tunisians etc – also go there to study.

29　The principal achievements of this alliance include the embargoes on Iraq and Libya, the isolation of the Sudanese regime, unconditional support of the US Administration for Israel and the priority given to the Jewish State in the Western media.

30　Cf. for example the acidic chronicles of international politics by Mohammed Jalal-Abadi, under the auspices of the Literary Circle of Bangladeshi Muslims in Great Britain.

31　Michel Foucault, *Dits et Ecrits III*, Gallimard, Paris, 1996, p. 708.

32　Abdessalam Yassine, *Islamiser la modernité*, Al-Ofok impressions, Rabat, 1998, p. 13.

33　A French writer and politician, writing in *L'Evènement du Jeudi*, Paris, 22–8 January 1998, p. 90.

34　Cf. Burgat, *L'Islamisme au Maghreb; la voix du Sud*, Payot, Paris, 1995, expanded edition. In the economic field, Bjorn Utvik has shown that from the 1980s onward the ideas of the Muslim Brotherhood were far from incompatible with the process of modernisation: see *Independence and Development in the Name of God: the Economic Discourse of Egypt's Economic Opposition 1984–1990*, Faculty of Arts, Acta Humaniora, University of Oslo, 2000. In the field of law, the work of Baudouin Dupret has demonstrated the highly diverse meanings of references to 'Islamic law'. See his *Au nom de quel droit: Répertoires juridiques et référence religieuse dans la société égyptienne musulmane contemporaine*, Maison des sciences de l'homme, Paris, 2000.

35 Especially in *Middle East Quarterly*, of which he is chief editor.

36 Martin Kramer, 'Islam versus democracy', *Commentary* 95, 1, pp. 35–42, and *Arab Awakening and Islamic Revival: the Politics of Ideas in the Middle East*, Transaction Publishers, spring, 1996.

37 John L. Esposito, *The Islamic Threat*, Oxford University Press, New York and Oxford, 1992, and *Political Islam: Revolution, Radicalism or Reform?*, Lynne Rienner, Boulder, CO and London, 1997.

38 John Entelis, *Islam, Democracy and the State in North Africa*, Indiana University Press, Bloomington, IN, 1997; cf. Graham Fuller, *Algeria: the Next Fundamentalist State?*, Arroyo Center for the United States Army, Rand Corporation, 1996.

39 Basma Kodmany Darwich and May Chartouni-Dubarry, *Les Etats arabes face à la contestation islamique*, IFRI, Armand Colin, Paris, 1997.

40 *Idem.*

41 This is according to the phrase coined by the Egyptian academic Saadeddin Ibrahim, imprisoned in 2000 by Mubarak's regime, apparently for having taken the civil and human rights objectives of his Ibn Khaldoun research centre a little too seriously.

42 Tareq Ramadan, *Aux sources du renouveau musulman: d'Al-Afghani à Hassan al-Banna, un siècle de réformisme musulman*, Bayard, Paris, 1998, and *Islam, Occident: le face à face des civilisations*, Tawhid, Lyon, 1995. His latest work, *L'Islam en question*, Actes-Sud, Arles, October 2000, is the result of a debate with Alain Gresh, the chief editor of one of France's most read monthly publications, *Le Monde diplomatique*. For another 'counter-reading' cf. Ibrahim Abu Rabi', *Intellectual Origins of Islamic Resurgence in the Modern Arab World*, State University of New York Press, New York, 1996.

43 Olivier Roy, *L'Echec de l'Islam politique*, Seuil, Paris, 1992.

44 Gilles Kepel, *Jihâd: expansion et déclin de l'islamisme*, Gallimard, 2000; Antoine Basbous, *L'Islamisme, une révolution avortée?*, Hachette Littératures, Paris, 1999.

45 Olivier Roy, 'Le post-Islamisme', *Revue des Mondes Musulmans et de la Méditerranée* 85–6, pp. 9–30.

46 In the complete bibliographical omission of any reference to the work whose problematic he largely engages with – Roy, *L'Echec de l'Islam politique* – the social sciences are – in the case of France at least – well relegated to the category of 'soft' sciences.

47 Gilles Kepel *La Revanche de Dieu: chrétiens, juifs et musulmans à la reconquête du monde*, Paris, Seuil, 1992

48 Gilles Kepel, *Jihâd: expansion et déclin de l'islamisme*, Gallimard, 2000; Antoine Basbous, *L'Islamisme, une révolution avortée?*, Paris, 1999.

49 Besides Esposito, Binder, Entelis, Fuller etc already cited, cf. amongst others Baudouin Dupret, 'La problématique du nationalisme dans la pensée islamique contemporaine. Introduction', *Égypte-Monde arabe* 15/16, Cairo, 1993; Augustus Richard Norton (ed.), *Civil Society in the Middle East*, 2 vols,

E. J. Brill, Leiden, New York and Cologne, 1995; Amani Qandil, 'Le courant islamique dans les institutions de la société civile: le cas des *orders professionels* en Egypte', in *Egypte Turquie: Modernisation et nouvelles formes de mobilisation sociale*, CEDEJ, Cairo, 1992; Fariba Adelkhah, 'Logique étatique et pratiques populaires: la polysémie du hijab chez les femmes islamiques en Iran'; Nilüfer Göle, *Musulmanes et modernes: Voile et civilisation en Turquie*, translated by Jeannine Riegel, La Découverte, Paris, 1993.

50 Roy, 'Le post-Islamisme', p. 88.

51 Cf. François Burgat, 'Les héritiers islamistes', *Libération*, 17 October 1988 (Rebonds); 'Des Fellaghas aux intégristes', *Le Monde*, 3 January 1991 (Débats).

52 Nouchine Yavari d'Hellencourt, 'Le Féminisme post-islamiste en Iran', *Revue des Mondes Musulmans et de la Méditerranée* 85–6, p. 99.

53 Fariba Adelkhah, *La Révolution sous le voile*, Karthala, Paris, 1991.

54 In Palestine, the prime minister's comments on the 'terrorism' of Hizbullah earned him a rough reception from the students of Bir Zeit University in February 2000.

55 The most recent of the testimonies to these massacres, the responsibility for which two French philosophers, Bernard Henry Lévy and André Glucksman, opined was 'obscene' to question, makes no less of an impact: cf. Nasroulah Yous, 'Qui a tué à Bentalha?', *Postface to François Geze et Salima Mellah*, La Découverte, Paris, October 2000; Habib Souaïdia, *La sale guerre Le témoignage d'un ancien officier des forces spéciales de l'armée algérienne*, La Découverte, Paris, 2001.

56 Burgat, *L'Islamisme au Maghreb*.

INDEX